C000083319

IF YOU'RE PROUD TO BE A LEEDS FAN

TOM PALMER

IF YOU'RE PROUD TO BE A LEEDS FAN

MAINSTREAM
PUBLISHING
EDINBURGH AND LONDON

Copyright © Tom Palmer, 2002
All rights reserved
The moral right of the author has been asserted

'v.' by Tony Harrison © Tony Harrison, 1987
reproduced by kind permission of the author

First published in Great Britain in 2002 by
MAINSTREAM PUBLISHING (EDINBURGH) LTD
7 Albany Street
Edinburgh EH1 3UG

ISBN 1 84018 574 0

No part of this book may be reproduced or transmitted in any form or by any
other means without the permission in writing from the publisher, except by a
reviewer who wishes to quote brief passages in connection with a review
written for insertion in a magazine, newspaper or broadcast.

Copyright permissions cleared by author. The author has tried to trace all
copyright details but where this has not been possible and amendments are
required, the publisher will be pleased to make any necessary arrangements at
the earliest opportunity.

A catalogue record for this book is available from the British Library

Typeset in Berkeley and Blur

Printed in Great Britain by
Mackays of Chatham plc

FOR REBECCA

Acknowledgements

I would like – most of all – to thank my wife, Rebecca. If it wasn't for her faith, love, patience and financial support this book would never have been written.

I would also like to thank Martyn Bedford for his generous support and friendship, without which – again – this book would not have come about.

Thanks also to Jon Buck, James Nash and Philip Davis; Mark McIntosh and Dave Veitch; Brian and Chris the Chelsea fans and Matthew Wing; Ken Hall; Dom Page; Dan Jones; Stuart Brumhill; and my wife's parents, John and Kate Page.

Thank you to Leeds Libraries' 2001 innovative Writer in Residency programme, part of the Arts Council of England's Year of the Artist project. The residency I enjoyed at Pudsey Library and Leisure Centre led directly to the commissioning of this book and I am very grateful to them, in particular to Jan Cryer. Also to Dani Louise and Jane Stubbs.

Thanks to Radio Leeds, Radio Five, the *Yorkshire Evening Post*, Ceefax, *The Square Ball*, *Panorama* and the many other media organisations who have been so free with their opinions about Leeds United over the past 12 months.

Thank you also to Tony Harrison – the author of the poem 'v.' – for allowing me to reproduce it in this book. Thanks also to Gordon Dickerson.

And finally thank you to my editor, Deborah Kilpatrick, and all the staff at Mainstream Publishing.

Preface

This book is about one fan's experience of Leeds United's 2001–02 season, an often turbulent and relatively disappointing ten months.

So much happened off the pitch – and in the end so little 'happened' on it – that the season threw up hundreds of opinions about the club, so much so that the author witnessed at least two fights caused by those differences of opinion.

But for a football book to be half-decent it has to be from one person's point of view. This is mine.

At the end of the book there is a poem by the Leeds poet, Tony Harrison, called 'v.'. It's set in the graveyard on the hill overlooking Elland Road. It's the story of an argument between a man visiting his parents' grave and a Leeds United fan. Tony Harrison has been generous enough to let me use it in *If You're Proud to be a Leeds Fan*.

If you're proud to be a Leeds fan clap your hands
If you're proud to be a Leeds fan clap your hands
If you're proud to be a Leeds fan
Proud to be a Leeds fan
Proud to be a Leeds fan clap your hands . . .

[applause]

The Gelderd End, Elland Road

LEEDS UNITED v SOUTHAMPTON Premiership
Saturday, 18 August 2001

Every morning it's the same: I stand in front of the mirror, staring at a tired face, singing: 'We are Leeds, We are Leeds, We are Leeds' in a throaty whisper, telling myself it sounds like the Gelderd End at Elland Road. 'We are Leeds. We are Leeds. We are Leeds.' My stubble stands on end like a cartoon electrocution, and I take up the razor and run it across my face.

I have to keep it up: 'Marching on together, We're gonna see you win, Na na na na na na.' I've done both cheeks, my chin, my moustache. 'We are so proud, We shout it out loud, We love you Leeds, Leeds, Leeds.' My throat. Any solitary bristles I might have missed. And it doesn't matter if I'm using one, two or three blades, a swivel head, a lubricating strip, whatever . . . this is the best shave a Leeds fan can get.

The bathroom door is open and my wife – Rebecca – stands watching me from the landing. Some days she thinks this is funny. Even charming. She loves me, doesn't she? Other days – like today – she thinks I'm pathetic. It's 18 August. The sun is shining. And I couldn't sleep because this is the first day of the football season.

I'd had a dream: I was taking a corner in front of the Kop. They were all waiting in the penalty box: Viduka and Kewell and Smith. I fired it into the box and it sailed over the lot of them, over the keeper's back-pedalling and into the net. I woke up cheering, my fists clenched.

I'm waiting for Martyn in Wetherspoons, the pub on the new station concourse at Leeds. It's bright and airy, the doors open, the floor to ceiling windows letting in the summer light. Outside, hundreds of Leeds fans are standing in the sun, drinking pints and watching women get out of taxis.

I have been to Wetherspoons several times during the close season. Whenever I drink in Leeds I like to start here. Something about it excites me. Even rushing past it to catch a train on a workday gives me a thrill. There are no posters of Leeds players on the walls, no LUFC flags behind the bar, but this is without doubt a Leeds United pub. Leeds United everywhere. In the pools of beer on the counter when they put your glass in front of you. In the weight of the toilet door when you hold it open for someone. In the familiar faces of the bar staff. This is not just another city-centre chain pub. Not today.

Before I came out my wife was not happy: I had to get away from the house early so I could be sure to meet Martyn on time. She was used to the way things are on summer weekends: a long lie in, breakfast in bed, read the paper, then a trip out or a bit of DIY. This morning I was off at 11 a.m.

'Why do you have to go so early?' she said.

'It's the first game of the season. I'm having a pint with Martyn. There's a lot of catching up to do.'

'But you only saw him last week.'

'I know. But that wasn't the football.'

'We could have had a nice morning.'

'I'll be back at seven.'

'Seven?' she said. 'That's all day. That's a whole day lost.' And she was right. I've never been able to work out why one football match takes up as much time as a working day, but it does.

And I got that familiar feeling that going to the football is a joke. That I'm spending £40 – even £50! – and eight hours of the weekend for what could be – and often is – a frustrating experience. I could have told her I've been doing it for 20 years, that it's part of me. But sometimes I wonder what it would be like if I stopped going, stopped looking at Ceefax, stopped caring about something so unimportant as a group of overpaid prima donnas putting one over on another group of overpaid prima donnas in front of an angry mob.

'I'll see you later,' I said. 'I love you.'

Martyn arrives. This is the moment I've been waiting for: a few pints before getting the R2 bus to Elland Road. Talking about how this is going to be *the* season. Going back over last season. Going back over previous Southampton games. Like the one two years ago when his mate – Andy – came up all the way from Southampton and they beat us. Outside the ground, instead of exercising control and restraint, he'd taken the piss, thinking it was funny that Southampton had won at Leeds.

Martyn puts his bag down. He smiles apologetically. It's not good news: Andy is on his way. He's coming again. That puts an edge on things. I can't just enjoy the game now. When you play teams from the south you don't usually have to worry about someone mocking you after the game. He's due at 1 p.m.

Martyn has followed Leeds for over 30 years. His dad wanted him to support Crystal Palace and took him to dozens of games at Selhurst Park. But Martyn was a Leeds fan. He would always support the team Palace were playing, just to make sure he didn't become a Palace fan. He says he's a Leeds fan because he saw the 1968 Inter City Fairs Cup final on TV, Mick Jones scoring the winning goal. But his mum said it was seeing Jack Charlton in the 1966 World Cup final that did it for him.

From when he was nine, his dad took him to Leeds away games in London. Leeds didn't win any of the first 12 games he saw. He had to wait until his first game at Elland Road. Four–nil. With his dad. Home to Palace. After a few years his parents let him go on his own. Home and away. His dad took him to Kings Cross, put him safely on the train, then collected him at the end of the day, plucking him out from under the noses of London fans looking for someone to beat up.

Martyn's dad was an FA referee and – at one Leeds game – managed to wangle getting Martyn into the tunnel so he could see his heroes. Martyn was 14. February 1974. The players filed past. They'd just lost to Stoke, the first league defeat for 30 games. Martyn saw Norman Hunter throw a sock tag against a wall. He picked it up and kept it. Then he saw Billy Bremner in the changing-rooms. Naked. But Billy Bremner threw a boot at the door and it slammed shut. After the players were changed Martyn was still in the tunnel. He saw Allan Clarke – his big hero – and asked him for his autograph.

'Fuck off,' said Allan Clarke, storming past.

Undeterred, Martyn went to 30 games home and away the next season. He joined the London supporters' club. It was easier to get tickets that way. He got a part-time job to pay for his trips and worked all summer in a factory so he could get a season ticket.

Halfway down the pint, Martyn's mate phones. He's stuck in a traffic jam south of Sheffield.

Shame, I think.

'He'll try and get to us before two,' Martyn says.

Don't fucking bother, I think.

In 1975 Martyn's dad wrote to the French FA. He was a referee, he said. He'd like to take his son to the European Cup final, Leeds United versus Bayern Munich. Two tickets arrived. Martyn's dad put them in an envelope above the fireplace. Martyn checked them every couple of hours.

In Paris Martyn remembers being furious that Leeds had been cheated by the referee and wanting to rip his seat up and throw it onto the pitch like the other Leeds fans. But he was with his dad. It was exciting to see all the trouble. The police in riot gear. The dogs. A full-on fight between the English and the Germans. And a Leeds fan smashing a bottle in a Munich fan's face. All the blood. His dad ushered him to safety, running the gauntlet of riot police, keeping him away from the dogs' teeth and the batons.

In the '70s and '80s Martyn suffered a series of girlfriends who hated football. They'd not like him to go away for a whole day just for football. Weekends were sacrosanct, he was told. One of them wouldn't even tolerate him watching *Match of the Day* and would find ways of stopping him reading the sports pages. Football became clandestine. If she was working on a Saturday he'd slip away to the football or watch *Match of the Day* if she was on the late shift.

Then work took Martyn to Cardiff and Oxford and it wasn't so easy to get to Leeds games. He saw the odd game in London. That was about it. Then Damaris, his wife, got on a course in Sheffield. Yes, he'd love to move there. Then she got a job in Bradford. They moved again. And he started going regularly. To Elland Road. Living in Leeds.

When Martyn's mate arrives he's a nice man, not the demon I had created in my head. He's with his new girlfriend. He's chatty and amiable. They've only been going out a few weeks. He asks me how I'm doing, remembering some detail about my life. Nice touch. He could be me, just another man halfway between 30 and 40, supporting the team from where he was born. It's just that he makes me feel vulnerable. If Southampton beat Leeds he'll be better than me. And he'll know it. It's as simple as that.

REASONS TO HATE SOUTHAMPTON
1 Martyn's mate.
2 Leeds 0 Southampton 3 in 1981.
3 Alan Shearer used to play for them.

Back in Elland Road for the first time in two or three months, you feel immediately at home. It's bright. Warm. You remember all the brilliant nights of the season before. Milan. Madrid. Barcelona. Here, you are happy. This is Elland Road. A new season about to start – a season in which Leeds could win something.

You feel like this at the start of every season. Over the summer you begin pleased to have a few football-free weekends to go on holiday, visit friends. You don't miss it in May and June. It's been a long season. You're ready for the break. But in July and August you get twitchy. Something missing. Not just the football, but being at Elland Road. There's something about it. Something – that if you stopped coming – you'd never be able to find anywhere else. And when the players come on the pitch – sparkling white shirts in the sunshine – you realise that this is going to be the year.

Leeds start well, passing it around. Moving off the ball, like a good team.

Southampton sit deep – predictably – barely capable of breaking out of their own half. With Leeds all over them, it's just a matter of time.

Then it rains. Sheeting down. Killing the game. People come from the front rows of the stands to shelter undercover. And the play tires in the heavy ground. Suddenly it's as if George Graham has been put back in charge. You'd expected goals. A couple by half- time. But it's nil–nil when the whistle goes. The players stride off and the people around you look disappointed. They've come to expect something more than this.

Martyn is glad to be back at Elland Road, but he remembers his mate's reaction to the defeat a couple of years ago. He's got a lot invested in this game. Andy is staying at his house tonight. Another Southampton win would be hard to take. Watching The Premiership *would be very hard to take.*

The second half begins cold and everything points to a 0–0. Southampton's spoiling tactics are doing the trick. Their bottom-half-of-the-table caution could get them the point they've come for. But as the game goes on it begins to show that Leeds are the fitter team. Spaces open up. Patience. That's what O'Leary calls for. Play the game for 90 minutes. And be patient.

Lee Bowyer scores. One–nil.

A few minutes later Alan Smith beats the last defender with a Cruyff turn (so it says in the press the next day) and slots it home. Two–nil.

And from then on it's champagne football. Harte hits the woodwork. Smith comes close again. Leeds are capable of getting more. And 40,000 will go home happy. It doesn't matter if two-thirds of the game was tedious. That's football.

You resist the temptation to meet up with Martyn and his mate. You'll go back to Rebecca. She's been decorating all day. You feel guilty.

Leeds (0) 2 Southampton (0) 0

Martyn; Mills, Ferdinand, Matteo, Harte; Bowyer, Batty (Bakke 60), Dacourt, Kewell; Keane (Smith 65), Viduka.

Scorers: Bowyer, Smith

1	Bolton	1	5–0	3
2	Arsenal	1	4–0	3
3	Leeds	1	2–0	3
4	Man U	1	3–2	3

[Key for league tables: the first column refers to the club's position in the league; the third column refers to the number of games they have played; the fourth column denotes the total number of goals they have scored compared to the total number of goals conceded; and the fifth column refers to the number of points they have.]

LEEDS ANNOUNCE STADIUM STUDY
www.lufc.com (22.5.01)

As the 2000–01 football season came to an end, Peter Ridsdale dropped the bombshell: Leeds United were considering leaving Elland Road. This is a crucial point in the history of the club, he said. The world of football is changing. The time has come to look to the future. Elland Road's illustrious history may have to be put behind us. The fans were sent a letter offering two options: rebuild or move.

Leeds's top club fanzine – *The Square Ball* – printed an amended version of the letter, translating the LeedsUnitedspeak:

> Option one is to try and improve Elland Road. What can I say? Only a moron would vote for this. It would be expensive and disruptive to income and capacity, and would cost a fucking fortune. Option two is to build a new state-of-the-art stadium. 50,000 capacity and the possibility of building it even bigger. It would be cheaper. It would be easier to police and steward . . . It would feel better for me when I'm entertaining directors of clubs from Europe to be able to show them round a nice ground. It would look good on the telly in the credits at the end of *The Premiership* with a fast-moving sky behind it. I don't want to influence you one way or the other, but please, please vote for this option.

When you got the slip through the post you decided you would vote. You didn't know which way, but you would vote.

There were good reasons for voting both ways.

The *Yorkshire Evening Post's* unconcealed backing of Leeds United's intention to move annoyed you at first and made you feel like voting NO. But maybe they were right. Maybe it's okay for the media to take a strong line on something. And it's not like they hadn't given the other view: there'd been dozens of letters and phone calls from NO fans.

But Jon – an off and on Leeds fan for 25 years – said he thought we should stay at Elland Road. Sometime soon – his theory goes – a big club will buy a big new stadium just as the football market collapses, just as it loses its imagined right to a Champions League place. Then there'll be trouble. That could be Leeds, he says. Look at Bradford's stadium, big and empty, as they slip towards Second Division nothingness. They're having to ditch all their decent players to make up the shortfall. He said this in August 2001, nine months before Bradford were put into the hands of administrators.

But we don't want to get left behind, you're thinking. We're already falling down the league table of attendances. Teams like Newcastle and Sunderland forever above Leeds until we do something. It doesn't feel good.

And this nutter who's been sending Peter Ridsdale hate mail, threatening his family, driving down his street and putting up posters. That makes you want to vote YES immediately.

It's not easy. Do you hold on to 20 years that have represented the most sustained range of emotions in your life? You love Elland Road! All other stadia are concrete and plastic. Or do you look to the future: 50,000 fans and enough toilets and burger bars and car parks and merchandise outlets to keep everyone happy? What's best for Leeds United? What's best for you?

You vote YES, unconvinced.

ARSENAL v LEEDS UNITED Premiership
Tuesday, 21 August 2001

REASONS TO HATE ARSENAL

1 Arsène Wenger.
2 1983. Second Division Leeds are beating top-flight Arsenal 1–0 with a few seconds of extra time to go in a 1983 FA Cup fourth round replay. Graham Rix scores.
3 George Graham.
4 Since we blew the league for them in 1999, matches between Leeds and Arsenal have been supercharged, hatred off the pitch and on.

Arsenal away and you're listening to Radio Leeds. It's not easy, especially as Arsenal tear into Leeds from the start. You hate listening to matches on the radio: you really need to see what's going on. You're three seconds behind the game. Each howl of the crowd or round of applause speaks more to you than words. The commentator and Norman Hunter are doing their best to put you at ease: Leeds are soaking up the pressure. They can do this, they say, they got used to it in Milan and Rome. It's part of the modern game. You have to be able to defend. But it doesn't sound good. Leeds have had 4 players booked in the first 17 minutes. At this rate of bookings, you calculate – giving yourself something to take your mind off Arsenal's relentless pressure – Leeds will have one player left on the pitch by the end of the game, that's as long as there's no injury time.

This is too much. You've tidied the entire house, switching radios on in each room you enter. You're winding your wife up. You feel sick with anxiety. So you switch all the radios off: Leeds are going to lose anyway. And if they win, it won't matter if you've missed it. A win is a win. But Leeds aren't going to win at Arsenal, are they? They haven't won there in the league for 21 years. You settle down with your wife to watch soap. It drains your mind, numbs your imagination. You forget that Leeds are playing. Occasionally.

She looks away from the screen.

You flick on Ceefax.

'Stop it,' she says.

But you are saying 'Harte! Harte's scored!'

You put Radio Five on to listen. It will be easier to listen to the radio now. Wiltord scores immediately. You switch it off.

'I knew I shouldn't have done that. It's bad luck.'

'What's bad luck?' Rebecca says.

'Switching the radio on and off during a game.'

In the second half you are still annoying her. You are watching Ally McBeal together. You can't get scores on Channel Four Teletext, so the only time you are allowed to look is during the ad breaks. The first ads are at 9.20 p.m. Ally McBeal is about to get off with Robert Downey Junior. You're mildly interested. The idea of Ally having a steady boyfriend is . . .

'FUCKING HELL, WE'RE WINNING AGAIN!'

It's too much for her. She banishes you. You take the radio into the bathroom and listen for the last half hour, immersed in water. But it isn't as torturous as you thought it might be. It's 2–1. Batty has come on. The midfield is more secure. You go back to Radio Leeds. You want to listen with other Leeds fans, not worry about Alan Green and his terrible candour. There's an incident as soon as you flick over. Bowyer has fouled someone. He's off!

Ten men will never hold out, you think. You don't allow yourself to believe that Leeds can win this game. Once you believe that, Arsenal will score.

Then there's laughter. Mills has tried to win a throw-in off a prostrate defender. He's tapped the ball against him. But Norman Hunter isn't laughing. He's enraged because the referee has sent Danny Mills off. Nine men now. The bath water around you chills several degrees.

Five more minutes of tension, crouching in cold water with a serious look on your face. It's painful, but eventually the final whistle goes. Arsenal 1 Leeds 2.

'WE WON! WE WON AT ARSENAL!' you shout to your wife.

But she is busy with Robert Downey Junior. You know she fancies him. You can tell by the way she wants to talk about what a tragedy it is that he's got those problems in his personal life. Drugs. Alcohol. Rage. But what do you care? Robert Downey Junior is not part of real life . . . and Leeds have won at Arsenal.

You flick between Radio Leeds and Radio Five desperate to hear the wise words of Arsène Wenger, but he's nowhere to be found. You wish you could see his face. Just to see his face now! It would make you so happy. This is what football is all about.

Arsenal (1) 1 Leeds (1) 2

Martyn; Mills, Ferdinand, Matteo, Harte; Bowyer, Bakke (Kelly 89), Dacourt, Kewell; Smith (Batty 47), Viduka.

Scorers: Harte, Viduka

1 Bolton	2	6–0	6
2 Leeds	2	4–1	6
3 Everton	2	3–2	4
4 Arsenal	2	5–2	3
5 Man U	1	3–2	3

Two days after the Arsenal game the FA's chief executive Adam Crozier speaks. He is concerned about the spiralling tension at Arsenal–Leeds games. 'The Arsenal–Leeds game has developed an edge that isn't entirely desirable,' he says. 'It is something the two clubs have to do a little bit of work on . . . It is not healthy to have that kind of rivalry going on.'

And you think: Bollocks! Every fan you know – Leeds or Arsenal – would prefer that sort of game to a tepid 0–0 draw. The game is about being behind your team, being cheated, being outraged, then getting your own back, seeing the stiff smile on the face of your opponent's manager in the post-match interview. Everyone wants to see fights on the pitch, players getting sent off. They want to feel injustice has been done and want to burn with hatred. They want to see opposition players get long bans they don't deserve. It's football. It's about feeling something more vital than the vacillations of *Ally McBeal*.

Adam Crozier also explains that both Lee Bowyer and Danny Mills will be investigated by the FA. It is alleged they spoke out of turn to the match officials. You watch a video of the game the next night. It's possible – reading Lee Bowyer's lips – that he may have suggested to the referee that he 'fuck off'.

At the end of the video you see an interview with Wenger. His face is straight. He doesn't want you and all the Leeds fans watching to know he's gutted. You smile.

The next day *The Guardian* reports that 'Lee Bowyer and Danny Mills were yesterday charged with misconduct by the Football Association for their use of foul and abusive language towards the referee Jeff Winter.' They have two weeks to respond.

O'Leary isn't surprised. 'I will not,' he says, 'tolerate my players running 50 yards to swear at a referee.'

CONFESSIONS OF A LEEDS FAN – PART ONE
1975–79

My earliest memory is going down into the cellar of our house in Leeds where my dad stacked old copies of the *Yorkshire Evening Post*. On top of the stack that day was a special pullout: the 1975 European Cup final, Bayern Munich versus Leeds United. I remember taking it back upstairs thinking it was important.

A few days later we were on holiday by Lake Ullswater, camping. There was a party. Lots of children stood around in cagoules, cheery women, men wearing yachting gear but without yachts, several of those eight-pint cans of beer on a table. And a radio. I remember the radio: one of those clunky boxes with a grill on the front. I can't remember much about the game: the disallowed goal, the cheating referee, the riots afterwards. But at the end – when Leeds had lost – I remember running off and going into our tent to cry. May 1975. Seven years old. I was a Leeds fan.

No one in the family had been into football before, no trace of it on my dad's side or my mum's. No one liked sport. But it didn't become an issue that I liked Leeds United: it was a childish fad, like my obsessions with dinosaurs, quarries and setting fire to Airfix aeroplanes stuffed with paraffin-drenched cotton wool. It wasn't like I was going to the games or anything. All I was doing was reading the football scores and collecting Frosties packet tops so I could send off for a free Leeds United scarf and bobble hat. That's where my Leeds United supporting would start and finish. I would grow out of it and move onto something more fitting for a son of Roundhay: playing a musical instrument, the school chess club, that sort of thing.

When I was ten my grandmother died. She left each of her grandchildren £200. We were allowed to buy one thing for up to £10 and save the rest until we were 16. I bought a clock radio from a shop in the Merrion Centre. Every Saturday afternoon I'd listen to Radio Two's football commentary, staring at the luminous green numbers on the front of the clock radio.

I can remember one game clearly. Liverpool at home. I had all my pieces of paper ready: a league table, records of home and away performances, and the full analysis of a dice football game played between the two teams that morning. But the commentator was laughing: Terry McDermott, Kenny Dalglish and Graeme Souness were playing the ball in triangles and the Leeds players were running around in circles. Leeds couldn't get the ball off them. We were going to lose to Liverpool again. And I knew I would have to face the legions of Liverpool supporters at school the next Monday.

The Leeds United of the '80s were about to be born and I'd come along just in time. But it didn't matter that my team was rubbish: it mattered that my team was Leeds.

When we went over to my parents' families at Christmas, I didn't need to sit mute in the corner watching my sister grab all the attention. That's because I wasn't there. I would send 'Leeds United Fan' instead. He would take along pictures of Brian Flynn and Trevor Cherry from *Shoot!* and show them to people. He would talk about all the players. He could list them. He knew where and when they'd been born. He knew the scorers of all the goals Leeds had scored in cup finals. He had a hand-written league table he would show to people, along with a list of games over the Christmas period. He could demonstrate how this or that set of results meant Leeds reaching 7th position or 15th. He would encourage people to guess the scores of all 11 games on Boxing Day and emerge successful as the one who got most right. Aunts, uncles and cousins – and sometimes sisters – would flock around him and nod their heads before making for other rooms.

When I was 12 they took me to my first game. This Leeds United thing had been going on for four years now. It wasn't a passing fancy. It was something that gave the boy self-esteem, the only thing that animated him.

Wolves at home. The 15th of December.

My first dad took me. We drove to the ground and parked on a side street of terraced houses, Leeds fans pouring off the hills and down every street. I'd never seen so many people in one place before. They were dressed in varieties of Leeds scarves I'd never seen. And some of them had real Leeds United tops on. And the floodlights were bigger than I'd ever imagined. They towered over everything. They were the biggest in Europe. I knew that before my first visit, just like I knew the proportions of the pitch, the biggest win, the heaviest defeat and the largest attendance.

I remember coming up the steps inside the stadium and seeing all the stands and the big patch of green. I'd seen the inside of the ground on TV, but it had never looked like this. We sat in Block E of the West Stand. Right next to the Kop. Thousands of people stood singing and waving their arms about. The noise was amazing. I wanted this. I wanted to be here every week, every month, every year. I was hooked even before the players came on the pitch.

WEST HAM UNITED v LEEDS UNITED Premiership
Saturday, 25 August 2001

REASONS TO HATE WEST HAM
1 They're from London.
2 Trevor Brooking.
3 In 1982 West Ham beat Leeds 4–3 and for some reason the result has always stuck in my throat.

After two wins Leeds go to West Ham. You expect a third win. Leeds turn them over there every year. You're convinced it's three points. You're convinced we'll be top of the league when The Premiership *comes on at 7 p.m.*

You listen on the radio. You can't afford to go to away games. Well, you could . . . if you didn't want to have a nice life with your wife, holidays, people coming round for dinner at the weekend, a job that sometimes stops you going to matches anyway. And could you really be arsed spending all those hours on motorways and in trains? All the home games, a couple away and one in Europe: that's the agreement you've made with yourself. And cup finals, when required.

The commentators are on form, even if the players aren't. 'Oh that's an outrageous tackle. The West Ham defender should be off for that . . .' and 'Why's Matteo getting booked for that, Norman? I can't believe it. It wasn't even a foul . . .' Radio Leeds. Putting Leeds United first.

After a strong start by Leeds, West Ham come more and more into the game. Di Canio and Cole are hammering away at our defence. But the defence look solid. The thought enters your head that you'd be happy with a draw, Leeds aren't going to win this. And when Rio clears a late West Ham chance it's clear West Ham aren't either. An honourable draw. Nil–nil.

Disappointed, your mind tacks around for a line on it: a draw away, that's okay, isn't it? Two out of three wins, seven out of nine points. That's good. Better than Man U. We'd be top if it wasn't for Everton. And they'll fall away soon. They might be top now, but that's an aberration.

West Ham (0) 0 Leeds (0) 0
Martyn; Mills, Ferdinand, Matteo, Harte (Woodgate 76); Bowyer, Batty, Dacourt (Maybury 76), Kewell; Keane, Viduka.

1 Everton	3	5–2	7
2 Leeds	3	4–1	7
3 Arsenal	3	9–2	6
4 Bolton	2	6–0	6
5 Man U	3	6–5	5

LEEDS MOVE EMBRACED BY FAITHFUL
Yorkshire Post (7.9.01)

It's early September and Leeds United announce the results of the Elland Road poll. Should we stay or should we go? Of the 28,250 voting forms sent out, 18,577 have been returned. 87.6 per cent of those said YES. Peter Ridsdale is relieved. It would have been hard to sanction the move if the vote had been closer. 'I wouldn't have been able to split our fan base like that,' he says. A few weeks before, the fans were being told that the vote was not the be-all-and-end-all, just part of a larger consultation process. But now, says Ridsdale, 'It gives us a clear mandate for making this move.' The consultation process is clearly over.

Ever the democrat, Peter Ridsdale says that the fans will have a full say on the design of the stadium and the services around it. But first he must turn his mind to finding a stadium sponsor. Yorkshire Bank and Coca-Cola are mentioned. It will not, he reassures the fans, be a tobacco, alcohol or sportswear company.

You cast your mind back: Leeds *are* Elland Road. The one constant thing. With your mum. With your dad. With 10,000 at home to Wimbledon in the Second Division and 40,000 on the first night of Champions League football. As a child. Then older, doing the first real thing on your own without your parents. On your feet. Sitting. Singing. Shouting. Silent. Forgetting all the things going on in the outside world. For 25 years Elland Road has been there. When your dad died. When your mum died. When your first long-term relationship fell apart and you were the scum of the earth. Whatever was going on in your life, it was nothing once you were inside Elland Road. You could forget the worst nightmares and the most passionate affairs. And when you walked out of the ground it would shock you that you could forget such important things just watching a game of football.

LEEDS UNITED v BOLTON WANDERERS Premiership
Saturday, 8 September 2001

This is Dave's first trip to Elland Road for 27 years. His dad used to bring him, but stopped coming when Brian Clough was sacked. Dave is now a third part-owner of the season ticket next to mine. Originally it was Mark's. But Mark moved to Cambridge, so now Mark shares it with Dave and Martyn.

Dave is 5 ft 11 in., dark hair, jeans, trainers, just like he said. I said I'd be in a black T-shirt and I'm worried that I'll miss him because I'm in a white T-shirt. But I stand in the place I said I'd stand, at the door to Wetherspoons, a pint of Stella in my hand.

A man comes up to me. 'Are you Tom?'

It feels like a blind date: two strangers brought together by friends for mutual pleasure. Unlike the blind dates I might have gone on when I used to do things like go on blind dates, this is okay. There is something to talk about straightaway.

REASONS TO HATE BOLTON
1 You know they're going to put 11 men behind the ball.
2 They are from Lancashire.

A dull game against a bottom-of-the-table side. This is what you have to expect when teams have respect for Leeds. Bolton: five midfielders packing the middle of the pitch, a deep defence, and the hope of hitting Leeds on the break. The perfect game plan. Is this why Bolton are top of the league?

Leeds don't show the guile to get round the back of Bolton and it's 0–0 at half-time. During the break Dave says he thinks things look very different to when he came here 30 years ago. Everyone sitting, no one moving around in the Kop. He doesn't say whether it's good or bad. But he agrees that the adverts on the twin screens and the idiot with the microphone are really annoying.

In the second half it's more of the same. Boring. You are deep inside yourself. The beer you had two hours ago is dragging you down. The Bolton fans out-sing Leeds throughout the game. You try to join in with the Kop two or three times: 'We are Leeds' 'Marching on Together'. But there is no passion in the crowd, the singing is not travelling down to the front of the Kop.

Then suddenly Robbie Keane is on the ball. Ninety minutes on the clock and the safest pair of boots is clear through on the keeper. But he toe-pokes it and the keeper scoops it up. The first really exciting moment of the game. In the 90th minute! And suddenly it's important. Now you want it. You're switched on. If we win we go top. And there we were, just waiting for the time to pass in silence, as the Bolton fans took the piss.

Kewell goes down. PENALTY! Everyone is cheering. But it's not a penalty. It's a free kick. And Ian Harte punts it into the Bolton fans behind the goal.

Leeds United (0) 0 Bolton Wanderers (0) 0
Martyn; Kelly, Ferdinand, Matteo, Harte; Kewell, Batty, Dacourt, Wilcox (Bakke 59); Keane, Viduka.

1	Bolton	4	8–1	10
2	Man U	4	10–6	8
3	Leeds	4	4–1	8

Leaving the stadium you and Dave talk about a scuffle that went on behind you in the Kop. It's a surprise. There's not much trouble in the ground any more. But Dave wouldn't know this. The last time he came, throwing punches and sharpened 50ps were the done thing.

Early in the game, a lad of 16 or 17 attracted everyone's attention. There was some trouble. When you looked round he had a fierce look in his eyes and, at first glance, you thought it was him who'd caused it: a wannabe hooligan. But it turned out he was the one crying, he was the victim. The-men-behind-you were supportive. And the girl next to him. The trouble was the man on the other side of him: 40s, hard-faced, a Service Crew man 20 years on, still full of venom, but no outlet for it now he has to sit nicely at the football. This man had been picking on the kid.

Even though the man had disappeared, the boy would not be comforted. If he looked at the girl or took up the offer of swapping places with the-men-behind-you he might start crying again. So he stared ahead with a look of determination – or desperation – on his face, his eyes bloodshot, tear tracks down his cheeks.

'I can't understand why that man was having a go at that lad?' you say to Dave outside, just as the lad moves in front of you in the crush to get the bus back to town. Dave points him out.

Someone says to the lad, 'Where's your old man?'

'I dunno,' he says, 'He started on me. Then he fucked off.'

LEEDS WILL MEET FANS' TRAVEL COSTS
Yorkshire Post (13.9.01)

'UEFA have announced that all the UEFA Cup games this evening, including United's clash with Maritimo, have been postponed in the wake of yesterday's terrorist attacks in America,' reports the Leeds United website. The Leeds United team were airborne when the news came through. They turned the plane round and headed back for Leeds–Bradford airport. There is no dissent. Even the Leeds supporters already in Madeira take it in their stride. Leeds United say they will recompense all those who travelled with the official club trip. And they offer to help those who went under their own steam to claim money from UEFA.

Images are replayed on our television screens. A plane smashing into the South Tower of the World Trade Centre, then the North Tower. The two towers collapsing, one after the other.

LET'S ALL LAUGH AT MAN U – NUMBER ONE
Newcastle United 4 Man U 3

The first defeat of the season for Man U is always a pleasure. You watch *The Premiership* knowing they have lost 4–3 to Newcastle. You sit back and enjoy every goal. You can even enjoy the celebrations around Man U's equaliser when you know that it will all come to grief. When Shearer scores the winner you are – for a moment – quite pleased for him.

What you didn't know was that at the end, the season's first exquisite moment would come: Man U win a throw in, Shearer tries to stop Keane taking it, Keane throws the ball at Shearer, then lashes out at him and has to be restrained by his team-mates from making a full assault. You wish that Beckham had not reached Keane in time. You would have liked to see Keane laying into Shearer. Keane sent off. Shearer stretchered off.

CHARLTON ATHLETIC v LEEDS UNITED Premiership
Sunday, 16 September 2001

REASONS TO HATE CHARLTON

1 The play-off final, 1987. Nil–one at Charlton. One–nil at Leeds. A replay at Birmingham, Leeds one–nil up with a few minutes of extra time to go. Then two goals from Charlton.
2 Peter Shirtliffe, the scorer of the two goals.

Sunday afternoon. You meant to go and find a bar to watch the Charlton game, Leeds due to go top if they win.

You ask Rebecca, 'Shall we go to Leeds and watch it somewhere?'

She says not. She's been away all week. Since Monday. Only getting back the previous night. She wants to do something nice. You need some time together. A bit of fresh air. So as Leeds kick off against Charlton you are walking in a place called The Valley of Desolation, north of Bolton Abbey. You're worried. The Valley. Desolation. It doesn't bode well.

You try to catch the time on people's watches as they go past among the trees, next to the River Wharfe. It could be half-time already, you think. You wish you'd brought your mobile. You could have checked the score on Clubcall every – say – ten minutes. Your wife would have agreed to that. She's a reasonable person.

You reach a café by the river. It's in the middle of nowhere. There's no satellite dish on top, you checked that from half a mile off. But still you go inside. It's a long shot, but they might have cable. Nothing. Just cups of tea, ice creams and old people. And anyway, the game would be finished now.

In the car on the way home you listen to the Blackburn–Ipswich commentary. They will mention the Leeds result eventually. The commentary is irritating after the calm of the riverbank, but Rebecca tolerates it. You've had a nice time together. This is her concession. You wish you could just turn the radio off. It's just noise. If only they'd just tell you the Leeds score you could turn it off.

After ten minutes the result comes through: Leeds have won 2–0 and are now top of the Premiership. You punch the air. Leeds have leapfrogged Arsenal. Again, you think of Arsène Wenger. He must be squirming, you think. He must hate Leeds even more.

That night you stay up to watch The Premiership. *They show Spurs–Chelsea for half an hour, then a couple of minutes of Charlton–Leeds. Robbie Keane slips past a ponderous defender to make it 1–0. You are delighted. He's had a slow start to the season: the goal will boost his confidence. Then Danny Mills buries one from 30 yards. Two–nil. You have already checked Ceefax to see the league table. It was the first thing you did when you got in from the walk.*

Charlton (0) 0 Leeds United (1) 2
Martyn; Harte, Ferdinand, Matteo, Mills; Bowyer, Batty, Dacourt (McPhail 65), Kewell; Keane, Viduka;
    Scorers: Keane, Mills

1 Leeds	5	6–1	11
2 Arsenal	5	13–4	10
3 Bolton	5	8–2	10
4 Newcastle	4	10–6	8
5 Man U	5	13–10	8

MARITIMO v LEEDS UNITED UEFA Cup
(First Round, first leg)
Thursday, 20 September 2001

Top of the league, Leeds United turn their attention to Europe. It's an annual event for supporters now. In the 20-plus years after 1975, Leeds got into Europe twice. Since you've been a fan Europe is something other teams did. But now it's every year. And not just the first couple of rounds until we come up against a decent club. Now we're contenders. Two European semi-finals in two years, Leeds are the team people look to avoid in the draw these days. And you love it. You love seeing the world's best players come up for corners ten yards away from where you're standing in the Kop: Raúl, Roberto Carlos, Rivaldo, Figo, Maldini. You love the memory of beating Deportivo 3–0 when they thought Leeds would be a walk-over. Of beating Milan. Even the memory of the last-minute Rivaldo equaliser when Barcelona broke your heart for a week. And you love European away days. You try to go once a year. It's expensive, but fantastic. Travelling with hundreds of other Leeds fans, drinking in bars, hanging around outside the stadium, out-singing some of the most famous fans in the world.
    You used to think Man U fans were arrogant saying they cared more

about the Champions League than the Premiership. You thought it was outrageous. Now you feel just the same.

REASONS TO HATE MARITIMO
1 They beat Leeds in the away leg of the UEFA Cup in 1998.

You've been at work all day; 12, 13 hours. Maritimo versus Leeds is on Channel Five. Kick off, 9.45 p.m . Exhausted, you can hardly be bothered to watch. Later you'll wish you hadn't.

There is a minute's silence. There have been several minute silences in the last few days. And two- and three-minute silences.

At kick-off you notice a banner on the fencing by the pitch, saying 'FUCK YOU BIN LADEN'. The next time the camera pans past the banner has gone.

The football is terrible. Maritimo are a poor side, but look at least like they are awake. Leeds slot the ball out of play unchallenged every couple of minutes. No Bowyer, Dacourt or Smith means no passion. The only highlight of the first half is the name of one of the Maritimo players: Quim. And it's not that funny.

After 35 minutes of the second half, Maritimo get a free kick from 40 yards out. Their player hoofs it into the box, the last defender backs off, leaving a sudden inexplicable yard between Martyn and the far post. The camera follows the Maritimo players' excited celebrations. They are beating the Champions League semi-finalists. Joe Royle – helping out the commentator – says 'This isn't Leeds United'.

Maritimo come forward again and their striker misses an easy chance to make it two. Leeds are jittery. The passing. The passion. Everything. The final whistle goes. You go to bed. Your wife is already asleep. You turn off the light and think that the way things are going Leeds could be out of Europe and your annual trip to watch Leeds play where people speak a foreign language and use foreign money might not happen.

Maritimo (0) 1 Leeds United (0) 0
Martyn; Mills, Ferdinand, Matteo, Harte; Kelly, Batty, McPhail (Wilcox 58), Kewell; Keane, Viduka.

LEEDS UNITED v DERBY COUNTY Premiership
Sunday, 23 September 2001

Mark has always been a Leeds fan. That's who his dad supported. But they lived in Guernsey, so he didn't get to see Leeds much. His first game was when the family went to visit his aunt in Leeds. Burnley at home. (But not the one where Eddie Gray played the game of his life.) When the family moved to Lincolnshire the man next door found out Mark liked football. He started taking him to home games. Grimsby's home games, not Leeds's. But Mark was still a Leeds fan. When Leeds came down to Division Two Mark went to Blundell Park, but this time in the Leeds end. He was shocked. It was different being among the Leeds fans. They were all thugs. Every one of them. And there was some trouble, fans rocking on top of fences, a pitch invasion. But he liked it. He was a Leeds fan, wasn't he?

Then he moved away from Lincolnshire and Grimsby Town: three years at University in Nottingham, watching Forest decline. Then to Newcastle to follow his wife's career. He saw very little of Leeds over the years.

When his wife was relocated – and seeing as Mark had done his bit following her up to Newcastle – he decided that he should have a say in where they moved to. They moved to Leeds and he got a season ticket.

A few years later his wife got offered another new job. A brilliant job. And they moved again. To Cambridge. But Mark didn't give up his season ticket. Three kids, his wife's career and a deputy headmastership in the East of England and he'd still come to a few matches. But it wouldn't be easy.

REASONS TO HATE DERBY
1 They are another 11-men-behind-the-ball team.

You meet Mark by the Billy Bremner statue along with around 400 people stood peering into the crowds 20 minutes before kick-off. He looks well. In the ground you try to catch up. Has he found a house in Cambridge? Are his kids settling into their new school? How's his wife? Sociable stuff. A nice chat before the game.

But it's difficult. The noise over the stadium speakers is so loud it breaks into your thoughts. And you have to ask him to repeat himself because you can't concentrate on what he's saying. As well as the Tannoy, there are the screens at the other end of the ground: two huge TVs showing images of goals and adverts for Carling and Strongbow. It's hard to draw your eyes away from those screens and not listen to the empty chat of the man with the mike. It's hard not to get angry that the club muscle in on the time you used to talk before the game. But you try. You haven't seen Mark for months.

You want to say to him that the club is conspiring against fans, trying to cut out terrace chatter, so that we all stare passively at their screens and have no time to plan insurrection, so they can sell us their products and their sponsors' products. You want to suggest we're all consumers now. Not football supporters, but consumers on a conveyor belt, taking in images and messages to buy this and to buy that, and information about how we must behave: no standing, no plotting, no sudden outbursts. Just sit still and watch. Don't even think about talking to each other.

The Kop is muted. This is Derby, not Deportivo la Coruna. The Kop needs a reason for getting into the game. Ravanelli dives. An innocuous challenge, but he's rolling on the floor like he's been bayoneted.

You join in the singing: 'Die you bastard, Die you bastard, Na, na, na-na-na-na.'

It's been a minute at least and he's still writhing in agony. No one would take feigning injury so far, no one would think they'd get taken seriously.

'Same old Itis – always cheating!' sing the Kop.

You join in. It's good there's someone to have a go at, a reason to get engaged. Everyone's laughing as Ravanelli hobbles to the edge of the pitch with the Derby physio. You can see his furrowed brow. Maybe he is hurt. You hope so. He's the only one of their players you fear. Him and a young player, Seth Johnson.

Back on the pitch, Ravanelli goes in for a challenge on the Leeds keeper. There's confusion. The ball bounces into the net. Derby have scored. An own goal? But no, the linesman has his flag up. Ravanelli rushes across the pitch to the linesman. Fifty yards in four or five seconds. An incredible recovery. The Derby fans are livid. They've been doubly cheated. An unpunished foul on their superhero and a disallowed goal. They've been the best team so far and they've got nothing.

It's all so unfair.

You feel engaged with the game now. Everyone does. There's nothing like a bit of derision to get everyone together. The singing starts. 'We are Leeds', 'Marching on Together', the works. Leeds have the initiative now. The ball soars across the Derby box and Eirik Bakke leaps from the mass of players to head it home. The Leeds players run to celebrate in front of the Derby fans. A nice touch. Leeds 1 Derby 0.

You try to talk to Mark at half-time, but again it's a struggle. They have turned the Tannoy up: adverts, action replays from the first half, then Paul Reaney comes on to give his opinions about the game. You expect more LeedsUnited-speak, but he talks sense, even mocking the Leeds players for their performance in Portugal three nights before. Maybe Leeds United Football Club are okay, you think. Maybe they don't want to control your thoughts. Maybe football is still football after all.

Derby are as good as Leeds in the second half. It's end-to-end stuff. The-people-behind-you are talking. What they did last night. Where they might go on holiday. Their thoughts on Kewell and Viduka.

'I've never liked Kewell,' says the woman. 'He's shit. He's lazy. I don't know what the fuss is about.'

'And Viduka,' says the man, 'He's done fuck all in this game. He just stands there like a fat cunt.'

Kewell tries to break past the full-back. He's tackled.

'See what I mean,' says the woman. 'He's fucking shit. We should have sold him for 25 million while we had the chance.' You find yourself agreeing. Yes, we should have sold him. He's never been the same since his injury.

Kewell goes at the Derby defence again, beats two players, side steps another and fires the ball against the far post. It ricochets back against the near post and into the net. Two–nil.

'Bastard! I knew he'd do that,' says the woman after the cheering has died down.

Leeds are on top. Three minutes later Kewell leaps in the box and heads the ball past the Derby keeper. Three–nil. The-woman-behind-you remains silent. She's fuming. This will only make her hate Kewell more. Leeds United are back on top of the Premiership.

Leeds United (1) 3 Derby County (0) 0
Martyn; Mills, Ferdinand, Matteo, Harte; Bowyer, Batty, Bakke, Kewell; Keane, Viduka.
  Scorers: Bakke, Kewell 2

1	Leeds	6	9–1	14
2	Bolton	7	10–4	12
3	Arsenal	6	14–5	11
4	Man U	6	17–10	11

CONFESSIONS OF A LEEDS FAN – PART TWO
1980–82

My mum took me to my second game. I had been piling the pressure on since my first dad took me to the Wolves game. She was divorced from my first dad and I probably used underhand tactics to persuade her. Something like: 'He took me to the football – why don't you?'

So she took me.

Aston Villa. April 1980. The first of 50 games she took me to over the next four seasons. My mum – who had never liked football, especially its supporters – became a Leeds United fan. She knew which player was which and why each manager needed to be sacked. She always got at least seven out of ten in the Leeds United quizzes I set her. She even read the *Yorkshire Evening Post* football pages every night. Me and my mum were Leeds United fans. We knew everything about everything.

Later she told me that she'd only read the football pages so there was something she could talk to me about. Unless she talked about Leeds United, I didn't talk. I was 13 . . . 14 . . . 15 and I didn't want to sit on her knee any more. I didn't want to go swimming with her. I didn't want to do anything with her. The only place I would willingly go with her was Elland Road.

The Villa game ended 0–0. At the ground they were advertising tickets for the last home game of the season. Manchester United.

'I want to go to that game too,' I said.

My mum didn't fancy it: Manchester United fans were known better for their thuggery than their Surrey residences back then. It was a risk. She talked to my second dad about it. They knew I was desperate to go.

So he took me.

There'd only been 15,000 at the Villa game. At Manchester United when I walked up the steps to Block E, I saw the Lowfields packed with red, the Kop with white. Elland Road was stuffed. And the noise was incredible. Forty thousand people bellowing at each other. And the songs. I couldn't believe it. It was a full-on 90 minutes of 'Who's that Dying on the Runway' and 'We hate Man U'. I loved it. And it was an important game: if Man U won and Liverpool lost then Man U would win the league. I think. That's how I remember it. That's all I remember, except that Leeds won 2–0 and Man U didn't win the league.

The next season I saw us lose 3–1 at home to Stoke, 3–0 at home to Southampton and 5–0 at home to Arsenal. We lost every game I picked. And badly. Even so, I spent all my money on Leeds United stuff. I had both kits. I had patches that I'd sewn onto my jeans, one saying 'Follow Me and Leeds United'. And two metal badges. One said: 'Jesus saves . . .but Arthur Graham nets the rebound', the other: 'Never mind the bollocks . . . here's Leeds United'. Rosettes with pictures of Brian Flynn and Byron Stevenson at the centre. A hand towel. Pennants with a list of all the trophies Leeds had won before I supported them. Silk scarves. Woollen scarves. A satchel.

Photos of family holidays – Paris, Pompeii, Hadrian's Wall – all have me wearing white with my chest puffed out, like I'm on the official team photo. There's a picture of me and my dad sat in front of the Eiffel Tower, me in the RFW pinstripe Leeds home top. And another of me in the Admiral top, kneeling with the dog in front of my mum and grandpa, and behind us a bus with red, white and blue bunting. Jubilee Day, 1977.

My mum took me to half the games in the 1981–82 season. She was getting into it. It gave her credibility at the school where she taught, Seacroft Grange. Mrs Nokes (that was her new name) was a Leeds fan!

Our final game together at Elland Road was the last home game of 1981–82 when Leeds beat Brighton 2–1 and it looked like we might stay up. Leeds, West Brom or Stoke were going down. Leeds had to play at West Brom. Then West Brom were going to Stoke.

Although my second dad had left the football largely to my mum, he realised that the West Brom game meant something. 'We'll go,' he said to my surprise: the three of us would go to Birmingham to watch the game. He phoned West Brom and asked them to post out three tickets. I couldn't believe it. I hadn't even asked. I was going to an away game. And it was the most important game in the world ever.

We sat in the main stand with the West Brom fans. I'd never been in a stand before where everyone else was standing up cheering while I was sat down. It happened twice. West Brom 2 Leeds 0. After that – and it was clear we were going to be relegated – the Leeds end erupted. My mum and I had seen the police wading into the Lowfields a couple of times, a pitch invasion. But nothing like this. I can remember the fences coming down. And the police piling into the Leeds fans. And all the West Brom fans stood around us shouting at the Leeds end. Things were being hurled onto the pitch. My dad said 'Right, we're going,' and marched me and my mum round the back of the Leeds stand ten minutes before the end. I'll never forget the noise coming out of the stand: the hammering on the corrugated metal, thousands of shouting voices. It was terrifying. And exciting. Especially the way my mum and dad were panicking. They wanted to get as far away from the Midlands as possible. I wanted to stay and watch.

My dad took us to the car and we drove off quickly. I watched the floodlights disappear.

'You are *never* going to the football again!' said my dad.

'I'm just glad we got out of there alive,' said my mum.

They were angry. They were scared. This was alien to them. This was not what their son should be interested in. They had made a terrible mistake bringing me down here. My dad drove stony-faced back up the M1, talking in a low voice to my mum. They calmed down after a while. I hadn't said a word since the second goal. They'd forgotten that Leeds had just been as good as relegated. It was the worst thing that had ever happened to their son.

We stopped for petrol at a service station in South Yorkshire. There were police everywhere. One of them saw my Leeds scarf and said 'Tha'll be playing us at Barnsley next year.'

When I was 16 I was allowed to spend the rest of the money my grandmother left me. I asked if I could get a season ticket in the Kop.

'No!'

'But I'm 16,' I said. I wanted to go every week. I wanted to be a proper Leeds fan.

They had a discussion after I went to bed. I heard their voices through the floor. I remember thinking: I'll go anyway. I'll go in the Kop. I'll say I'm out playing football. I'll go every week, home and away. Fuck them. I can do what I like.

In the morning they had a suggestion. Yes, I could get a season ticket. But in the South Stand. And I could go to home games only. Not away. Never away.

LET'S ALL LAUGH AT MAN U – NUMBER TWO
Deportivo la Coruna 2 Man U 1

It is not easy to watch Champions League football. The adverts, the banners, the silver stars, the music. You wouldn't watch, except you think there's a chance Man U might lose. Deportivo la Coruna, who Leeds beat in the quarter-finals last year. But you know they're good, capable of beating Man U.

It's end-to-end in the first half. Man U match the Spaniards and eventually score: van Nistelrooy. In the second half, even though Deportivo throw everything at Man U, it's not going to happen. This is a fine result for Man U. The rest of Europe will take seriously any team who can win in Coruna. You turn the TV off with five minutes to go. You don't like to see Man U win these games. It really gets under your skin.

The next day, surfing the Web, you see the final score: Deportivo 2 Man U 1. Deportivo scored twice in those last five minutes. The first must have been seconds after you turned the TV off. The second in the last minute.

You're gutted. And delighted.

LEEDS UNITED v MARITIMO UEFA Cup (First Round, second leg)
Thursday, 27 September 2001

MORE REASONS TO HATE MARITIMO
1 They beat us in the first leg.
2 They were supposed to lose.

The first crunch match of the season: Maritimo at home. UEFA Cup first round, second leg. It was supposed to be an easy tie: Leeds seeded and this lot halfway down the Portuguese league. But when you watched the first leg on Channel Five, Leeds were hopeless. Maritimo 1 Leeds 0.

After two seasons reaching European semi-finals you'd be gutted if Leeds went out in the first round. The season would be gutted. European football is part of being a Leeds fan now. You've got a taste for it. The night before, you watched Champions League on ITV. When the these-are-the-champions music came on, then Liverpool, you felt sick with envy. That's where Leeds should be. And Liverpool playing so badly, beating some no-team. Leeds would have done better. Leeds are a true Champions League team, not Liverpool.

You go to the match with friends: Martyn and Dan. And Matthew, your wife's cousin, going to his first game. You want him to be impressed. You want this to be one of those nights, not a bitter slanging match as Leeds slip out of Europe to a minnow.

After a few pints you are at the back of the Kop. Not your usual seat. Being deep under the stand reminds you of when you were 17. You used to stand here: on the right-hand side, arriving over two hours before the game so you could secure a place up against the boards at the back.

Leeds drive forward and Maritimo look weak. Leeds are passing the ball crisply, moving well. A machine. A good team. It's only a matter of time.

Keane scores. One–nil. Then Kewell. Two–nil.

Leeds are motoring. The season's first call of: 'We're all going on a European Tour' strikes up. And later: 'We are the Champions . . . Champions of Europe . . .'

At half- time a Formula One racing car is unveiled by Peter Ridsdale and four tall women who wave at the Kop. The fans sing 'Get your tits out for the lads' as the car shines Leeds United white under the floodlights. This is a unique opportunity for Leeds United, we are told. Leeds United are the first club to have their own F1 racing car. And it won't cost a penny, Peter Ridsdale assures the fans. Someone behind you shouts, 'What's it for?' as the crowd sings: 'One Peter Ridsdale, there's only one Peter Ridsdale.' Peter Ridsdale waves. Other chairmen must wonder how he does it, haunted by the ghosts of Manny Cussins, Leslie Silver and Bill Fotherby, who suffered a campaign of abusive graffiti around the stadium in his last months: 'FOTHERBY IS A CROOK' and worse.

Martyn comes back from the toilet, having missed the unveiling of the car. In the toilets he saw two black men being abused by a group of white men.

'What are you doing here?'

'You're not fucking Leeds fans!'

That sort of thing.

The black men, Martyn says, did nothing, said nothing, just kept their heads down. 'Any response and they'd have got a beating,' he says.

The second half kicks off. Matthew is enjoying himself. The crowd is singing. There's a positive atmosphere. Leeds are two up and looking for more. Eirik Bakke obliges: 3–0. It's all over. Leeds are through to the next round. Later in the game, with the players clearly taking it easy – reserving energy for Sunday's trip to Ipswich – a Mexican wave gathers pace, doing four laps of Elland Road.

After the game I ask Matthew what he thinks. He must have heard all the stories about Leeds fans. What did he make of it, being among 35,000 of us?

He loved it, he says. He'd come again. He'd bring his family – when he has one. He was worried he might not like it, that he'd be put off by drunks and racists, but everyone was friendly. And although you prefer a more aggressive atmosphere, tension on the pitch and off it, you are pleased he's had a good time, pleased about the Mexican waves and the upbeat singing.

Leeds (2) 3 Maritimo (0) 0
(Leeds win 3–1 on aggregate)

Martyn; Mills, Ferdinand, Matteo, Harte; Bakke, Batty, Dacourt, Kewell; Keane, Viduka
   Scorers: Keane, Kewell, Bakke

TROYES RETURN TO ENGLAND
www.soccernet.com (28.9.01)

The draw for the second round of the UEFA Cup matches Leeds with Troyes, an unfashionable French team. The team that knocked Newcastle United out. They will come to Leeds first, then Leeds will travel to France. Another uncomplicated draw. You could say it was easy, but that would be tempting providence. Last season Leeds drew Barcelona and Milan in stage one of the Champions League, Lazio and Real Madrid in stage two. That, after having to qualify against 1860 Munich. This year the draw is on our side.

   Troyes, you discover, looking at a map over the shoulder of a man wearing an Alan Smith top in a remainder bookshop in Scarborough, is south-east of Paris. Not so far away. You start to do the groundwork with Rebecca. There and back in a day? Or a few days out there, taking in Paris? The two of you?

UNITED IN £60m LOAN
Yorkshire Evening Post (29.9.01)

Late September 2001 and Leeds United announce their annual figures. It looks good, if absurd. A turnover of £86.3m compared to last year's £52.4m. An operating profit of £10.1m. Last year it was £2.7m. The playing staff are worth £198m, up £90m. But – taking into account wages and transfer fees (you wonder why they weren't in the figures anyway) – a loss of £7.6m.

   But not to worry. On the same day the club announce they've taken out a £60m loan over the next 25 years. This will help pay off old loans and outgoings Leeds United have committed to. This added to the income we'll be getting from the Champions League – which we're going to qualify for every year now – means the only way is up for Leeds United.

Something Jon said to you comes back: some time soon a football club is going to move to a big stadium, puffed up with its own importance, just as the football market crashes. A recession, perhaps. The collapse of the TV football market. Fans' willingness to pay out £30 a week goes down, people tightening their belts. Jon used the image of a beached whale: Leeds United, stuck out on the M1 with a new stadium to take 50,000, but only 25,000 fans. Just like the good old days in Division Two. It's a worry. What if Leeds do fall away and never get into the Champions League again? There's Villa, Newcastle, Tottenham, a dozen teams that could overtake.

But Leeds are in the big time now. Let's be positive.

IPSWICH TOWN v LEEDS UNITED Premiership
Sunday, 30 September 2001

REASONS TO HATE IPSWICH
1 One of Rebecca's best friends supports them, which makes you vulnerable.
2 All last season they matched Leeds, spending nothing compared to Leeds's millions. More embarrassing than outrageous.
3 All that Tractor Boys bullshit.

Having intended to watch Ipswich v Leeds in a Scarborough pub – part of a weekend break at the seaside with your wife – you are exhausted and go to bed in the cottage you've rented instead. You wake up just as the game should be ending and go downstairs to put on Ceefax.

Ipswich 1 Leeds 2. A Keane equaliser and an own goal by Venus at the death. Leeds are back on top of the table. Again.

You're glad Leeds got the three points, but something is making you feel uneasy. You're guilty that you just slept while Leeds were playing. What sort of a fan are you? You could have watched it in a pub or listened to it on the car radio. Even just followed it on Ceefax. Instead you slept.

But you're on holiday, another voice is saying. So what if you missed it? You're not duty-bound to follow every game. Sleeping through a Leeds game is good. You can wake up, slip downstairs, and as you come round with a cup of tea, the three points are in the bag. No tension. A result. And you can always tell people you watched it. But tell who? No one cares if you watch games or not. Just you. No one cares if you're a five-star or a two-star Leeds fan. It's just you. You've always been like this, trying to prove to yourself – in case you have to prove it to someone else – that you are a good Leeds fan. Whatever that means.

Ipswich (1) 1 Leeds (0) 2
Martyn; Mills, Ferdinand, Matteo, Harte; Bowyer, Batty, Bakke, Kewell; Keane, Viduka.
  Scorers: Keane, Venus (og)

1	Leeds	7	11–2	17
2	Arsenal	7	16–5	14
3	Man U	7	22-13	14

There will be a break in the season now. England are gearing up for their all-decisive World Cup qualifier against Greece. A win and England will be going to Japan and South Korea. Martyn, Ferdinand and Mills are all in the squad. Three Leeds players. There were whole decades when Leeds didn't have a single England player.

And Leeds will remain top for a fortnight. When the domestic football restarts Leeds will have to play Liverpool away, Chelsea home and Man U away. Three of the four other so-called big teams. The fourth – Arsenal – are already beaten. Leeds might be top now, but it will be hard to sustain. October could be a cruel month. Even though Leeds are three points clear, it's hard to imagine they'll still be top by the end of it. If they are then you might start to get excited, might start to think Leeds could win something. But for now you'll play it cool. Pretend you'll be happy with fourth place and Champions League qualification.

Then, out of the blue, you see a brief paragraph on Ceefax 312. Miscellaneous news: the retrial of Leeds United players Lee Bowyer and Jonathan Woodgate will start tomorrow. They are both charged with GBH with intent and affray.

LEICESTER CITY v LEEDS UNITED Worthington Cup (Third Round)

Thursday, 9 October 2001

REASONS TO HATE LEICESTER

1 Robbie Savage.
2 Matt Elliot.
3 Your wife's dad and his family support them. You're vulnerable again.
4 They knock us out of the Worthington Cup every year. Normally . . .

After work you travel down to Warwickshire to stay with your wife's parents. You've an early start in Birmingham the next day: a course. Leeds are at Leicester. You could have gone, but – on balance – having just shelled out £185 for a trip to Troyes you decided not to. Something you are regretting already.

Radio Five are covering Coventry–Chelsea. Normally you'd flick over to Radio Leeds but, south of Barnsley, there's no reception. You'll have to listen to Coventry–Chelsea and wait for the 'And-now-let's-go-over-to-Filbert-Street' and the subsequent five seconds of torture, knowing there's been a goal, but not who for.

From the M1 you see floodlights. Hillsborough on the hill over Sheffield. What could be Derby's ground, or maybe Burton Albion's. In an hour or so you might be able to see Leicester's floodlights . . . Then it dawns on you. You're stupid! You don't need Radio Leeds. You can have Radio Leicester. You can listen to the game.

You scan the channels. Nothing on medium wave. Then Barnsley–Newcastle, Coventry–Chelsea again, a French game. Then you get it: Century Radio. Leicester versus Leeds. They're talking about Gary Parker, Leicester's stand-in manager. The club sacked Peter Taylor a few days before. The commentator, with the same voice as every other football commentator on commercial radio, is saying how the Leicester team will be up for this one. A new manager about to come in – they'll be fighting to impress. They'll not roll over today.

Your wife's dad supports Leicester. He was born and bred there. He likes Villa too. That's his adopted team, having lived on the outskirts of Birmingham for 30 years. For some reason, every time you visit your wife's parents Leeds have either lost to, or are about to lose to, Villa or Leicester. Last year, the four of you had a day out in Stratford and listened to Leicester–Leeds on the way home in the car.

Rio Ferdinand's debut. Leeds were three down at half-time. You could hear the Leicester fans singing 'WHAT A WASTE OF MONEY'. Of course, your father-in-law was very good about it. He was probably more concerned for your feelings because Leeds were losing, than that his team were winning. Still, every time you stopped at traffic lights you wanted to jump out of the car and run for it.

Now, weaving between lorries, you have to brake: Keane has scored. Leeds 1 Leicester 0. You punch the roof of the car. Immediately you feel dizzy and move into the slow lane. You might faint. Never listen to a Leeds game while driving. You should have learnt that lesson by now. You remember going off the road when Leeds went 1–0 up in the 1987 FA Cup semi-final.

Three minutes later Keane gets a second. You shout something out loud, but keep your hands on the wheel. You are enjoying the commentary now. They have to admit that Leeds are a fine team. After the first goal they weren't too worried. But at 2–0 the commentator asks the expert (who, it turns out, is Gary Birtles) if he can see Leicester coming back from this. No, he can't. That's it as far as he's concerned. It's about damage-limitation now. Leicester need to tighten up, play for self-respect. They don't want to let in five or six.

In the service station you hesitate at the till and put the Walkers crisps back. A golden rule: never buy anything connected with another football club, especially mid-game. For years you have been prepared to pay more for electrical goods, avoiding Sharp at all costs. Now it's Vodafone.

Back in the car you find out it's 3–0. Bakke has scored. You were right not to buy the crisps.

In the second half you come off the M1 and start down the A42 towards Birmingham. You're worried the reception might fade leaving the Leicester area. You might have to stop in a lay-by, phone ahead and say you're going to be late. As you drive slowly down the A42 and M42 Keane completes his hat trick. You open the window and make gestures with your arms: you want the other drivers to know you support Leeds. Then Viduka scores. And Kewell. The commentators are going on about what a superb team Leeds are. You like it. This is unbiased opinion. They think Leeds look good for a trophy this year. You have to slow down, over-excited again. You are laughing, shouting out loud. This is brilliant. Leeds are through to the last 16. Leicester 0 Leeds 6!

Leicester (0) 0 Leeds (3) 6
Martyn; Mills, Ferdinand (Duberry 68), Woodgate, Harte; Bowyer, Dacourt, Bakke (McPhail 60), Kewell; Viduka, Keane (Smith 56).
  Scorers: Keane (3), Bakke, Viduka, Kewell

CONFESSIONS OF A LEEDS FAN – PART THREE
1983–84

My mum stayed at home when the 1983–84 season started. I had my season ticket now. And anyway, I'd be safe in the South Stand. That was the deal. As long as I didn't join the animals on the terraces I could go on my own. Newcastle at home. I was excited. Nervous. This was a big game. Two of the favourites for promotion head-to-head on the first day of the season.

They put the Geordies in the bottom of the South Stand. I was in the top. Their keeper broke his arm in the first minute so they had to put a defender in goal. It was looking good. And there I was on my own at Elland Road: a proper Leeds fan now. I could shout what I wanted and if there was any trouble I could stay and watch it.

'What shall we do?' I said to the man sat next to me – the same age as my dad – as plastic seats started flying back at us from the Geordies.

'Just sit tight,' he said, as the police piled into the Geordies and more seats came back at us, injuring people nearby.

The noise was terrifying.

Meanwhile, in front of the Kop, Kevin Keegan was dodging missiles. On the Monday the *Yorkshire Evening Post* published a photo of all the coins, nuts and bolts and ball-bearings that had been thrown at him. I hid it from my mum. She went to the newsagents the next day to complain that the paper hadn't been delivered . . .

But thinking about it – and looking back at the newspaper clippings – I can see I've got this all wrong. The ball-bearing game was the year before. I watched it from the South Stand, alone, just like I watched the QPR and Shrewsbury games a month later, the terraces empty, Elland Road's standing fans banned for two games for crimes against Kevin Keegan. I must have had a season ticket the year before too. My first solo game would have been against Wolves. It ended 0–0 . . . I think. I'm not sure. I can't remember it.

That's the thing about football memories: they're like all memories. Jumbled. If I look too closely at the stories I tell other people about myself, I will always find contradictions. Two seasons' games against Newcastle will blur into one because it sounds more dramatic if my first game without my mum was a full-scale riot. I could even take it further and say Keegan got baseball-batted after the game too, even though that was years later. Or earlier. And these stories come out more and more twisted when I'm drunk or with people who don't know so much about football and can't pick you up on it. Maybe that's part of the reason I've had a season ticket at Leeds for 17 years: because I want people to think I'm hard. When I'm not. Or that I've got something about me. When I haven't. Maybe I *haven't* had a season ticket for 17 years. If I look closely there was the season I played for a pub team. And the first season I was at university. Maybe I'm not the big Leeds fan I let people think I am. And the main person I've fooled is myself.

And that moving story about my mother? Did she really take me to 50 games? Wasn't it more like 10, 15? Did I really cry in 1975? Why would I? I didn't even know the names of Charlton, Clarke and Bremner. I don't even know if they all played that day. And – at the time – didn't I used to say to people who asked that I supported Leeds and Liverpool? Isn't there a picture of me in a sandpit – aged eight – wearing a red football top? Or did I remove it from the album and tear it up?

My stories are full of holes.

Maybe Martyn's story is full of holes too. Maybe he did go to the final in 1975. But maybe he didn't see a Munich fan's face slashed open. Maybe he made that bit up the day he came back. It would have made him look good at school, and now he's told the story so many times he's stopped disbelieving it himself.

That's what it's all about.

I tell people I've seen Leeds play European away games in Belgrade, Madrid, Troyes and Eindhoven. But the Belgrade game was played in Holland. And I couldn't get a ticket for the Eindhoven game, even though I travelled. Half-truths. You can twist things – even invent things – and no one's going to pick you up on them. No one cares about how many times I've seen Leeds play in Europe, how many different countries I've seen them in. Except me. What's important is what I think of myself. That's what it's all about really.

LIVERPOOL v LEEDS UNITED Premiership
Saturday, 13 October 2001

Noon kick-off. Liverpool away. From the time you started supporting Leeds this was always the game you dreaded. In recent years Leeds have done well against Liverpool. Last season we beat them home and away. But it wasn't always like that.

At school there were Leeds fans and there were Liverpool fans. Late '70s, early '80s: on Monday mornings it was always the same. Liverpool had won and Leeds had lost and the Liverpool fans would take the piss. They were the best. They won the league every year and nobody ever beat them.

And you? You supported Leeds. And Leeds were shit. And it followed – at school – that if your football team was shit then you were shit too.

Liverpool supporters. They were always the weakest of the weak. People without character. You can see that now you're 34. It didn't occur to you then that they were so weak they needed to attach themselves to something strong to have any sense of self-esteem, to get themselves through their childhood.

You were weak too. You were somewhere around 13th out of 15 boys in class-credibility. But you would still come to school with your Leeds United pencil case. There were other Leeds fans of course, but most of them were too high in credibility to have anything to do with you. You were insignificant. You were among the weak. But the rest of the weak supported Liverpool.

Monday morning. You'd go into school. On the Friday, the last time you saw your 'friends', they'd said:

'We're gonna thrash you tomorrow, Leeds fan!'

'Three–nil.'

'I can't wait to take the piss out of you on Monday.'

And on the Saturday you'd listen to the match on your clock radio, a sick feeling in your stomach. One–nil. Two–nil. Three–nil. The final whistle. It was inevitable.

You hated Liverpool more than anything in the world. You hated all their players, their fans, the First Division titles they won year after year. You really could not see an end to it. This was the status quo. When they lost it was unnatural, like a crack had opened in the sky and you could see the backdrop for a moment. Even today, playing Liverpool, it seems part of the order of things that Leeds should lose.

After Leeds got promoted back to the big time, normal service was resumed. Leeds went to Liverpool and lost 3–0. At Elland Road Liverpool were 4 up within 20 minutes, although the game ended Leeds 4 Liverpool 5. Throughout all the years you had seen Leeds grab the odd draw, but never a victory over Liverpool. But early in the 1991–92 season, Steve Hodge having scored the only goal, you were surprised by the final whistle. You'd expected an equaliser. It was impossible that the game could end 1–0, impossible that there weren't another 20 minutes to play, impossible that the newsprint the next day would say Leeds 1 Liverpool 0. But that was how it was. And it was the best feeling, the most important game you'd ever been to. The world had turned on its head.

Less than a year later Leeds beat Liverpool 4–3 at Wembley. You were behind one of the goals. Like the rest of the Leeds fans there, you couldn't believe it. Leeds beating Liverpool at Wembley? What the fuck was going on?

Since then there have been more victories. The Double last season. And you'd never forget the day you met your wife: Alan Smith scoring on his debut. Liverpool 1 Leeds 3.

You decide to watch the match in Ilkley. You have to be there right after the game. For work. But you should have left earlier. In the traffic jam that snakes a mile into Ilkley you listen to the match. It's appalling. You feel anxious. This is not how you wanted to follow the game. Edging forward a few yards a minute you are becoming more and more frustrated. You need to get to the pub. You're missing everything. You have the feeling of distress you always have when you can't see what's going on. There is a man trying to get across the road in his Jeep. You slow down so he can cut in. It's Eirik Bakke! Definitely Bakke. But Bakke is taking a throw-in at Anfield and this is just an ordinary man. This happens to you all the time: you see Leeds players everywhere. The car in front has a sticker. You thought it was Leeds sticker, saying Leeds United. When you look closer it says 'Lease Direct'.

REASONS TO HATE LIVERPOOL
1 World domination throughout the '70s and '80s.
2 All the Liverpool fans I had to tolerate at school in Leeds.
3 They have Leeds's Champions League place.
4 They knocked Leeds out of the FA Cup last season.
5 I have hated them longer and more deeply than I have hated any other team.

In the pub you get a pint and stand at the back of 40 or 50 fans watching a large screen. The game is 25 minutes in. You put your pint on the side of the pool table. Rio Ferdinand scrambles to reach a wayward free kick and hoists the ball back into the box. You take your jacket off. The ball skims off the head of a Liverpool defender and falls to Kewell's feet. You stop taking your jacket off. It hangs from your arm. Kewell hits it. The ball deflects off two Liverpool players and settles in the back of the net. And, like most of the others, you shout like you're at the football. The camera is not on the referee. It even says 1–0 on the screen. And Liverpool are taking the ball back to the centre circle. It's real. It's 1–0.

Two groups of three lads by the pool table do not cheer. They look angry. They must be Liverpool. The bar is now thick with smoke as you watch the game on the small TV screen above the pool table. You can't see the big screen for people, some eating as they watch, all drinking. There is an easy atmosphere. It's not like watching Leeds in a city-centre pub where it can be fierce, everyone pissed up, part of a mob of 500.

You wonder what would happen if Liverpool scored. The six lads by the pool table would go up and cheer. You'd have to step back from them, disassociate yourself, just in case something happened. You've been in pubs – admittedly for Leeds–Man U games – where celebrating Man U fans have had to hide under tables from a shower of glasses and stools.

The half-time whistle goes. Liverpool 0 Leeds 1. The two lots of Liverpool fans swear and head for the bar.

During the break you sit outside on the benches. You hope the game carries on like this. You and your wife are meeting a friend and her boyfriend tomorrow. The boyfriend – Dom – supports Liverpool. If Liverpool turn it round you'll have to feel all those feelings again. Just like when you were a kid. You'll be thinking about him all day and night, what he's going to say. It'll be subtle. We're not kids any more. But knowing anyone who supports a team Leeds are playing is hard, especially if you have to meet them the next day.

You have to pass through the main part of the pub again to reach the screen. There are still 50 people crammed in at one end, watching the match. The rest of the pub is laid out with tables. A dozen old couples are eating Saturday lunch. A day out in Ilkley. The place stinks of boiled vegetables.

Back at the football end there is a hubbub of voices. Laughter. The odd shout of 'Come on Leeds!' But Liverpool are more in the game now. Phil Thompson is on the sideline shouting at them to get stuck in. It's inevitable, you think: it's Liverpool. It is right – it has always felt right – that Liverpool are superior. The ball hits the Leeds bar. Murphy pops up and heads it back into the empty net, Martyn on the ground. Four of the six lads by the pool table go up. One races to the TV screen and tries to touch the image of the celebrating Liverpool players. Then he turns to the Leeds fans and makes a mock Leeds United salute. But everyone has their back to him. Except you. You stare at him. He knows you're watching, but doesn't catch your eye. Then a boy of 10 or 11 runs through the bar, wearing a Liverpool top: 'LIV-ER-POOL . . . LIV-ER-POOL . . . LIV-ER-POOL . . .' You feel like you are being haunted by someone from your primary school. At the last minute you resist the temptation to stick your foot out and bring him down as he passes you.

Liverpool (0) 1 Leeds (1) 1

Martyn; Mills, Matteo, Ferdinand, Harte; Bowyer, Bakke, Dacourt, Kewell; Keane (Batty, 88), Viduka.
　　Scorer: Kewell

1 Leeds	8	12–3	18
2 Arsenal	8	18–5	17
3 Man U	8	25–14	17

On the radio, after the game, you hear that the Liverpool manager, Gérard Houllier, had been taken away from the stadium at half-time with chest pains. He's gone to hospital for surgery. The next day the papers are full of it. He's had an 11-hour operation on his aorta. Serious stuff. He could easily have died. But he's recovering now.

There are two voices in your head. The first is hoping that he gets better. This is just football and a human life is worth more than a stupid game like football. The second voice is denying that. It's saying that really you don't give a shit about Houllier. You don't want him to die. You wouldn't wish that. You've seen pictures of his wife going into the hospital. But – the second voice goes on – wouldn't it be good if he had to retire? Wouldn't it be good if Liverpool fell away? Leeds would have a much better chance of getting into the Champions League. We might even pick up one of the cups with Liverpool out of the way. But this is wrong, says the first voice, this is a man's health. The second voice comes back and says that one man's health might be worth Leeds United winning something. It's not like you have to press the button. It's not like you have to announce that's what you think. You can't deny it: a part of you is glad that Gérard Houllier is having trouble with his heart. And part of you is disgusted with yourself.

You don't say any of this to Dom the next day. You've met in the Cow and Calf in Ilkley. He says a 1–1 draw makes a change from the usual 4–0, 5–0 thrashings Liverpool give Leeds. You remind him that Leeds did the Double over Liverpool last year. He smiles. He's a Liverpool fan. He's thinking about the three trophies they won, that they beat Leeds on their way to winning the FA Cup, that his team is in the Champions League and yours isn't. He doesn't even need to mention it.

You're not so bothered because you can't keep your eyes off one of the men in the pub: he's 20 or so, good-looking, wearing a blue top. 'That's Paul Robinson!' you say. You remember seeing Eirik Bakke in Ilkley yesterday while he was in Liverpool playing for Leeds. It's happening again. What's that matter with you? Are you sick? You ask Dom: 'Is that Paul Robinson?' He thinks not. He goes to have a better look.

'I don't know,' he says. It is though.

Your wife thinks it is too.

CONFESSIONS OF A LEEDS FAN – PART FOUR
1983–84

My first away game without my parents was in the 1983–84 season. Shrewsbury. On the football special. Me and a mate went into Leeds and queued at the side of the station. The police and their dogs walked up and down the queue watching out for deviant behaviour, but not spotting all the cans of lager in bags that were banned on football specials. I had borrowed my dad's silver hip flask and filled it with the only drink from his cabinet that I could swallow: a sweet liqueur called Grand Marnier. I kept it in my inside pocket, shitting myself that the police would know, or that my dad would draw up in his car and point at the lower level of his liqueur bottle in front of hundreds of Leeds fans.

When the police let us on the train there was a mad rush by people who knew what they were doing and where they were going. We went to find seats in one carriage and were told 'Not here.' Everyone had their cans out, cards on the tables. The next carriage was half empty. When the police came down the train, cans went under seats and everyone looked out of the windows or studied their cards. I didn't dare get my hip flask out in the carriage. I was so terrified I'd be found out by the police and arrested. I decided to ditch it, so I went to the toilet and started to unscrew the cap. I'd get rid of the drink at least. Hide the empty bottle in my jacket lining.

There was a knock on the door.

'Open up! Police!'

This was it. I was 16 and I was going to be arrested for the first time. I opened up, frozen with fear, to see my old boss and half a carriage of can-waving Leeds fans laughing at me.

My old boss was my hero. He didn't know it, but I modelled my late teenage years on my idea of what he was. He went to every Leeds game. Home and away, a proper Leeds fan. And a hooligan. He'd been arrested for fighting. He had scars. I wanted to be like him. When Leeds were away in London we would have to get the milk delivered before 6 a.m. so he could set off with his mates to the match. We could do it in half the time if we wanted. While we were delivering he used to tell me stories about what he used to get up to at the football, stories about his mates getting arrested and his famous assault on Chelsea's new electronic scoreboard with a brick. He was a superman, everything I wasn't. But at least I knew him. And all my mates knew I knew him.

One Christmas I was looking for presents in Lewis's and I found him in the Leeds United department. He was a bit funny with me, like he didn't want to see me, so I left it. Maybe he only wanted to be associated with me on the milk-round. That was fair enough. I was only a kid, after all. He might not want to be seen talking to a kid in Leeds: one of his proper mates might see him. I knew that. A few days later – after we'd done the Christmas Eve round – he brought a present out from under the seat: a Leeds United tracksuit in a Lewis's bag. I wore it all Christmas. All January. All February.

When I was a bit older he started to let me go to away games with him and his mates. We'd finish the milk-round and head down to Salford Van Hire. He'd hire a furniture van then drive it up to City Square where 30 or 40 of his mates would pile in, all with off-licence bags full of lager and cider. And one bloke who used to drink Matteus wine. Then we'd be off.

On the way it'd get louder and louder in the back of the van. Occasionally the police would stop us and everybody would give false names and addresses. Except me. I was too scared to lie. If anyone needed the toilet they'd open the back doors of the van and put on a display for whoever was in the car behind.

Once we reached the town where Leeds were playing, we'd find a pub on the outskirts. Some would go to the pub. Others would go off, to come back later, a few of them bruised, a few of them missing. Then we'd go down to the ground. Everybody pissed. Except my old boss. There'd be a few skirmishes, but always someone there to look out for me.

One time in Grimsby two of their fans came after me and my old boss's second in command – who'd normally have nothing to do with me – jumped on them, banged their heads together and ushered me towards a turnstile. Inside, we'd hang on the walls, sing the worst songs, sometimes climbing over the ten-foot fences to invade the pitch. Then it would be back to Leeds. To the pubs where they drank.

I'd go along too. I'd just started drinking. They introduced me to the pubs. Yates's, when it was still on the other side of Boar Lane. The Whip. The Mucky Duck. The Madhouse. Places round The Calls and the market. And my favourite: The Precinct. Here I was, drinking in Leeds United pubs with the hardest Leeds fans in town. Now I really was a proper Leeds fan.

It was never a smooth ride on the football specials, but I liked it.

On the way back from Shrewsbury we stopped in a station packed with Chelsea fans, screaming at us and throwing stuff at the train.

Then at Newcastle they kept the Geordies in the pubs as they marched us through the town. You could see them in the bars, raging at us like caged animals. After the game we were ambushed, bottles and bricks flying over a wall at us.

At Barnsley the police herded too many of us into a pen and several people were nearly suffocated as they kept us waiting before letting us on the train. My jacket was torn to shreds on barbed wire up the side of the pen. I told my mum the truth about it, but she didn't believe me. They'd already had words with me for being a liar.

But I was never in real danger. When there was any proper trouble I would step back and watch, or run away. Once a coward, always a coward. After a while you could read it, see it coming: in pubs, at away games, everywhere. I was so terrified of getting hurt I would watch everyone just in case it was about to kick off. The two times I was in confrontations, I ran before anyone got within ten yards of me, racing halfway across town, out in front of buses to get away. But I liked to watch it. If there was somewhere good to watch from I'd be there.

Eventually my boss had to go away for a while and he sold the milk-round. Without him there it didn't seem right me hanging around with his mates. And I was scared of some of them. A family member told me later that my parents were relieved: they thought I was keeping bad company.

He sent me a letter when he was away. I kept it for years, like it was a used cup final ticket.

But me and my mates were still under his influence. Even after he'd gone away. We based our weekends on his model: bottles of Pils in The Precinct on Friday nights, then on to Yates's and all the rest. Screaming Leeds songs in the streets as we went, chants echoing from other streets in the city. Then Saturday. A few pints before Elland Road. The match, crammed into the Kop, riding up and down the steps. Then Friday night all over again: The Precinct, with its boxing ring at the far end, Yates's and the walk home through Harehills, writing 'Leeds United' on walls, screaming 'We are Leeds', 'Marching on Together' and 'Who's That Dying on the Runway?' until we got within hearing range of our parents' Roundhay houses. We were full-on Leeds United supporters then.

On the pitch meanwhile, Leeds were shit. It was hopeless. It came to a head in the FA Cup in 1984. We had to play Scunthorpe three times to decide who would get through to the Fourth Round. Once at Leeds, then two replays at Scunthorpe. My mates and me went to all three games. Leeds 1 Scunthorpe 1. Scunthorpe 1 Leeds 1. And finally, Scunthorpe 4 Leeds 2.

Leeds United '80s-style.

THIS TRIAL BEGINS NOW
Yorkshire Evening Post (16.10.01)

'This trial begins now,' says the prosecution in the second trial of Lee Bowyer and Jonathan Woodgate. Again the images of Bowyer and Woodgate fill the newspapers. And for several more weeks the evidence will be reported for a second time in the so-called Leeds United trial. The witnesses, the confusion over who bit who, who gave who a victory hug, whether Michael Duberry lied and – of course – the story of what happened to Sarfraz Najeib that night in January 2000. But there is less coverage, especially in the nationals. This is a story that has already been told. Only when the verdicts and the sentences come out will this grab the nation's attention again.

LEEDS UNITED v TROYES UEFA Cup
(Second Round, first leg)
Thursday, 18 October 2001

REASONS TO HATE TROYES
1 They are French.
2 They are an obstacle.

Troyes at home in the UEFA Cup, £12 a seat. You look around you. The stadium is full of families: mums, dads, kids. Every other kid is wearing a Leeds United jester hat: £15 from official retailers, or £5 from a couple of men outside the ground. Important merchandise to create the full experience for those coming to the game. The pitch of the support is several octaves higher than usual, like those schoolboy internationals they used to show on Grandstand.

You're not used to kids at the football. Behind you two girls are hanging from the front row of the upper tier, singing along with the Kop: 'Marching on together . . . We're gonna see you win . . .' It's nice. A party atmosphere. The kids' parents are smiling, talking to each other. And when Leeds score the first goal the kids scream and shout, throwing their bodies about. Then, the entire stadium – brought up on high-tech TV football – turns to watch the replay on the giant screen.

Leeds score a second before Troyes get one back. When Troyes score, a man emerges from the rows of children to reply to the celebrations of a small pocket of French supporters with a two-handed gesture. The stewards close in on him. This is not the South Stand as he knows it, they tell him. Today it is a family stand and they'd expect him to behave appropriately. No gestures. No aggression.

Leeds score again. At half-time it's 3–1.

In the break you go to the toilets, standing alongside boys half your height, as their fathers stand watching you. On your way out you see a familiar face: a Leeds fan you used to know. One of your old boss's mates from the '80s. He was a nutter back then, the one who smashed two Grimsby fans' heads together on your behalf. Today – like everybody in the South Stand – he is with a child. He catches your eye and looks away.

Back in the stand you see Seth Johnson leaving the pitch, dressed in a suit. While you were stood at the urinals, he signed his contract to join the cause.

'For when Bowyer goes down,' a voice behind you says.

Leeds score a fourth in the first minute of the second half. That's two goals for Viduka, two for Bowyer. A French player is sent off but it passes as if it hasn't happened. It's only fun to see a player go off when you know him: Ginola, Keown, Le Saux, Shearer, someone like that. Then you can abuse them as they make the long walk, look to see them turn round and gesture at the referee. But this sending off is meaningless. You don't know the player and the tie is over.

Leeds are cruising, saving energy now for Chelsea on Sunday. Time passes. Children around you are fidgeting, kicking the backs of their seats, empty plastic pop bottles around their feet.

Then Troyes score a second. The tie is not over after all. You can't go to France in two weeks and just enjoy yourself. Now there's something to play for. It's the first time Leeds have conceded two goals all season. As everyone leaves the ground there is an announcement over the Tannoy: Tel Aviv 2 Chelsea 0. A big cheer goes up. Everyone heads for the car parks happy.

Leeds (3) 4 Troyes (1) 2

Martyn; Mills, Ferdinand, Matteo, Harte; Bowyer, Bakke (Batty 66), Dacourt, Kewell; Keane (Smith 70), Viduka.

Scorers: Bowyer 2, Viduka 2

LET'S ALL LAUGH AT MAN U – NUMBER THREE
Man U 2 Deportivo la Coruna 3

You catch another Champions League game on ITV. After Man U's defeat in La Coruna you think it might be worth watching their home game against Deportivo.

Man U take an early lead. You wonder what you might do with the rest of your evening if Man U get a second. Your wife goes to answer the phone. Deportivo score. You cheer loudly so she can share your joy. You run downstairs when Deportivo score their second a minute later. She must be kept in touch with the game. This makes for good viewing. A fine way to spend the evening.

Then Man U score and the commentator says: 'They never give up, this lot!'

But the Man U defence looks rattled. Deportivo are still finding outrageous amounts of space down the flanks. The defence looks shaky.

How many goals have they conceded this season? And Barthez looks dodgy most of all. That first goal. He just ran past it and the Spaniard stuck it in. Then it happens again. Beautiful. A moment to savour. Barthez runs out of his box and straight past the ball. The forward just needs to slot it home. Man U 2 Deportivo 3. You celebrate. The camera homes in on the faces of the Man U players. Defeated. And it occurs to you that sometimes you get more pleasure out of Man U losing than Leeds winning.

LET'S ALL LAUGH AT MAN U – NUMBER FOUR
Man U 1 Bolton 2

Your wife's friend, Stu – a Villa fan – picks the two of you up from Staines station. You're visiting Stu and Lucy to meet their new baby, Olly. You shake his hand and settle on the back seat. Stu's hand, not the baby's, who you've been assured has not been named after Olivier Dacourt.

'Bolton are winning at Man U,' Stu says. 'Five minutes left.'

You ask him the other scores. Arsenal are drawing. Villa – his team – are losing. Leeds play Chelsea tomorrow. A win and Leeds would go three points clear.

'It's a good set of results for your lot,' Stu says.

At his house, pretending to look at the new baby, you see the final scores flick up on BBC1. Man U 1 Bolton 2.

And later that evening you catch the tail-end of *The Premiership* at another friend's house. Rickett's winning goal. You punch the air. The Bolton fans are singing: 'Can we play you every week?' to the Man U fans. The commentator picks up on it, laughing.

Twice in a week, the nation celebrates.

LEEDS UNITED v CHELSEA Premiership
Sunday, 21 October 2001

In the run-up to the Chelsea game, sections of the tabloid press brand six of the Chelsea players 'yellow'. Desailly, Le Saux, Petit, Gallas, Ferrer and

Gudjohnsen had all – given the choice by the club – chosen not to go to Israel to play Harpoel in the UEFA Cup, even though the battlegrounds of the Gaza Strip and the West Bank are a long way from Tel Aviv. Some players were allowed excuses: young babies, pregnant wives, toothache. The Chelsea manager, Ranieri, says, 'All the world is strange at present; no city is very sure.' Ken Bates – the Chelsea chairman – is not so impressed: 'I think we will have a bigger problem at Elland Road when we play Leeds than we'll face out here; more intimidating, probably.'

Chelsea played in Israel without the regular 'Fly Emirates' message on their shirts. A wise move. At home the press berated the six, but the Tuesday murder of an Israeli cabinet minister compounded Chelsea's anxiety.

In *The Telegraph* Giles Smith was behind them all the way:

> The question still remains: should Chelsea travel to Leeds tomorrow? My feeling is it's a matter of conscience for the individual . . . If he decided that, from his point of view, the dangers of the trip to Leeds were too great and the potential consequences too awful, then I think one would have to sympathise, or certainly respect his right to that opinion . . . [but] it's all very well to make out that Leeds is a special case. The problem is, one then sets a precedent. Before you know it, people will be refusing to go to perfectly nice places like Southampton and Derby . . .

Leeds City Station is busy when the London train arrives. It's just gone 1 p.m. There are a few men hanging around, in baseball caps with L.U.F.C. sewn gold on blue. The atmosphere is not normal. There's a tension in the air, police watching from the corner. People read the tabloids: 'FOWLER CAN LEAVE FOR £10M' and 'LEEDS BID £10M FOR FOWLER' on the back pages. Apparently Viduka is set to move to Roma and Fowler is being lined up at a cut-price fee, even though he scored a hat-trick for Liverpool the day before.

Groups of men make their way through the barriers from the platforms, most dressed in shirts and jackets. Quality stuff. Dark colours: slate grey, black. Some in yellow and blue shirts, 'Fly Emirates' across their chests. They have blank expressions on their faces, dead eyes: a pose, but it's effective. If one of them catches your eye you look away. Two or three stand to check text messages. They'll be meeting up with mates. Mates who've come on earlier trains or by car. There's nothing to say they're Chelsea fans. But it's obvious they're here for the football.

The police watch from a distance. There is no noise in the station. Only footsteps. There are no friends embracing at the barriers. No children dancing round their parents' feet. No teenagers in the Body Shop, Claire's Accessories, Paperchase. They have all moved on.

The men have made their way out of the station, some in Coopers, most down the concourse to Wetherspoons, suddenly full.

A blue Hackett T-shirt with a number three on the shoulder and back.

A red-and-white checked shirt under a Lacoste open-neck sweatshirt.

A blue baseball cap with logo. No lettering.

Four men in black jackets, all zipped up to the throat.

Burberry on shirts and scarves and baseball caps.

Tan jackets. Unzipped.

A discreet England crest on a baseball cap.

All the right clothes.

All the right colours.

All the right logos.

More trains arrive. Local trains. Leeds fans. Some in Strongbow shirts, some in the same clothes as the Chelsea fans. Small groups of men walk through the station without talking, out of the sliding doors and toward the pubs. One group stands under the awnings of the station, the rain falling inches from their polished shoes, staring out like a pack of lions on raised ground. Every one of them in a blue or check baseball cap. Every one of them silent, determined looks on their faces. A couple of nods and they step out into the rain. They walk across City Square and are gone. Other men jog through the square, stuffing sandwiches into their mouths, getting the hassle of food out of the way before they reach the pub.

Two police on foot make their way to Wetherspoons. They look purposeful. The bar manager meets them round the corner, out of sight of the drinkers. They are concerned about a group in the pub, in Stone Island jackets and jumpers. And one man with 'Fly Emirates' blue on white across his chest. He's huge: built like an oversized Kray twin, his chest puffed out. He stares hard at every face in the pub, blowing smoke into the air, waiting for each person to look away before he eyes someone else.

Another group of lads come in. Puffer jackets. More England baseball caps. An England logo on a blue sweatshirt. Again no words. Just gestures as they gather at the bar. They could be Chelsea. They could be Leeds. The bar is full.

REASONS TO HATE CHELSEA
1 Leeds hate Chelsea.
2 Jimmy Floyd Piggybank.
3 The 1970 FA Cup final, when I was three.

4 Their fans.
5 Their players.
6 Their chairman.

Even before kick-off the Leeds fans are having a go at the Chelsea players. They're soft southern bastards. They're a bunch of cowards. There are a few muted replies from the Chelsea end. Then the classic starts up, everybody's favourite:

> When I was just a little boy
> I asked my mother what should I be.
> Should I be Chelsea?
> Should I be Leeds?
> Here's what she said to me:

> 'Wash your mouth out son
> And go get your father's gun
> And shoot the Chelsea scum.
> Shoot the Chelsea scum.'

Everyone sings along with gusto. And before Chelsea get a chance to respond – maybe with their own favourite 'Ten men went to mow' – the Leeds fans are singing again:

> Six men wouldn't go, wouldn't go to Israel.
> Six men wouldn't go, wouldn't go to Israel.

Everyone in the Kop is laughing. There's no response from the away end. On the pitch Leeds are on top, coming at the Chelsea goal. After a booking for Le Saux (for a brutal tackle on Danny Mills) more songs: 'Le Saux takes it up the arse, Le Saux takes it up the arse . . .'

Nil–nil at half-time. For some reason David O'Leary is up in the director's box. The big screen shows him settling down to watch the second half. You learn after the game he'd been sent off. He'd objected to Le Saux's tackle on Mills and had a go at the referee.

The second half is equally tight: no space in midfield. Chelsea are getting to most of the 50–50 ball and Hasselbaink comes close to scoring. There's clearly no chance of a repeat of his visit last year when Leeds won 2–0 and the Kop sang 'Let's all laugh at Jimmy!' and 'Jimmy? What's the score?', much to everyone's – except Jimmy's – amusement.

After the final whistle, the Chelsea fans sing 'Small team from Yorkshire . . .

You're just a small team from Yorkshire.' The Kop replies 'When I was just a little boy . . .' And you look at the expressions of determination and hatred on the faces of those singing. There's a lot of tension today. It's Chelsea and you half expect something to kick off in the car parks. The fans have a history.

Outside there is something wrong. You see a few Chelsea shirts squeezing their way past the mass of Leeds and expect to see them attacked. At least goaded. But there's something else going on. A huge group – several hundred – is gathered around a big car. A Jeep or an Espace. It's hard to see. Thirty men and boys balance on top of a wall watching. At first you think it's Chelsea fans trying to get away early. Some men are banging on the windows of the car and shouting. But this is not regular football unpleasantness. There's been an accident. People are injured. The people in the Espace look nervous. Someone shouts 'FUCKING KILL THEM!' and there is a surge from the crowd – an eagerness. A police van is trying to force its way through several thousand people caught in the crush. Ambulances follow.

In the paper the next day there is not much to report. An accident. Three football fans were taken to LGI after the game. A 'fleet of ambulances' attended. Thousands of Leeds fans were held up as the injured were attended to.

Leeds (0) 0 Chelsea (0) 0
Martyn; Mills, Ferdinand, Matteo, Harte; Bowyer, Bakke, Dacourt, Kewell; Keane (Smith 76), Viduka.

1	Leeds	9	12–3	19
2	Arsenal	9	21–8	18
3	Man U	9	26–16	17

After the game David O'Leary expresses regret that the Le Saux tackle went unpunished. It should have been a red card, he says.

Ranieri – the Chelsea manager – disagrees. It was, he says, 'a normal English tackle between two English players', a statement that might explain why his squad is packed with foreign players. O'Leary takes the comment in good humour: 'He's a nice man,' he says of Ranieri, 'and his English is getting better, but maybe he needs to improve it a little bit.'

Two days later the FA have received referee Paul Durkin's report. They decide O'Leary was sufficiently punished spending the second half in the directors' box. And Durkin goes so far as to express regret: he 'misinterpreted' Le Saux's tackle. Le Saux, in the meantime, has written to both Mills and O'Leary. Letters of apology. He is a nice man, a sensitive man. He tells the press: 'I regret my actions after what has been a difficult week for me and everyone at Chelsea Football Club.'

CONFESSIONS OF A LEEDS FAN – PART FIVE
1989–1992

When I went away to study I went as far as I could from Leeds. My mum always said that you needed to get far away from your hometown if you wanted to get the best out of higher education. She was starting to regret saying that now: soon after I signed up at a college in Reading my second dad died. I was the last child at home. With me leaving, my mum was going to be on her own. But I still went to Reading. Not the university: some college where they took people who weren't good enough to go to universities. Full of failed home counties types. A Middlesbrough fan. And me.

It's only when you leave something behind that you realise how important a part of your life it is. The first night in a concrete hall of residence, while Leeds were about to play Oxford, I was meant to be in the bar getting drunk with my new friends, making sure I had some so I didn't get left out. But at 7.30 I slipped out. I managed to get an Oxford channel on the radio. This is the first home game I haven't been to for six or seven years, I thought. But it felt more like a punch in the stomach than a thought.

I could hear the noises of the Kop, all the songs, all the abuse aimed at the Oxford players. And I thought, what the fuck am I doing in Reading? I lived in Leeds. I lived in Leeds and I went to the football. That was what I did! That's who I was! But here I was in Berkshire. Why hadn't I got a season ticket? Here I was amongst a load of soft southern bastards – all guffawing in the bar, already getting off with each other, already making 'plans for the weekend' – and I was listening to my mates and all the other 24,000 Leeds fans on the radio singing 'We are Leeds' without me.

At half-time I went back to the student bar and tried to join in. People were closer, arms round each other. Everyone had a friend. Except me. I was alone and everybody knew it. Did everybody hate me? I didn't belong with them. I should be on the Kop, shouting abuse at southerners, not drinking with southerners. I had to get a refill several times to steady my nerves.

Back in my room the radio was recording the second half of Leeds versus Oxford. I'd go back at closing time and listen to it like it was live. But it was no good. You have to know the score, so at full-time I phoned my mum and got her to put Ceefax on.

'It was 2–1,' she said. Full-time.

At least we'd won. That was the main thing. But I felt bad too, not like I was used to feeling when Leeds had won.

'How are you settling in?' she said.

'I love it,' I lied.

The first term, up to Christmas, I probably only went back for four games. I had to be tough with myself. Enforced withdrawal. Make my mum think I was happy, so she only had herself to worry about. But going back for Christmas, back to Elland Road, back to the pubs in the centre, back to my mum, I knew there had to be a change. I hated Reading. I hated everybody there. I would save all my money and drive back to Leeds every other week. I had a car. Petrol was cheap. I'd work like fuck for ten days, not go out, then go back to Leeds and spend my grant there.

I made friends with the Middlesbrough fan. He was even more desperate to get out of Reading than I was. Mick. The one sane person in the asylum. We travelled back up the M1 together. Shared the cost. It was routine. Every other weekend we'd head north. He'd go and watch Boro. I'd go and watch Leeds.

Two-thirds of the way through the season – with Leeds chasing for promotion – my mum called me. The club had put tickets for the last six home games on sale. The ticket office would open the next day. What were we going to do? There was no way I could get back and queue tomorrow. And she was ill, coming down with something. But I needed tickets. The next day she stood in the queue with the rest of them for three or four hours so I could see Leeds's last six games in Division Two, so I didn't miss out just because I lived in Reading.

I got a season ticket for my second and third years at Reading. There was no point trying to pretend to her that I was going to integrate at college any more. Stuff that. I wanted to be back in Leeds as much as I could. And Leeds were back in the big time now. I'd never seen a Leeds team finish fourth. I'd never seen a Leeds team win anything. I hadn't thought it was part of the deal. Supporting Leeds was about being a Leeds fan, about worshipping players like Ian Baird and Glynn Snodin, not about winning.

I'd been to every home game in 1991–92, but we won the league away: at Sheffield United. Still, I had to be in Leeds that weekend. Just in case it happened. And I wanted to see my mum. She'd been ill for some time. Something to do with her eyes. And she was losing weight. After all the years of going to Elland Road together, we sat down and watched Sheffield

United versus Leeds. End to end and in the end satisfying. A 3–2 win. Then it was Man U at Liverpool. If Man U blew it we were champions.

My mum knew how much this meant. Like every other Leeds fan, I'd been waiting years for this. Eight years in the Second Division and suddenly Leeds were ninety minutes away from winning the title.

The game kicked off.

Liverpool scored early. But you couldn't get your hopes up. It had to be two. Two–nil and you could start to celebrate.

My mum was sat quietly on the sofa next to me when Liverpool scored again. The dog left the room: it didn't like excitement. My mum hugged me. This was the moment I had been living for for years. And I was glad she was there with me. After all those games together watching Leeds lose to Stoke and Sunderland and Shrewsbury . . .

And there I was, crying again.

Two months later my mum was dead. There hadn't been anything wrong with her eyes after all, it was liver cancer.

'I'D RATHER NOT KNOW ABOUT FOOTBALL ANY MORE . . .'
Yorkshire Evening Post (26.10.01)

A former Leeds fan tells the court that after seeing the assault on Sarfraz Najeib he no longer goes to Elland Road. He doesn't think he'll be welcome. He wishes he'd never heard of Leeds United. He was unhappy giving evidence, and he's unhappy that his sons have been getting grief at school because their father is trying to do the right thing in court. He saw Jonathan Woodgate that night. Now he wishes he'd never heard of him.

The Yorkshire press are still covering the trial in depth. You have to admit that it doesn't look good for Bowyer and Woodgate. Half of you feels like they should get what they deserve. If they did it. The other half wants the trial over, the players free and Leeds United unfettered and champions.

But the trial would come to an end soon. Just before Christmas. And you wouldn't believe the impact it would have once it was over. You'd have thought things could only get better once the two-year saga was over.

MANCHESTER UNITED v LEEDS UNITED Premiership
Saturday, 27 October 2001

'Which pub are you going to? The Rose and Crown?' Damaris, Martyn's wife, wants to know where we're going to watch the noon kick-off: Man U v Leeds from Old Trafford.

'No. It's unlucky,' says Martyn. 'We'll be in The Star. We always lose when I go to the Rose and Crown.'

'Yes,' she says. 'I'm sure it's because of which pub you watch the match in, nothing to do with David O'Leary.'

REASONS TO HATE MAN U
1 Their supporters.
2 Their players.
3 Their manager.
4 Their stadium.
5 Their city.

The curtains are closed in The Star. The lights are off. It's hard to acclimatise coming in from the bright street, leaving behind day-trip families and couples walking by the river. A thick fog of smoke already, there are 30 or 40 stood at the bar. You get two pints each and sit at a free table next to the screen.

The game starts badly, Man U at Leeds from the first kick. But Leeds defend well. They've learned how, playing all those fancy European sides last year. And they did it at Arsenal, soaking up an hour of pressure before snatching the three points.

You look around the pub. The Star is different to The Rose and Crown on the other side of the road where you watched Liverpool away. No old couples eating their Saturday lunch. No smell of boiled cabbage. Here there is a sign on the board saying NO FOOD. This is a serious pub where you come to watch the match and nothing else.

At half-time Martyn talks. During the game he was quiet, just staring at the screen. There was nothing to say. You tend to witter on through matches, trying to find an outlet for your nervous energy. He sits there like an unexploded bomb. But the break gives him a chance. He was worried at the beginning. Man U were all over us. But as the game went on Leeds got more and more into it. He's saying what you're feeling: maybe we won't lose.

Two more pints each and the second half is better, Leeds taking the initiative. And Man U are hesitant. The fans in the pub are getting behind the team. Every time a Man U player screws up there are hand gestures. Every time Beckham comes on the screen, shouting. A row of five children – two boys and three girls – sit watching the men watching the screen. You wonder whether their mother has brought them here as part of their education.

Beckham scythes Robbie Keane down. Keane is not happy and lunges at Beckham, pushing him to the ground. The Leeds fans show their approval. But the referee is talking to Keane. It looks dodgy, a sending-off offence certainly. But he gets away with a yellow card and Leeds are still in the game.

It might be end-to-end stuff, but it is difficult to watch. You feel tense. However much lager you drink you can't shake your unease, even though Leeds do look the better team.

Leeds get a free kick. You expect to see Harte lining it up, but Keane lofts it quickly over the wall. It's there. GOAL! Somehow you have prised yourself from behind your table, climbed over some seats and are in the middle of the pub dancing around with the other fans. Leeds are one up at Man U. You search for Martyn's face. Why isn't he celebrating? You spot him frowning, still sat down.

'The ref hadn't blown,' he says. 'It has to be taken again.'

Everyone sits down.

'YEEEEAAAAAAHHHHHHHH!' This time it counts. Viduka finds a bit of space and hits it past Barthez. Goal! A real goal. There is more dancing. Prolonged dancing. You, Martyn and 40 others.

Then the tension kicks in.

'Twelve minutes,' says Martyn.

Forty fans sit with serious looks on their faces. It's as if there hasn't been a goal at all, as if Leeds have gone one down. The seconds tick away. Leeds try for a second. Maybe we can kill the game. But this is Man U and you know what will happen next. Everyone knows really. Solskjaer comes on and Man U come at Leeds. More like they were in the first half. Every attack is painful. You can feel it in your guts, in the muscles under your stomach fat. You feel sick. No one is drinking. They are just staring at the screen.

Two minutes to go. A cross from the left. And there is little Solskjaer. A foot taller than the 6 ft 3 in. Leeds defenders. The ball loops over Nigel Martyn. You have your hands over your face. You can hear the cheering of the Man U fans on the TV. You hope that Martyn will tap you on the shoulder, tell you it's been disallowed and that it's the Leeds fans cheering. But he doesn't. One–one.

Man U come at Leeds again. This is just like them. They do it week after week, year after year. They play for 95 minutes. Another cross. Matteo heads it towards his own goal. It hits Nigel Martyn's shins and somehow he gathers it.

Again and again. It's just a matter of time, you think. Where did the referee get four minutes of injury time from? Did he have to consult Alex Ferguson first?

Yet another attack. The ball travels at the same angle and pace as Solskjaer's goal. But Nigel Martyn touches it away and Danny Mills shepherds it to safety.

The final whistle brings disappointment and relief. A draw at Man U is a draw at Man U. And it could have been worse.

Man U (0) 1 Leeds (0) 1
Martyn; Mills, Ferdinand, Matteo, Harte; Bowyer, Bakke, Dacourt, Kewell (Smith 90); Keane, Viduka (Batty 71)
   Scorer: Viduka

1	Villa	10	17–8	21
2	Leeds	10	13–4	20
3	Arsenal	10	22–9	19
4	Liverpool	9	17–9	19
5	Man U	10	27–17	18

TROYES v LEEDS UNITED, UEFA Cup
(Second Round, second leg)
Thursday, 1 November 2001

The moon hangs over the runway at Leeds–Bradford airport. Inside people wander aimlessly, staring at the departures board, browsing in WH Smith. Some are here for the London shuttle. Some wheel holiday suitcases through the departure gate. One group is gathering at the check-in desk: women in their 30s, men in their 40s and 50s, their voices filling the airport concourse. Several solitary men watch from benches or half-hidden behind pillars. Four men go by, dressed in expensive suits and ties, walking in step with each other. Commuters. Confident.

'Leeds United?' one of the suits says. The others nod and smile.

The recommended check-in time has passed, but people are still arriving. So far there are no hordes of drunken beasts. No young men shouting. A man walks through one of the doors. He looks like Des Lynam, well groomed, wearing a poppy and a navy-blue scarf, a subtle Leeds

United badge. He holds the door open as a small woman pushes her husband into the departure hall. He is wearing the Leeds United blue away kit, a scarf hanging from his wheelchair.

These are the supporters of Leeds United. From places all over the UK: Bristol, London, Cumbria, Guiseley, Denholme, all converging on Leeds–Bradford airport to join a day trip to northern France, to watch Leeds United. A man, dishevelled and tired, with a brilliant white Leeds scarf draped around his neck. Two younger men who look like Oxford dons: tall and uneasy, one with a Leeds United scarf stuffed in his duffel coat pocket. Three fat skinheads in baseball caps getting coffee from the Klix vending machine. A middle-aged couple in matching Leeds tops.

You're not quite as relaxed as the rest of them look. You don't like airports. You've had bad news at airports. And you don't like flying. You always have to grip the hand of the person next to you, be reassured by them that you're not going to die in a narrow tube of fire thousands of feet above the world, that you're not going to have to scramble over people's seats, punching them out of the way, when the captain says 'BRACE! BRACE!' But you can't grab anyone's hand today. Your mother is not here. Nor your wife. And – surrounded by 200 Leeds fans in front of whom you have to look laid back – you won't be able to whine or sweat or watch the wings for cracks and the engines for flames. You're going to have to sit tight and tell yourself you're more likely to get killed crossing the road, or that it would be better to die in a moment of extreme pain and fear than waste away for months or years unvisited in a care home.

You never liked flying.

And now there are some younger men. The kind of people you might expect to see following Leeds in Europe. The kind you saw in Heerenveen and Madrid. They look determined, some in Leeds tops, some displaying logos: Duffer, Quiksilver, Stone Island. They head straight for the check-in.

A woman with a Leeds United jester hat. A tall man, shaven-headed, wearing a Burberry baseball cap. A man and his two grown sons. A boy with his mother and father. An overweight lad with a Leeds United holdall. Lads with mad eyes. Another man in a wheelchair. Two girls walking close together. A lone man standing on the fringes writing in a notebook. All queue to join flight BY802A to Reims.

In the lounge – airside – there are dozens of Leeds supporters having breakfast, buying newspapers and magazines, playing the slot machines. Others stare out across the tarmac. It's light now, a cold grey morning on the first day of November.

A mobile phone goes off to the tune of 'Here we go with Leeds United . . .'

Leeds fans – still half asleep – slump in the seats, leafing through the pages of the *Mail*, the *Telegraph*, *The Sun*. People have been up for hours. Some have driven overnight to be here.

It's only 7.30 a.m. but the bar is filling up, men knocking back bottles of Budweiser and pints of Guinness. Theirs are the only audible voices in the sleepy departure lounge.

A policeman surveys everyone, holding his machine gun firmly with both hands, security tight after 11 September. They are about to call the passengers to flight BY802A.

A writer waits for his plane to take off. Outside the snow is heavy, but he's not worried. He's sure the aircrew have everything under control. The first take-off is abandoned. The writer watches through the window, a huge arc of slush cast across the runway as the plane makes its way back to the terminal. They try a second time, but have to abort again. And the writer joins the rest of the passengers back in the terminal building. There will be a delay. It is not safe to take off yet.

Eventually – its passengers back on board – the plane makes its third attempt, this time accelerating down the length of the runway. But the writer knows there's something wrong. They should be in the air by now. He speaks to the man next to him, glimpses the perimeter fence of the airfield coming towards them through the snow and feels a blow to the back of his head. At first he thinks someone's playing a trick on him, fooling about. Then he hears a terrible sound. A crack. The plane is shaking violently, something crashing through the floor of the fuselage. He watches, confused. The noises are appalling. He tries to make sense of them: hammering, tearing, grinding, but these are noises far louder than he has heard before. He loses consciousness.

The plane overshoots the runway and hits a house. A wing is torn away and the house catches fire. The next obstacle is a hut: the back of the plane is sliced off along with the remaining wing. The main body of the plane moves forward at high speed. Some of its passengers are already dead. Some unconscious. Some have their eyes wide open. A man is thrown forward through the plane, somersaulting. Another man is flung from the plane, still strapped to his seat, 100 yards away in a field.

The undercarriage is torn away and the plane is battered and punctured by trees as it spins until it finally stops. Smoke rises from the house, the hut and the pieces of shattered fuselage.

The plane reeks of petrol – it could go up at any moment. Those alive and able to move are on their feet, stumbling and confused. They have got out, but they know there are others still in there, so they go back. The first of them goes in to emerge with a child of two, its face bruised and bleeding. Its mother appears beside him and takes her child. She holds it to her chest and sobs. It's a miracle!

But nearby are the dead and dying. One man trapped under a wheel of the plane. Unbearable pain.

The writer remains unconscious. His head has been cracked open. Several of his bones are smashed, his tibia and fibula sticking out through his trousers, his knee bent back grotesquely, his elbow pulped. He will probably die.

Those on their feet pull broken bodies from the wreckage as fire crews desperately try to stop the plane blowing up.

Later, at a nearby hospital, 11 arrive in a line of ambulances. Some will live and some will die.

Back in their hometown word is out. Mothers, wives, girlfriends, fathers, children and friends of the dead and dying (and those lucky enough to be alive) are fraught. They know there have been deaths, but they don't know whose.

A woman is told her husband – the writer – is not on the list of survivors. She sits with her two sons. Then she is told that he is alive. Unconscious, but alive. Another miracle!

A man in Leeds hears of the disaster and is told that his brother is dead. He travels home to Tyneside to be with their mother, only to see a newspaper sign saying his brother has survived. He and his brother will go on to help England win the 1966 World Cup. His brother is Manchester United's Bobby Charlton. He is Leeds United's Jack Charlton.

Matt Busby survives too. Just. He is under the knife for hours, needs constant care and oxygen. He lies in a plastic tent for days then weeks. When he is well enough they tell him that eight of the team that he built – the team which won the English Championship in 1956 and 1957 and reached the European Cup semi-finals in 1957 and 1958 – are dead.

The last man to leave hospital in Munich is the writer. He can go home to his wife and two sons. His book *The Day a Team Died* has you in tears. You, the one who sang 'Who's that Dying on the Runway' and 'Always Look on the Runway for Ice' with gusto. The one who (at 13) wrote the names of 8 dead footballers on your plastic football as a joke: Geoff Bent, Roger Byrne, Eddie Colman, Duncan Edwards, Mark Jones, David Pegg, Tommy Taylor, Billy Whelan.

You, who can be 99 per cent sure you'll not sing those songs again.

In 2000 history nearly repeated itself. The young and promising Leeds United team were seconds away from a similar fate.

'Everyone on board could see the flames and the explosion,' says Peter

Ridsdale, 'and everyone seemed to be shouting "There's a fire!" . . . we had just taken off.'

A hundred and fifty feet up, the right engine on fire, a plane full of fuel. Forty passengers, eighteen footballers. But history would not repeat itself.

The pilot had struggled to bring the plane back onto the runway. He had half a minute to land it. He would say the next day, 'I dread to think what would have happened.' If he hadn't got the plane down, he means. 'You would have been talking about a major explosion and I think almost certainly fatalities.'

The plane hit the tarmac, left the runway, bounced two or three times before stopping. The nose wheel and undercarriage collapsed on impact. The plane came to a halt just 300 yards from the perimeter fence.

David O'Leary was on his feet, trying to force the emergency exit, hurting his shoulder, but managing to marshal everyone to safety. Fuel from the tanks spilled out onto the grass. The plane could have gone up at any moment.

'I could feel the heat on my right shoulder,' says Ridsdale, describing his escape from the plane.

The next day the papers are full of images of the plane off the runway, nose down into the earth, the front wheel broken away, the charred engine of the small plane just a few feet from the row of empty oval windows.

'After seeing the pictures this morning,' says Ridsdale, 'it makes me feel even more shaken at the thought of what could have happened.'

Your plane is in the air: a smooth take-off, 300 Leeds fans en route to Troyes. The man across the aisle is talking to you. He's had – he says – three pints in the bar already. He's a graphic designer and a big Leeds fan. He's sharing his opinions with you. He thinks Duberry is a welsher and that £185 for this trip is a rip-off. He wants to know how you feel to be the only white man from Keighley and whether you have to keep lots of copies of the Koran at Bradford Library, where you work. He talks to the two women in front. They work for Leeds United. He wants to know if they're single. They're not, they tell him. After everything he says, he laughs, cackling in their faces. They look uneasy, but they tolerate him. He turns to you again. He's pointing at the stewardess.

'Look at that!' he says. 'Have you seen her tights?'

She is only two yards from him, no doubt listening.

When his attention is with the women again, the man behind you leans forward and mutters, 'You'll not be wanting to sit with that cunt all day.'

Reims airport is tiny, like landing in a farmer's field, the terminal no bigger than the south stand at Elland Road. There are three buses and a police escort waiting for you.

The buses move off. Two police bikes at the front, a police car at the rear. The Leeds United representative hands out our match tickets and asks the fans to listen to some points he has to make. This, he says, is the biggest match in the history of Troyes. They're not used to this level of football. And the police, he has been led to believe, are a little edgy: they've heard about Leeds fans. They're a bit like the Italian police, he says. There's a general murmur and someone shouts from the back of the bus: 'Act first, ask questions later.'

The man nods. 'That's right,' he says. He wants us to have a good time, so the best thing we can do is not give the police a chance to react. Then he hands out 'The Leeds United Travelling Fan's Guide to Troyes'.

The week before the club trumpeted the guide on their website, firing press releases out to the media: 'Whilst the media has obsessed about a minority of fans causing trouble, the vast majority of Leeds fans act sensibly and are there to enjoy the football and the culture of wherever they are playing . . .' It is a guide to what Troyes has to offer, seeing as the club will be dropping us in the town centre seven hours before kick-off. It recommends the cathedral and some of the churches, art galleries, the better buildings of Troyes. It offers solutions to the fan who might find himself in trouble: there are local phone numbers and ideas on what to do if you lose your passport. There is also a message from Peter Ridsdale. 'Whenever we travel abroad,' he says, 'we take the good name of Leeds United with us . . . Please have respect for the people and culture of Troyes.'

Everyone is reading the guide. The man at the front draws our attention to the map. He points out the station, the stadium, the place where the most bars will be open. There are noises of approval. The Useful Phrases section draws particular attention. Leeds fans practise their French.

'Une biere . . .'

'Pardon.'

'Une biere s'il vous plaît.'

'Ou est la toilette?'

'Je suis un supporter de Leeds.'

'Nous sommes les Champions . . . les Champions d'Europe.'

'Qui a mange tous les pâte en croute?'

During the rest of the coach journey several cars with English number plates overtake, beeping their horns, right-arm salutes through open windows. An electric road sign informs drivers that they should take Junction 32 for the Troyes–Leeds football game.

As we pull up at the ground – a small but tidy modern stadium – four cars empty and a dozen or more men stand in the street staring into the coaches. None are wearing colours. They are waiting for their mates. They look hard, arms folded, hands in pockets. But the bus moves on. We are going to be dropped in the town centre. The men get into the four cars and follow.

The streets of Troyes are quiet. It's a bank holiday: All Saints Day. There are few people about: couples out walking, people with dogs, families staring out of restaurant windows, their first sight of the guests of their city. And a woman in her 80s, dressed head to foot in black, sitting on a park bench drinking from a bottle of lager.

Like it said in the Leeds United Travelling Fan's Guide to Troyes, this is a nice place: narrow cobbled streets, half-timbered sixteenth-century houses. Like York. From the main shopping streets you can disappear down narrow lanes into small courtyards to find gardens and churches surrounded by tightly packed houses. A canal cuts through the town and the cathedral stands huge, catching the sun. This is a place with a sense of history, the streets named after writers – Zola, Barbusse, Hugo – and politicians – de Gaulle and Clemenceau.

There is little sign of a Leeds United presence on the streets of Troyes. Nor is there much sign of a local presence. None of the shops are open. Few of the bars. No cars, no trucks, no bikes. In the odd back street, clusters of Leeds fans are gathering. They talk in loud voices that break the silence in the narrow meandering lanes. They are making their presence felt. The French walk by, interested, but not alarmed. At least three camera crews are trawling the streets, looking for action.

In the Place Alexandre Israel there is already the sound of chanting. It's 2 p.m. Two large bars are spilling Leeds fans out into the street, tables covered already in empty plastic glasses and beers. This is the meeting place, fans embracing with exaggerated gestures, calling out in loud voices. Some locals, driven to the edge of the square, stand and watch. Others talk to the Leeds fans. There are friendly gestures. It's good humoured, a happy atmosphere.

On another side of the square a large black bus – its screens down – waits. Inside, 20 to 30 police are resting. Next to the black bus, two mini-buses. Again full of police. One waiting officer reads a copy of *Le Monde*. Another leafs through a porn mag.

Troyes Cathedral is spectacular. Instantly calming. Huge pillars stretch up and arch across to support the ceiling, a beautiful round window casting multicoloured light through the dusty chasm above. The two Oxford dons – one with a Leeds scarf still hanging out of his pocket – are walking round, gazing up. A family of four, with two young children, the boy wearing a Leeds United top, point out the icons and pictures in the half light: a family holiday to watch Leeds United in France. And a man you saw on the plane over here lights a candle at the feet of the Virgin.

Back in the main square the Leeds fans have been at it for hours. Some are having a piggyback race. Some are in a circle, chanting: 'Glory, glory, Leeds United. Glory, glory, Leeds United . . .' The locals – more of them out on the streets now, taking the bank holiday air – watch in amusement: couples, old women, girls, families, groups of lads in zip-up jackets. They watch from the benches on the other side of the square, from the steps of the Hotel de Ville, from shop doorways. The sun has gone down behind the buildings, lighting only the spires of the cathedral. Everything else is in shadow. The air has gone cold.

One fan can feel the beer kicking in. He's been drinking for a couple of hours and he doesn't feel as keyed-up as he did for the first hour and a half. He wants something to happen. He's watching the vans of police on the other side of the square. He likes to see a bit of trouble when he comes all this way for the football. He'd like to start goading the police, encourage a few people to throw bottles. Then there'd be a confrontation. They've come all this way. They've been drinking together for hours. They're on foreign soil. It's inevitable, he thinks. And he wants it to happen now. He's noticed that the tone of the singing has changed. No more 'We are Leeds' and 'Glory, Glory Leeds United'. Now it's:

> We fucking hate the French
> We fucking hate the French
> We fucking hate
> We fucking hate the French.

And he thinks it's just a matter of time before his wish comes true.

But not every Leeds fan is in the main square drinking. Restaurants up and down the streets around the square are packed with small groups of English – men, women, children, eating over bottles of wine. Some still walk round the cathedral, disappointed that all of the other churches are shut. Likewise the museums and art galleries. Some wander the streets taking photos of buildings, the elegant police HQ, the Hotel de Ville. Some sit by the canal talking.

The locals still watch with amusement in the main square. A group of tourists on a guided tour can't hear their guide for the noise from the bars full of Leeds fans. And something is going on in the pub on the near side of the square. The police are on their way. A man in another bar calls his mate there. There's a couple of police vans coming your way, he warns. But it's only the Police Municipal. They are not as mean as the Police National.

They're there to keep the peace. That's all. They talk to a few of the Leeds fans, make gestures – like a referee – that the fans should cool it. There are a few words, then the shaking of hands.

The Police National – the heavy squad – watch from the other side of the square. They have put down what they were reading. It could be about time: this is, after all, what they are here for. Their *raison d'être*.

Two groups of North African-looking lads watch from the steps of the Hotel de Ville and a shop doorway. They are dressed in similar gear as some of the Leeds fans, but it's all Puma. No one from Leeds wears Puma. The lads are winding each other up, cocky. But they are kids. They look tough on their own, but when one of the Englishmen walks by, they appear suddenly wiry and boyish. They will watch. That's all. They might learn a thing or two. And they like the buzz in the air. It's exciting.

The two main bars have stopped serving. They have closed their doors and are sweeping up the debris inside. Half-a-dozen Leeds fans are despatched to find beer and come back with huge turquoise bags full of cans and bottles, like heroes returning with the kill. A hundred men gather in a large circle, holding their cans and bottles in the air: 'We're All Going on a European Tour' . . . 'Stand Up if you Hate the French' . . . 'Glory, Glory Leeds United' . . . 'Super Leeds' . . . 'We are Leeds'. . . 'Marching on Together'.

The French – before leaving – have their photographs taken with the Leeds fans in the background, sightseers in their own town. But the crowds are thinning out, fans making their ways to smaller bars near the stadium, flags no longer tied to the scaffolding by the bar, now draped over shoulders. Some stand up alleys, a stream of piss coming back into the square. There is nowhere to drink here. People are on the move. Just like the last time Leeds United played football in France.

It's 1975. Leeds are playing Bayern Munich in the final of the European Cup, in Paris. The game started well for Leeds as they overran the Germans. But a bar hit, a disallowed goal and a dead cert penalty turned down all colluded against Leeds and Munich went on to score twice, leaving a sour taste in the mouth of the Leeds fans and accusations that the referee was bent.

During the match, plastic seats and flagpoles, bottles and lightbulbs from the state-of-the-art scoreboard are hurled down from the stands.

After the game, as the Leeds fans leave the stadium, some have running battles with the Germans – overturning cars, smashing up coaches, looting a local supermarket – still thinking about the Lorimer offside, how Leeds had been cheated again. A boy of 13 tells a reporter: 'I smashed a few shop windows. I was so mad at being cheated out of the Leeds goal.'

Whatever anybody said, Leeds fans had taken part in one of the worst cases of football hooliganism seen in Europe. But the Leeds manager, Jimmy Armfield, defended the rioters: 'There has been a trend,' he said, 'in recent years towards over-enthusiasm, because football in England to a lot of people is a way of life; they get involved and support us from the heart. European competitions just bring out the exuberance in them.' Echoes of Bill Shankly's famous 'Some people think football is a matter of life and death . . . I can assure them it is much more serious than that,' dismissed on Merseyside after Heysel and Hillsborough.

Leeds fans are seen returning to Leeds City station, their anxious parents, wives and girlfriends standing at the gates. In Calais there are more supporters waiting to catch boats home – trapped by the striking French – hundreds of them, sleeping on the ground like a retreating army.

The final score: 300 seats broken, 1 TV camera beyond repair, a looted supermarket, 13 complaints from the public, 80 treated for injuries. The reports of two dead German fans are unfounded.

The *Yorkshire Post* concludes its coverage with 'There is one corner of a foreign city which may, alas, be forever sorry that Leeds United's lunatic fringe paid a visit.'

The Bar L' Agora – Troyes – is one of the few not packed with Leeds fans. It's ten minutes from the main square, on a dark street of parked cars. There is a scarf on the wall: 'Troyes–Leeds Tour Coupe 2001–02' and singing from a dozen men at the bar: 'Estac! Estac! Estac!' Esperance Sportive Troyes AC: the name for the Troyes football team.

It's a North African bar. Except for two Leeds fans, who look young and small compared to the men in the square. They've had enough of the singing and the aggressive man at the bar shouting 'AL-GE-RI-A! AL-GE-RI-A!' at the top of his voice. They get up to go, but a man stops them.

'You go to the match?'

'Yes,' says one of the lads. He points to his shirt. 'Leeds United.'

'You cry today. After Estac.' The man gestures tears running down his cheeks.

The Leeds fans smile and edge towards the door.

'After the game you come back here. We drink. Yes?'

The Leeds fans nod. But their faces betray fear and the men let them go.

With the Leeds fans gone, the men turn on each other, playfully pushing and shoving until a fight breaks out between two of the older men. An unexpected explosion of violence. They are pulled apart. One is the man who was shouting 'AL-GE-RI-A'. His friends sit him on the pool table and tell him to calm down. After a minute, he approaches his adversary and kisses him gently on the lips. Then suddenly they are all chanting again: 'ESTAC! ESTAC! ESTAC!' An older man, apart from the main group, dances in the middle of the room, moving like a belly dancer to the sound of their chanting. Behaviour more insane than anything the visiting hundreds from Leeds have served up so far.

Back in the main square the two large bars have long been shut. There is debris everywhere: cans, bottles, bags, cigarette butts and packets.

An old couple come round the corner and see the mess.

'Mon Dieu!' says the woman.

A girl slips on a heap of discarded chips. Her father catches her.

From somewhere comes the sound of Leeds fans singing. Muted. It could be a memory of the chanting before, like music still playing in your head after you've left a club. On the corner of the square 300 Leeds fans are packed into a bar with full-length windows. This is where the chanting is coming from. Everyone faces a man who is stood on a chair at the centre of the bar, leading the singing. The flags from the scaffolding are pinned against the windows. And the tone has changed again.

> Fuck' em all
> Fuck 'em all
> The long and the short and the tall
> For we are United
> And we are the best
> We are United so fuck all the rest.

Inside it's so loud the staff look startled as they serve men who stay at the bar and pass back a stream of beer. It's hot. Impossible to get served unless you are part of the system, each bartender monopolised by one person apparently buying drinks for 10 . . . 20 . . . 30 people. The air stinks of beer and cigarettes. The atmosphere is good-humoured. This is a celebration. No one has started any trouble.

Outside French families stand and watch. Some have their faces right up to the window so they can peer inside, as if they are looking at an exhibit in a zoo. This is a new attraction on their evening promenade, different to window-shopping and greeting friends. The Leeds fans stare out, clapping in perfect synchronisation, seamlessly delivering song after song:

> Rule Britannia
> Britannia rules the waves
> Britons never never never shall be slaves.

Outside tickets are changing hands, two Frenchmen the centre of attention.

You order two beers. 'We are Leeds' fills the bar. In the stadium we will point emphatically at the opposing fans: 'We are Leeds [POINT], We are Leeds [POINT], We are Leeds.' Now we point at the men behind the bar. They look terrified. You notice the top of a tree outside moving from side to side on the far side of the crowd.

A man appears next to you, the first person you've spoken to in two hours of drinking. He tells you he's Romanian and shows you a picture of three children. He wants money to send home to his family. You ask him how long he has been in France, but he doesn't understand. He can speak French, Spanish and German, but his English is not strong and you speak only English. You give him some money. He is delighted. He repeats that he is from Romania and asks if you know Hagi. Hagi: the greatest Romanian footballer ever, one of the best European players of the last decade. He says it again, louder: 'Hagi.' You urge him to be quiet, not to mention Hagi. He smiles. Georgie Hagi: seeing out his career with the Turkish Champions Galatasaray of Istanbul, who Leeds played in 2000 and where two fans were murdered the night before the game. You tell him again: 'Don't mention Hagi. Galatasaray! Galatasaray!' Behind you they are singing:

> Give me George in my heart, keep me English.
> Give me George in my heart, I pray.
> Give me George in my heart, keep me English.
> Keep me English 'til my dying day.

They are not referring to Georgie Hagi.

> No surrender,
> No surrender,
> No surrender to the IRA
> SCUM.

The man says goodbye and moves onto the next people in the crowd. He is saying 'My children in Romania . . .' The man he is addressing refuses to look at him, but his mate is staring straight at the Romanian as if he's going to hit him, saying 'Do one!' The Romanian vanishes.

The tree is swaying more violently now. It's only small, a few thin branches visible through the crowd. Hands grip its upper trunk, pulling then pushing, smiling faces around it.

You are back in the bar, queuing for a beer. Waiting, you pick out three or four faces and make out the words of songs you've not heard before: 'Never forgive. Never forget . . . Never forgive. Never forget' and 'Singing die, die Turkey, Turkey, die!'

Your first reaction is: how pathetic! However drunk you are, you don't want any part of this.

But you look at their faces, screwed up with emotion and remember seeing footage from Istanbul. On a TV in a hotel room in Granada. You saw your old boss among the images. You thought for 12 hours he could be dead, searching for his name in the newspaper the next day. And, having talked to people who knew the dead men, and thinking that these could be their friends stood here in Troyes, just like they stood in Istanbul two years ago with Christopher Loftus and Kevin Speight. Thinking: who are you to say 'You have to get over this?' Thinking: how you would feel if it had been your best mate? Remembering how for months after the stabbings, from the first night, if you let your mind slip, you would feel just the same: we should go over there and teach the Turks how to be civilised, chuck them out of the tournament, tell them to go fuck themselves if they want to join Europe. A country that slaughters animals by slashing their throats and letting them bleed to death, a country with the human rights record of a '70s South American dictatorship, a country of tumbledown buildings that thinks it deserves to play us at football and has the nerve to call itself European. You wanted to do something. You wanted to strike back. And you know how misplaced that rage was, but you felt it and meant it, and right now you can't feel anything but sympathy for these pissed-up men chanting 'death to Turkey' in this bar in France.

Another song builds among the crowd and you start to sing 'Give me George in my . . .' and stop yourself, confused as some of the others go on '. . . keep me English, keep me English to my dying day'.

Towards the ground there are several packs of Leeds fans looking for bars. One group come up to you. 'Excuse-moi. Ou err le bar? Is there a bar round here, mate? Do you speak English?' You tell them they'd best go back into town: there's nothing open near the ground. Other packs of men eye you savagely. They'd like to rip your head off. Given the chance. And you wish you had come in your Leeds top. This always happens to you. People think you're a native. It happened in Madrid. You were buying a McManaman Madrid shirt for your wife and two Leeds fans started hassling you. Until you started speaking and told them you were a Leeds fan too.

The lad who sat behind you on the plane appears. 'You got rid of your mate then?' He's just come from the town centre, he says. On the way he was jumped by a bunch of lads. He went through some blocks of flats and they came after him. They would have had him too, if some other Leeds fans hadn't come round the corner and scared them off.

On arriving at the Stadium d'Aube all the Leeds fans are frisked. This, after queuing at two security points, showing their tickets, standing as the police check them over. You have to empty your pockets and hold your arms out for a full check: missiles, weapons, alcohol.

In the ground several Leeds fans are putting up their flags: Tadcaster Whites, Cleckheaton Whites, Oslo Whites. Union Jacks, a Soviet flag, a Tricolour in yellow, white and blue. As the ground fills up you realise that this will not be a Leeds United walk-over. You can tell even before the players are on the pitch. The Troyes supporters are chanting and singing, every single one of them clapping their hands, stamping their feet, shouting out the names of the players, led by the-man-on-the-pitch. The Leeds support answers back with some of the old favourites, but it's hard for a few hundred to make an impression, such is the noise from every other corner of the ground.

When the Troyes players run on the pitch, Leeds fans give two-fingered gestures, perhaps unaware that it was a few miles from here that the first two-fingered salutes were delivered. Around the time of Agincourt, if the French caught an English archer, they would cut off the fingers he needed to draw back his bow. The English – as a sign of defiance before they let fly another volley of arrows – would hold up two fingers to show they still had them.

Both teams are on the pitch now. Leeds are all in white, but the regular Strongbow logo is missing.

'It must be alcohol,' someone says. 'UEFA don't allow alcohol or cigarette advertising.'

'But we wore Strongbow in the first leg,' says someone else.

'And against Maritimo, home and away.'

'It must be just the French then.'

That's what people agree on: the French don't allow alcohol advertisements.

Someone else says maybe someone has made the decision to respect the French memory of nearly 600 years ago: Agincourt, all those strongbows that brought down the French. But nobody listens to him.

MORE REASONS TO HATE TROYES

1 Their late goal at Leeds that means they aren't dead and buried.
2 Their fans are intimidating.
3 You have a bad feeling about the game.

When the game starts, Troyes are on top immediately. Leeds are without Rio
Ferdinand and it shows. The French crowd is more committed than any crowd
you have seen before, and the Troyes players feed off it. After eight minutes of
running Leeds ragged, Troyes score. A corner given away after a Duberry error
is struck to the back of the box and is followed by a fierce shot from 20-plus yards.
One–nil. The noise is deafening.

On the other side of the fence, a few feet away, a woman in her 50s is shaking
her fist. She is possessed, taunting the Leeds fans. Like every other Troyes fan this
is her biggest game ever. And with this goal, her biggest moment. Just as Leeds
were the passionate underdogs in the San Siro and the Bernabeu last season, now
Troyes are the underdogs playing the team to be beaten, a team with European
pedigree.

When Leeds equalise you can't resist going up to the fence and catching the eye
of the gesturing woman. You smile and wave at her, but are determined not to
make aggressive gestures. She turns away to look fiercely at the pitch. That's shut
her up.

At 1–1 Leeds are on top. You expect more goals. We've burst their bubble and
are at last out-singing the French. It's going to be okay. You allow yourself to think
that it's good Troyes scored – victory after a few minutes of worry is always
sweeter.

Then Troyes score again. Another long-range shot.

Now you look fiercely at the pitch, thoroughly aware that there could well be
a woman standing a few feet away from you on the other side of the fence waiting
to catch your eye. The Troyes fans drown out any hope of Leeds getting a few
songs together in response. We are struck dumb, not used to being favourites
under pressure. The game has defeat written all over it.

The second half picks up where the first left off: Troyes all over Leeds. There's
little singing in the Leeds end. You try to join in the odd chant but no one has the
stomach for it. The Troyes fans are too loud anyway. The whole stadium is
clapping, chanting, jumping up and down.

Then it's 3–1. Troyes are winning. Catastrophe! We were 4–1 up at home and
now we're losing on away goals, going out of the UEFA cup to a no-team.

Again, you choose not to look at the woman on your left.

The Leeds fans are shouting at the players.

'Come on you lazy cunts. Get your fingers out!'

'What are you fucking doing?'

'Get Smithy on!'

Then abuse towards Duberry and arguments break out.

'You can't slag one of your own players off. What's the fucking point in that?'

'He's a fucking welsher. That's what!'

Troyes attack again, their striker one-on-one with Martyn. If he scores, it's *curtains. But he balloons it over the bar. Nearly 4–1. Nearly all over. This is a disaster, you are thinking. You haven't felt this bad at the football for years. There's no singing from the Leeds end, just row after row of anxious faces and exchanged glances.*

A rare Leeds attack. Viduka makes what looks like a terrible attempt to shoot and the ball drifts across the box. But Keane is onto it. GOAL! Three–two. Leeds are winning again. On aggregate. The Leeds stand goes mad. You're pushed against the fence, just like the good old days in the Kop. You are dancing with the fat lad you saw at the airport. Everyone is clasping each other.

Keane does a double somersault and comes right up to the Leeds fans. He's so psyched up he looks insane. (You learn later that two minutes before his goal he said to Bakke 'We're still winning aren't we?' and Bakke said, 'No, we need another goal.')

Now the Troyes fans are silent. There's only a few minutes to go. They need two goals all of a sudden. You sing along with the Leeds fans, trying to catch the eye of every Troyes fan you can. You see them looking over. You gesture at them. This is beautiful, you think. Better than a 5–0 win. Let them think they've got the greatest result in their history, then break their hearts. There's no more singing from the home fans. It's all quiet. And Leeds hold out to win 6–5 on aggregate.

Troyes (2) 3 Leeds (1) 2
Martyn; Mills, Duberry, Matteo, Harte; Bakke, Batty, Dacourt, Kewell (Wilcox 46); Keane, Viduka.

Scorers: Viduka, Keane

On the plane the man who nearly got a beating in the blocks of flats comes back and rests his hand on the seat in front of you. He is wearing a ring, over a centimetre square, textured like a meat tenderiser. He gives you a nod. Behind him is the man who sat opposite on the way out. You shut your eyes and pretend to sleep. With your eyes closed you listen in on a dozen conversations.

The second Troyes goal was a deflection.

Three coaches of fans who came overland with an independent travel company all had forged tickets and weren't allowed in.

Jason Wilcox was our best player. That's how bad it was!

You fall asleep. You're exhausted, emotionally and physically.

The landing at Leeds wakes you up: the plane is caught in violent cross winds throwing the plane all over the place, then a bang as the plane hits the runway – the bloke next to you says its always like that coming into Leeds – and you expect to see the wheel come through the bottom of the fuselage.

Eighteen hours later, at 2 a.m. on a Friday morning, 300 Leeds fans disperse through the car parks.

CONFESSIONS OF A LEEDS FAN – PART SIX
1992–93

I didn't hate Man U until 1992, although Man U and Chelsea were the most loathed clubs on the Kop. I hated Liverpool. Even after we'd beaten Man U to the league I still didn't hate them. I laughed at them. They were a source of amusement. The songs we had for them were wonderful:

> Oh scum
> Look what we've gone and done
> We've won Division One
> We are the champions.

And 'Who's the champions now, scum? Who's the champions now?' and 'Let's all laugh at Man U, Let's all laugh at Man U . . .' The night we won the league I went out with a friend and we belted out all those songs, all around town, then in City Square with thousands of others. Town was packed. Everybody talking to everybody. Leeds was one big Kop.

It wasn't until the next year that I learned to hate Man U. Leeds went from champions to 17th. And Man U signed Cantona. I heard about it on the *Nine O' Clock News*: And finally . . . the sky is about to cave in . . . The pundits said that Cantona was the last piece in the Manchester United jigsaw, the catalyst that would turn them from a good team into a great team. They were right: a decade – or more – of disgusting success began.

I loved Cantona. I'll admit it here. That's why I hated him so much when he played for Man U – because I had loved him. In fact, even when he was at Man U, I still loved him. It was like losing a lover to a worst enemy. That's the closest I can get.

After he left people said he'd won the league for Leeds in 1992. I used to disagree. Vehemently. I fired out statistics. He'd only started six games for Leeds that season. The players that won the league were Lukic, Dorigo, Whyte, Fairclough, Sterland, Strachan, McAlister, Batty, Speed, Chapman and Wallace. Not Cantona! So what if he scored a good goal against

Chelsea? That was one goal out of 74. And he only scored three goals in total for us that season.

Back then I worked in a bookshop. People would leave newspapers all over the staffroom. I'd tear out the images of Man U players – or at least deface them. And people would know – on the numerous work nights out – that after three or four pints I was an easy wind-up. Early evening entertainment. Start talking about Man U and I'd go bananas.

On the shop floor where I ran the sports book section I refused to stock any of the Man U books. Every publisher produced at least one. We stocked none. For a while I got away with it. My floor manager – Jill – felt the same as I did. No books on scum. That was our policy. Then there was a reshuffle and I got travel books and the sports section started to turn an unhealthy shade of red.

At the time I watched every Sky game going. But if Man U were winning it had to go off. It made me feel sick to see Man U win. To see Cantona score. It made me want to kick the television down the street. I was furious.

At work there was a girl called Rosie. She was from Manchester. The morning after they won the 1992–93 championship she came up to me and said 'We've got your trophy now.' I was helpless with rage. How do you deal with that? What are you supposed to do?

Then there were the matches: Leeds United versus Manchester United. It wasn't like the other games of football. It was tense, painful, aggressive, almost too much to bear. I would be in varying states of rage, anxiety, fear and exhaustion.

Looking back I sometimes think it bordered on pathological.

But none of this was unusual. All over the city this was happening – and worse. Leeds had been struck by a malady, a collective mental illness.

LEEDS UNITED v TOTTENHAM HOTSPUR Premiership
Sunday, 4 November 2001

REASONS TO HATE SPURS
1 They knocked us out of the cup in 1982. Mickey Hazard scored the winner. You listened on the radio and have never forgotten.
2 They stole George Graham. (Although – on reflection – it all worked out rather well.)

Spurs come to Elland Road as the form team after three straight wins. And there are worries for Leeds. Ferdinand could still be out. But when the teams emerge, he's there. The Kop salute him: RI-O! RI-O! RI-O! Ferdinand – as ever – holds the defence together, striding about, an occasional burst of speed to head off a threat. It's immediately clear why Leeds were such a shambles in Troyes. Without Rio Ferdinand, Leeds United are going to win nothing this season.

Spurs play deep. They don't look like the Premiership's so-called form team. However many big names they have on the park – Sheringham (ex-Man U, booed every time he touches the ball), Anderton, Poyet, Ziege – they are playing it safe. The teams go in at 0–0.

But the second half is like a different game, Spurs coming at Leeds. They must have identified something about us. Or about themselves. Inevitably they score, Poyet pouncing to hammer one in from 20 yards or more: the third time Martyn has been beaten from outside the box in four days. The Spurs fans are briefly vocal.

There is grumbling in the Kop. This is the first goal we've conceded at home in the league this season. We've forgotten how it feels to see the opposition players peeling away to their away fans, hearing cheering you're not part of.

Nine minutes later – courtesy of a lucky bounce and a fumble by Sullivan – Harte equalises. A belter. Again from outside the box. On the big screen replay you see the ball hit Sullivan's chest, bounce onto the post, then off his shoulder and in. He moves uneasily in his goalmouth. The Leeds players (and the fans) are on top now. It can only be just a matter of time before Leeds go 2–1 up.

With less than ten minutes to go and the first early-leavers thinking about where their car is parked, a tame back pass bounces to Sullivan and his defender, Perry. Kewell bears down on them and sticks a foot out. It's always worth sticking a foot out: it creates the unexpected. GOAL! Somehow the ball has travelled between the two Spurs players and bounced into the empty net. Two–one.

The referee tries to usher the Leeds players back to the centre, but they are too busy celebrating with the Kop. At first Sullivan refuses to rise to the taunts of the Kop, but after the final whistle he comes back to his goal to collect his towel and is cheered like the scorer of the winning goal, which in a way he is. At last he looks up. He smiles.

And once again you can't quite believe that Leeds are top of the league.

Leeds United (0) 2 Spurs (0) 1
Martyn; Mills, Ferdinand, Matteo, Harte; Bowyer (Johnson 40), Bakke, Dacourt (Batty 81), Kewell; Keane (Smith 75), Viduka.
  Scorers: Harte, Kewell

1	Leeds	11	15–5	23
2	Liverpool	10	20–10	22

3	Villa	11	17–11	21
4	Newcastle	11	21–14	20
5	Arsenal	11	24–13	19
6	Man U	11	28–20	18

LET'S ALL LAUGH AT MAN U – NUMBER FIVE
Liverpool 3 Man U 1

During the Spurs game you overhear the man behind you. He's listening to Liverpool–Man U on the radio.

'Two–nil at half-time,' he's saying to his mate.

'Who to?'

'Liverpool.'

'Yes!' says his mate.

At half-time the score comes up on the big screen. A big cheer goes up. Then a few minutes later: 'Three–one! It's three–one!' Everyone goes home happy. They'll be watching *The Premiership* tonight. Leeds have won. Man U have lost. It's like a rare alignment of the stars, a must-watch TV night. On the way home in their cars they listen to Charlton scoring 4 in 18 minutes to beat Arsenal at Highbury. A perfect day. Even the defeated Spurs fans motoring down the M1 have something to laugh about tonight.

LET'S ALL LAUGH AT MAN U – NUMBER SIX
Arsenal 4 Man U 0

One day after the defeat at Liverpool, Man U are at it again in the Worthington Cup. Playing the Arsenal side who had lost 4–2 at home to Charlton, also the day before. You didn't even know it was on until you read about it in the paper the next day. Four–nil! A hat trick from Wiltord! It sounds good. But there are no familiar names in the Man U team: Jimmy Davis? Danny Webber? Nothing players. Not even fringe players. Still, Man U losing 4–0 is worth a small laugh. A chuckle.

SUNDERLAND v LEEDS UNITED Premiership
Sunday, 18 November 2001

For the first time in ages you manage to get a ticket for an away game. Sunderland. The Stadium of Light. You'll get up there early, find a bar. You've got a couple of mates who live round there. You could make a day of it. And a night.

But four days before the game, your house move date comes through: the day after Sunderland. Not good. Not good at all.

You address it with your wife. If you can get everything packed up on Saturday, you tell her, it'll be all right to go to the match. That's all right, isn't it? Box everything up. Get it all out of the way. Then she can have a nice rest on Sunday. Before the big move on Monday. While you go to watch the football.

At 11 p.m. on Saturday you're not even halfway through the packing. You could work through the night, then leave your wife to finish up. You'd come back straight after the game and work through the night again, if necessary. She'll go for that.

REASONS TO HATE SUNDERLAND
1. One of your first games at Elland Road: Leeds 0 Sunderland 3. A Paul Bracewell hat trick.
2. Every year – in the FA Cup previews – being reminded about Ian Porterfield scoring the winner against Leeds in the 1973 final.
3. You had a ticket to go today, but . . .

You tune into Radio Leeds on your way to the rubbish tip. The game's five minutes in and Leeds are all over Sunderland. Peter Reid's boys aren't doing so well this year. They're not the team they've been for the last couple of seasons. This should be easy. Three points. No fear of losing our unbeaten record.

Then the first flashpoint: Thome fouls Alan Smith, standing on him. The commentator is incensed: that's not right, that sort of thing. 'Thome is just a coward,' he says. 'He's a coward, standing on Smith like that!'

Back from the tip – filling boxes with books and pots and plants – it's the second half. You wish you were in the Stadium of Light. It sounds like Leeds are doing the business, even though it's still 0–0. But as the match goes on Sunderland come back into it. And the tone of the commentary has changed. You are starting to feel uneasy.

Batty scythes down a Sunderland player. 'Oh dear,' says the commentator, chuckling. 'You don't want to mess with David Batty like that!'

Then Sunderland score twice. Your wife goes downstairs and doesn't come back. You were never any fun to be around when Leeds are losing. Leeds's unbeaten record is slipping away. Eleven games: six wins, five draws and no defeats. In your head you say things like: Every team has to lose a few games . . . It pans out over the season . . . Sunderland were just lucky . . . there won't be the pressure that we're unbeaten any more. But it doesn't help. You think about turning the radio off. Why listen now we're losing? It's not like you can do them any good sat here surrounded by packing boxes. At least if you were there you could sing.

The game ends 2–0. Your wife comes back upstairs. She wants a break from packing. She says that this is supposed to be the most stressful thing you can do in your life. Moving, she means. But then she didn't support Leeds in the '80s.

Sunderland (0) 2 Leeds (0) 0
Martyn; Mills, Ferdinand, Matteo, Harte; Bakke, Batty, Dacourt, Johnson; Smith, Keane.

1	Liverpool	11	21–11	23
2	Leeds	12	15–7	23
3	Villa	12	17–11	22
4	Man U	12	30–20	21

CONFESSIONS OF A LEEDS FAN – PART SEVEN
1994–2001

After years of not going to away games, it started up again. The first was Villa in the league. A mate invited me down to Birmingham. We watched it from the Villa stand. Leeds lost 3–0. That night he got out a film he said I needed to see. *I.D.*: a policeman infiltrates a hooligan gang at a London football club. Except it turns out that the hooligan gang infiltrates him and he becomes obsessed. I thought it was the greatest film I had ever seen. It was exciting. I wanted to be like him, bellowing at the football, drinking in a pub where everyone has a pathological love of their football club. And a hatred of everyone else. Going to see Leeds away again switched something in me back on.

I started reading all those new football books that were coming out. *Among the Thugs. Steaming In.* All those. It was a new genre at the bookshop. Hooligan literature. I searched them all out, read about hooligans from Aberdeen to Watford. Stories of planned-out riots, ambushes, ways of taking football supporting to the next level. I went to Blackburn, Bolton, Port Vale and Chelsea. I wasn't a hooligan. I was too scared of getting hurt. But I liked to watch it when it happened. I liked the tension of being an away fan, being part of the minority hurling abuse at the opposition, walking through the streets, people eyeing me nervously. And I'd stay out drinking later and later in Leeds. Talking about football. Singing about football. Shouting about football. With anyone who'd have me.

But it wasn't the football. Not really. It was everything else. The football was a symptom. In the real world a relationship was collapsing. I'd been in it for ten years – that was what was really going on. It's just I didn't know the real world from the unreal world. All that drinking, all those away games, all the Sky watching. And the rest. One day she turned on me and said that I was 'scum'. She chose the word carefully.

But you don't want to be dragged through another mediocre break-up story. The point is that Leeds United were always there, from when I was seven. Always there, they fade in and out of your life, taking up 30 per cent of your free time to taking up 80 per cent. You can spend your adolescence hiding in your bedroom. Your girlfriends can leave you. Your parents can die. You can be a good man, a bad man, an indifferent man, but Leeds United are always there.

For a couple of years, Leeds United were my crutch. I lived alone. I watched Sky alone. I drank alone. I loathed myself. I had voices in my head telling me I was scum. I had damaged the world. I could never get away from those thoughts. Except at Elland Road. Every time I went into Elland Road – pissed – I would forget. It used to amaze me. I could go from days of self-indulgent self-loathing to the football and forget everything. Coming away after 90 minutes of excitement and rage I'd be amazed that I could forget all the unhappiness. It was like I didn't have to be me for a couple of hours.

And for that I am eternally grateful to Leeds United.

Then Rebecca. We met the day Alan Smith scored his debut goal and Leeds won 3–1 at Anfield. One problem was that Rebecca lived in London. (Bear with me. This is a love story, but it's a love triangle: me, Rebecca and

LUFC.) It would take six months to persuade her that Yorkshire was the place she should choose to settle down in. Before I met Rebecca I'd missed one home game – a league cup tie against Villa – in a decade. Now I would have to miss more. She came up two weekends a month. I went to London one weekend a month, missing two games. She'd let me listen to the matches I was missing on her mobile phone. And of course she didn't realise the sacrifice I was making, she didn't know that this was about as serious as I could be. I'd missed two games of football.

Eventually she moved up to Yorkshire. Her first game was Derby at home. Leeds won 4–1.

Then we got married.

GRASSHOPPERS ZURICH v LEEDS UNITED
UEFA Cup (Third Round, first leg)
Thursday, 22 November 2001

Now you've moved, getting home from work takes longer. It's already touch-and-go whether you'll get back for the match, Channel Five screening Zurich v Leeds. And your wife wants to drop in at the supermarket. This is not good. But what can you do? You have to eat. And she says she'll cook tonight: you can watch the match, she'll bring it up to you.

'Okay. If we're quick,' you say.

But neither of you are familiar with the layout of this supermarket and it's taking ages to find the few things you'd agreed to get. Time is marching on, the chances of missing the first minutes increasing. You go on missions to find things. Mushrooms. That's the last thing. Then you can get home to the football. You find some and bring them back to the trolley. But she says they're the wrong kind of mushrooms. You say you like this kind: these are the mushrooms you want. Your favourites. She says not. You say all mushrooms are the same, that supermarkets have created the illusion of choice to make you spend more money. She goes off to find the right sort of mushrooms and you stand there feeling angry and weak and pathetic.

REASONS TO HATE ZURICH
1 They're Swiss.

Again – because you have just moved – the TV is not tuned in. It's easy to find BBC1, BBC2, ITV, Channel Four, but not Channel Five. You go round the dial. Nothing. You were one of the few who could get Channel Five where you used to live. People would come round so they could watch the match at yours. Now you don't have Channel Five. The quality of your life has just slipped a notch. You won't get to see half Leeds's games in Europe. Half England's games.

Fuck it! You'll listen on the radio. Radio Leeds. You find medium wave, but it's covering something else. But the Leeds games are always on FM anyway. You tune in. Still nothing. You move the aerial about, put the radio on a stack of boxes. Still nothing. And it dawns on you: you have moved to Todmorden and you can't get Channel Five or Radio Leeds. What have you done?

Radio Five is available. They are covering Ipswich v Inter Milan, but have a man at the game in Switzerland. Almost as soon as you turn it on, an update: Zurich 1 Leeds 0. You go downstairs. You will not listen to Ipswich, who, to make it worse, are beating Milan. You'll devote the evening – or what's left of it – to your wife. Fuck football! Fuck Channel Five! To hell with the lot of them.

Ten-thirty. The sports news on Radio Five: Zurich 1 Leeds 2. After Nigel Martyn saved a penalty, Harte hammered in a free kick and Smith got the winner.

The next day at work a friend is describing the goals to you. He gets Channel Five. He's not a Leeds fan. He supports Liverpool. You should be lapping up his descriptions, asking him to expand, to say how well Leeds played, what character there is in the Leeds side. But you don't like hearing about Leeds from a Liverpool supporter. You're the Leeds fan! You're the one who should know everything. You change the subject.

Grasshoppers Zurich (1) 1 Leeds (0) 2

Martyn; Mills, Ferdinand, Matteo, Harte; Batty, Dacourt, Bakke, Wilcox; Smith, Keane.

Scorers: Harte, Smith

LEEDS UNITED v ASTON VILLA Premiership
Sunday, 25 November 2001

One-thirty, and you are waiting for Martyn at the Billy Bremner statue. A coachload of Villa fans has just been dropped off: families, adolescent lads, children, women. In party hats and scarves, they wait among clusters of Leeds fans.

Since he was erected, Billy Bremner has become the meeting place. A few yards from the memorial plaque for the two men murdered in Turkey, this is the spot where a mountain of flowers and scarves appeared overnight after that semi-final in Istanbul. Even today there is a bunch of yellow flowers lying between Billy Bremner's oversized bronze boots.

A group of six men, all wearing black suits, meet and make their way to the East Stand through the tall gates and up the steps to reception. Upstairs – through the window – you can see waiters and waitresses dressed in black and white and the outline of a huge row of wine bottles. Ninety minutes to kick-off and hospitality is in full flow.

A long queue of Villa fans waits patiently at the burger bar. Two men work the queue, blowing Du-du, du-du-du, du-du-du-du, du-du on luminous plastic trumpets, shouting 'Three pound each. Two for a fiver.' Some boys already have horns, winding themselves as they try to get a tune. A group of kids gets out of a minibus, holding McDonald's flags and balloons, grinning madly while staring up at the edifice of the East Stand, excited on E numbers. At the club shop there is a queue three wide and thirty long backing up from the IN door, and a second mass of people pouring out with official Leeds United merchandise in official Leeds United plastic bags. The brand is really performing today.

REASONS TO HATE ASTON VILLA

1 The 1996 League Cup final. My first and only cup final. Villa beating us 3–0. The Leeds team looking like they didn't give a shit.
2 The Villa fan on the train away from Wembley, shouting his mouth off about how shit Leeds were. Me having to be restrained from committing my first assault.

3 Benito Carbone scoring twice, putting Leeds out of the FA Cup in January 2000, after Leeds played them off the park.
4 Last Christmas – having just lost at home to Villa – visiting two of my wife's friends who support Villa.

Peter Schmeichel runs towards the Kop after Villa win the toss and force Leeds to change ends and gets the special welcome reserved for every Man U veteran. He looks as huge and invincible as he always did. But this must be a comedown for him: being a Villa player. Villa might be third in the league but they won't end up in the top six. Everybody knows that. Including Schmeichel.

Leeds are on top immediately, showing no sign of having played Zurich on a heavy pitch three days earlier, playing quick passing football, trying to get the ball to the feet of Smith and Keane. Smith playing his perfect game, short bursts of speed in the box, and winding up his marker, Alpay. Alpay deals with it well. This is an easier ride than a recent visit, two seasons ago, just after Galatasaray, when he was booed for his Turkishness every time he touched the ball.

Keane misses a couple of chances, but soon redeems himself, intercepting a Wright back-pass that leaves Schmeichel stranded at the edge of his box. Keane side-foots it to Smith, who hits it hard against the knee of Steve Stone. The ball ricochets into the net. The players celebrate right in front of you. This is going to be a good day. No repeat of last Christmas's difficult trips to the homes of Villa fans.

Then Smith is fouled from behind. The referee is holding up a red card. Alpay is on the ground and Smith is walking away. Next to you Martyn is incensed.

'What the fuck has he sent Smith off for?' It's only then that you realise that Smith has been sent off. Someone says he's elbowed Alpay.

Villa hit ten-man Leeds straightaway. You might have turned the TV over to watch a different game. Villa know they can win it now. And Leeds are showing the strain of a hard week. With only one striker left at the club – Viduka and Kewell away, Bridges injured, Smith off, no one on the bench to come on – Keane looks lost up front, unable to hold the ball up, losing possession however hard he battles.

'That's going to cost us three points,' Martyn says.

Then Villa score, Kachloul volleying it past Nigel Martyn. Impossible to stop. If we can just make it to half-time, you think, then O'Leary can sort this out.

'We're going to lose this 3– or 4–1,' says Martyn.

And you agree, thinking how odd it is to be watching Leeds and knowing they are going to lose. It's a long time since you felt so hopeless.

The Villa fans sing 'You're not singing any more . . .'

The Leeds fans turn their attention to Alpay: 'Shit Turkish bastard, You're just a shit Turkish bastard!' Booing every time he gets the ball.

The half-time whistle goes and like every Leeds fan you are booing the referee. You spend half-time contemplating defeat. This is going to be another Christmas of running into hundreds of Villa fans.

The second half begins. The fans are still flat. There's no singing, except at the back of the Kop. But it's not spreading.

Mills fouls Hendrie. Mills stands up. Hendrie pushes Mills over, hand to face. And Hendrie has to go. He knows it. The players know it. The crowd know it. But the referee needs to ask his linesman. And the result: a yellow card. O'Leary is on his feet. Forty thousand Leeds fans are on their feet. It's an outrage. The Smith sending-off is now ten times more unjust. One of Hendrie's team-mates has a hold of him. He's lost it. It's just a matter of time before he gets sent off. His next tackle. But John Gregory intervenes and pulls him off. Hendrie walks to the dressing-rooms. The fans around the tunnel are on their feet shouting at him as he leaves the pitch.

The game is explosive now, bad tackles flying in. And the Villa players don't like it. Their rhythm has gone. They recoil. It's Leeds, animated and aggressive, who take up the game. The Kop is singing. The Villa fans are quiet. The Leeds midfield – Bakke, Batty, Johnson – have the game by the scruff of the neck. Leeds make chances. Martyn stands idle. The 10 men of Leeds are so fired up they could be 20 against Villa's 11.

With the fans settling for a brilliant draw – an achievement after everything the referee has done – Harte lifts a free kick to the far post. And for a second, as Rio's header travels towards the goal and Schmeichel stands watching the flight of the ball, you imagine a win and how good it would feel to come out of this game with everything. But the ball comes back off the post and the game ends 1–1.

The referee is surrounded by Leeds players as they are applauded off the pitch.

Leeds (1) 1 Villa (1) 1
Martyn; Mills, Ferdinand, Matteo, Harte; Bakke, Batty, Johnson, Wilcox; Keane, Smith.
Scorer: Smith

1	Liverpool	12	22–11	26
2	Leeds	13	16–8	24
3	Arsenal	13	28–15	23
4	Newcastle	13	23–17	23
5	Villa	13	18–12	23
6	Man U	13	31–23	21

LET'S ALL LAUGH AT MAN U – NUMBER SEVEN
Arsenal 3 Man U 1

On the way home from the Villa game you listen to the second half of Arsenal–Man U. It was 1–0 to Man U at half-time. A draw would be the best result. When you get into the car it's 1–1, Arsenal having scored right at the start of the second half. Although a 1–1 draw would be best for Leeds and although you hate Arsenal, every time Arsenal come at Man U you want a goal. However logical it would be to want a draw, it's bollocks. You want them beaten. Whatever the circumstances the first thing must be for Man U to lose.

Barthez obliges. 'And it's back to Manchester United's man of the match, Fabien Barthez . . . Barthez . . . oh what's he doing? Henry has scored . . .' It sounds so good you commit to watching the Sunday *Premiership* programme, however late it's on.

That evening on *The Premiership* the Man U defence is a joy to watch – Blanc, caught out time and time again, is forced to pull players back or chop them down. Barthez makes save after save, then – in a moment of madness – taps the ball to Henry who slots it home. Then Barthez smiles. He's embarrassed.

Earlier on *606* the Man U fans were raging. Barthez must go! That's what they were saying. Ferguson should swallow his pride and accept he's made a mistake: they've got a dodgy keeper.

After Barthez's second error, fumbling the ball at the feet of Henry and a third goal conceded, the camera focuses in, looking for another smile. But Barthez looks confused. He can probably hear the Arsenal fans chanting 'Barthez! Barthez! Barthez!'

FOWLER SIGNS AMID INJURY CRISIS
Yorkshire Post (30.11.01)

After months of rumours, one of the great English strikers of the '90s, Robbie Fowler, became a Leeds player. 'Leeds United,' reported *The Guardian*, 'have agreed a fee, believed to be around £12m for Liverpool's iconic striker, Robbie Fowler.'

The press had a lot to say about the move. Fowler was not a happy bunny. He didn't like the Liverpool caretaker manager, Phil Thompson. Nor did he like the rotation system at Liverpool. Here was one of the best in the game – with possibly his last chance of going to a World Cup finals coming up – and he was sat on the bench.

The Liverpool fans found it harder to let go. In a Merseyside paper 79 per cent of those polled disagreed with the sale. (You suspect the other 21 per cent were Evertonians.) Fowler's nickname on the Anfield Kop was 'God'.

Phil Thompson – talking footballspeak – said 'It wasn't our decision to let Robbie go.'

Meaningless.

Either way, it was a huge signing for Leeds. Peter Ridsdale hit the nail on the head, saying, 'It's not long ago when the very thought of a player like Robbie leaving Liverpool to join Leeds would have been laughed off.'

'This club's going places,' says a player leaving one club for another, 'the ambition here is to finish as high in the league as we can and end up in the Champions League.' No mention – refreshingly – of Leeds fans being the best in the world. After his relationship with the Liverpool fans no one would have swallowed that.

David O'Leary is ecstatic. Here was a player he'd been after for over two years. He'd put him in the team straightaway. Give him 10 to 12 games to get fit.

LEEDS UNITED v CHELSEA Worthington Cup
(Fourth Round)
Wednesday, 28 November 2001

ANOTHER REASON TO HATE CHELSEA

1 That TV documentary where Chelsea players take the piss out of the Leeds team playing bingo with Don Revie.

It's raining in Leeds. It's been dark since 4 p.m. Winter in Yorkshire. You imagine the Chelsea players peering out of their coach windows as they approach Elland Road through the rush-hour traffic. And the Chelsea fans on the M1, windscreen wipers going, moaning about having to drive so far north on a horrible night like this. They're not going to like it and neither are the players. Especially the foreign ones. They like it after March, until August, when the sun's out and it reminds them of home. You can see Chelsea's season fading now the nights have drawn in and there's ice in the air. Foreign players don't thrive in the English winters. That's the theory.

But the cold seems to have got to the Leeds fans too. Even though this is the day Leeds signed Robbie Fowler, there's no buzz around the ground. It's like people have turned up because they have to, not because they want to. You feel a bit like that. Why did you bother coming? None of your mates have. There's no one you recognise around your usual seat in the Kop, just lots of girls and couples. All wearing gloves and hats.

There must be some regulars in the back of the Kop though. You can hear them: 'Le Saux takes it up the arse, Le Saux takes it up the arse . . .' and 'Chelsea rent boy, Chelsea rent boy, Wo-oh, wo-oh . . .' The two chants blend into perfect a cappella. The girls and boys around you smile. Maybe they can't hear the words. Maybe they can. They look like this is their first visit. Three girls – 14 or 15, maybe – are directly in front of you, each wearing a Leeds top, each with SMITH across their backs. They watch him warming up near the centre circle, stretching his thighs. Then it's back to Le Saux. 'Five men and a puff, Wouldn't go to Israel . . .' Some laughter. But you don't laugh. You're not in the mood. The game passes. There is nothing to get excited about. It's frustrating and you wish you'd gone straight home from work. It's like the Leeds players don't want to go through to the next round.

One–nil to Chelsea. Then 2–0.

You leave early, five minutes to go. There's none of the regulars there to rib you so you don't feel so bad. And, turning to go, you notice that half the seats around you are already empty anyway.

No one gives a shit about the Worthington Cup, you think. It's best to be out of it. Now Leeds can concentrate on the league.

Leeds (0) 0 Chelsea (1) 2

Martyn; Mills, Ferdinand, Matteo (Duberry 59), Harte; Bakke (McPhail 63), Batty, Dacourt, Wilcox (Kelly 77); Smith, Keane.

LET'S ALL LAUGH AT MAN U – NUMBER EIGHT
Man U 0 Chelsea 3

You knew the score before you started watching: Man U 0 Chelsea 3. That's why you thought you'd watch *The Premiership*, even though Leeds aren't playing until Sunday.

The first thing is Roy Keane playing at centre-back. The best midfielder in the country playing in defence? Ferguson must be desperate. He's got a touch of the Wilkos. This is a sign of decadence. The end of an era.

The first goal comes quickly. A Melchiot header. He celebrates by digging a double line in the Old Trafford turf with his boots. You try to pick out the faces of Man U fans in the background behind him. You've always liked seeing the faces of fans whose team have just conceded a goal.

The Man U defence is a shambles. The camera focuses on their faces. They look troubled. Then a close-up on Ferguson, just after Le Saux hits the bar from 25 yards. He is red-faced, how he looked the day Leeds whipped the title away from him in May 1992. His team is chasing the ball around like a pack of schoolboys as it is touched from Chelsea boot to Chelsea boot. The mighty Man U are second best.

Hasselbaink scores the second. It's exquisite in that the multi-million Veron scuffs the ball to Chelsea who rush up the pitch and score.

The game is up for Man U, their defenders pulling at shirts, cutting players down with Second Division tackles. You catch the faces of more Man U fans in the crowd again. They are thinking: What the fuck is going on? What the hell is this? You think of the Man U fan you know who told you that he gave up his season ticket because home games in the league were so boring – he always knew Man U were going to win. He must be gutted to be missing this!

When Chelsea get their third, the camera again picks out more Man U fans: hundreds of them streaming out of their seats, back to the car parks, no scarves hanging out of windows tonight as they head south.

Ferguson leaves the pitch after a handshake with Ranieri, a camera tracking him like he's got the ball at his feet and is about to deliver a cross, his face like thunder, chewing hard on his gum. After the game he will say that his team cannot win the league now. Five defeats is too many. No one has won the Premiership with five defeats in the bag before Christmas.

On *606* that evening: the unthinkable. Ferguson – say the Man U fans – should go now. They should get a new manager in. He's lost it. He should never have let Stam go. And Veron is shit.

But most Man U fans don't call up Richard Littlejohn. They won't want to listen to *606* tonight.

And what about all the kids who have worn the red shirts since they can remember? Their youthful confidence based on being Man U fans, that's always put them one up on everybody. How will they go on now? How will they live from day to day without their self-esteem being bolstered by the football team they have chosen as a crutch?

FULHAM v LEEDS UNITED Premiership
Sunday, 2 December 2001

REASONS TO HATE FULHAM
1 At the start of the season you believed the hype and feared they'd be vying with Leeds for a Champions League place.
2 They were mean to Micky Adams – ex-Leeds – when they sacked him to make way for Kevin Keegan.

Another game on Radio Five. It's on Sky in the pubs, but you can't be bothered to go out and watch it. You can do a few jobs at home while you're listening. Low-grade DIY. That sort of thing.

But as soon as the game starts you feel too tense to concentrate on anything else. You hate football on the radio. You can't see what's happening. You have to rely on the fall and rise of the commentator's voice, the noise from the crowd, knowing which part of the crowd the noise is coming from. It would be easier to watch it on Ceefax. Ceefax is honest. It doesn't get your hopes up. It doesn't have you worried that a goal against is inevitable. No suffering. No tension. Just 0–0, 1–0, a penalty miss, 1–1, 1–2, a sending-off, finish. A result – good or bad – and you can get on with your day. No need for detail.

Leeds have a decent team out at Fulham. Kewell and Viduka are back from World Cup duty. And Fowler is playing. His debut. Keane is on the bench. Smith on the right wing. But the game is not going well. Fulham are pressing. Kelly clears off the line. Smith is lost out wide and is eventually booked. Then Johnson. It does not make for good listening.

You lie on the sofa and stare at the ceiling. You are too depressed to do any of those DIY jobs you meant to do. This is why you shouldn't listen to Leeds on the radio. You get up off the sofa. You pace the room. You look at the stuff you need to do for work. No chance. You try to tidy up but you always end up on the sofa, staring at the ceiling. You feel sick.

The game goes on. You do not have to read between the lines of the commentator to feel bad: 'Leeds have been away from their best today,' he says, 'here comes a corner from Harte . . . oh, it's a dreadful one . . . some of these set plays! Poor corners . . . and poor throw-ins . . . too many unforced errors . . . Leeds United have hardly forced van de Saar into a save . . .' And you're thinking you're glad it's nearly over and that you will soon be able to get up off the sofa and do something else. Get yourself out of this mood. You don't mind if it's a draw. That's okay. At least it won't be a defeat. But there's still time: 'Last throw of the dice for Fulham . . .' says the commentator. You know what could happen now. As soon as you settled for a draw, you put a curse on the game. How many Leeds games have you listened to on the radio now? Five hundred? Six hundred? You've been doing it for quarter of a century. It could be a thousand. You should know better than to have a glib thought like 'I'll settle for a draw!' You should keep your thoughts in check.

The final whistle. Nil–nil. You switch the radio off and go downstairs. Back into your life.

It's warm. The fires have been lit. Your wife has finished dressing the Christmas tree. You have missed that. You feel pathetic. Life flows by and you sit in your attic listening to Leeds United games. Will you always do this? Will you do it when you have children? Will you always use up half your spare time doing this?

Fulham (0) 0 Leeds (0) 0
Martyn; Kelly, Ferdinand, Mills, Harte; Smith, Batty, Johnson, Kewell (Dacourt 69); Viduka, Fowler.

1	Liverpool	13	23–11	29
2	Arsenal	14	30–15	26

3	Leeds	14	16–8	25
4	Newcastle	14	24–18	24
5	Chelsea	14	19–11	23
6	Aston Villa	14	18–14	23
7	Man U	14	31–26	21

LEEDS UNITED v GRASSHOPPER ZURICH UEFA Cup
(Third Round, second leg)
Thursday, 6 December 2001

Having won 2–1 in Zurich, Leeds have what looks like an easy job to finish the Swiss off and reach the last 16 of a European tournament for the third year on the trot. You win away: you should win at home. And there'll be a big crowd, tickets only £12. You booked yours weeks ago. And you never miss a home game.

So why aren't you going to Zurich at home? You've got a ticket. You're not working. You've got a car to drive to Elland Road, but you're driving in the opposite direction.

'I don't want to go,' you say to your wife.

'My God,' she says, 'I never thought I'd hear you say that.'

You try and explain. You've been away for three days with work. You haven't had a free evening in for over a week. You haven't spent more than two consecutive evenings in the new house and you've lived there for three weeks. And – most importantly – you haven't seen your wife, haven't just sat and talked to her for what seems like months.

So, tonight, you don't feel guilt. You thought you would, but you don't. You just feel indifferent. Where's your passion for Leeds United gone? One day you can't get enough of them, the next you can't be arsed with them. You have to conclude that there's something going on, something about you and Leeds United that's not so intense any more.

MORE REASONS TO HATE ZURICH
1 They had the audacity to go one up on us in Switzerland.
2 They must – therefore – be punished.

Martyn runs you through the game on the phone the next day. Leeds were rubbish. They played without passion and Zurich could have nicked it at the end. They only needed another goal to put Leeds out. O'Leary – he says – stormed off the pitch after the final whistle. He usually congratulates his players. There's something going on there too.

Leeds (2) 2 Zurich (1) 2
Leeds win 4–3 on aggregate.
Martyn; Kelly, Ferdinand, Mills, Harte; Batty, Dacourt, Kewell; Smith, Keane, Viduka.
   Scorers: Kewell, Keane

LET'S ALL LAUGH AT MAN U – NUMBER NINE
Man U 0 West Ham 1

Another day: another Man U defeat. You watch it on *The Premiership*. As Fergie chews hard on the touchline, his players carry on from where they left off in their last game. Up front they look okay: pass, move, pass, move, but their attacks peter out. In defence they look woeful: a Blanc clearance sails over his own head. The Old Trafford crowd sounds taped. The only audible words are Cantona songs. You like that. You never thought you would, but he's been gone for years and they still sing his name as today's players stumble clumsily on the pitch.

   Early on Keane is booked for arguing. He eyes the referee as if he'd like to kill him. The referee misses a second bad tackle by Keane, definitely a bookable offence. Keane should be off.

   After the break West Ham get the goal, a header from deep by Defoe. The camera pans in on a Man U fan with his head in his hands. It's great. This is the way you've been wanting to see Man U for years. And the tackling has all but vanished, replaced by shirt-pulling, grabbing, tackles on the man not the ball. And assault: Keane on Joe Cole. Another sending-off offence. The referee misses it again. The commentator says 'He's a lucky boy.' Then Keane punches Repka. The referee misses that too. Keane should have been sent off three times.

   Ferguson storms off the pitch, grey-faced, still chewing, stomach full of bile and ulcers.

   You listen to *606*.

   First Man U fan caller: 'Sack Fergie.'

   Second Man U fan caller: 'He's lost the plot completely. Sack him.'

Richard Littlejohn: 'Good evening.'
Third Man U caller: 'Is it?'

BLACKBURN ROVERS v LEEDS UNITED Premiership
Sunday, 9 December 2001

REASONS TO HATE BLACKBURN
1 Alan Shearer played for them (winning the only honour he ever received).
2 They bought the 1995 title.
3 They poached David Batty away from Leeds.

After a bad run you're worried to hear the team news from Blackburn. Yet another Sunday lunchtime game and Smith and Johnson are suspended. Bowyer still injured and potentially going to prison before Leeds's next game. Kelly on the right in midfield. And Duberry. You have nothing against him, except his footballing skills.

But Leeds start well. You realise that Leeds have such a big squad we can accommodate injuries, suspensions and prison sentences. And for the first time in a long time you are getting into the game. Life has been busy recently: house moving, work pressures, your wife. She's not been well. It's been getting worse for months. On your mind all the time. But today you are more relaxed. She's downstairs and not in too much pain. You feel like you can care about the game today.

But the game changes: Harte, Kelly and Mills are all booked. And now Blackburn are coming into it. They are over-running Leeds's three full-backs now they can't make reckless tackles for fear of being sent off. And they have Gillespie, Jansen and Duff, all happy running with the ball at their feet. Then Batty is booked. The pressure is building in your head. For the first few minutes Leeds sounded great, now it's nervous and mistake-ridden. Another nervous afternoon listening to Leeds on the radio. If only you had Radio Leeds, at least you could listen to the excuses of the commentator, take comfort in the bias . . . then there's a goal. You weren't concentrating. You listen for the next word. Someone's name. Was it Leeds or Blackburn?

Then the commentator says 'Kewell . . . Kewell has scored.' One–nil to Leeds.

Now Blackburn are on the rack, Leeds hard at them. You've seen it so many times: Leeds unconvincing, lacking confidence, until they score, only then looking like a team that could win the league. This is good.

But it's time to eat.

And this is not just a normal Sunday dinner. This is the first meal your wife has cooked using and serving with all the wedding presents. You turn off the radio. You know the boundaries.

You are still swallowing the last mouthful as you tune in the radio in the kitchen.

'I'll sort some coffee,' you say.

'Leeds two to the good . . . ' says the commentator.

Kewell again.

This is it, you think. The season is back on the rails. Now we'll play catch-up with Liverpool. An easy win that looked difficult on paper. Three easy home games to follow. Maximum points in December?

Fowler fires two shots wide. Blackburn miss a chance. The match is in its endgame. The commentator admits that Blackburn have been unlucky. You think, you have to take your chances. That's the difference between the Blackburns and the Leedses of this world. Then Berg scores for Blackburn.

Two–one and eight minutes of tension to go. With every Blackburn attack you wait to hear Alan Green's voice fall to tell you it's safe. In five minutes you'll feel either elated that Leeds have got three points away from home, or depression that we've had another draw. For now: utter uncertainty and anxiety. And 28,000 Blackburn fans urging their team on. You want to turn it off, but you're stuck with it. It would be nice to sleep for five minutes then switch on Ceefax to see a 2–1 win, but this is what football's about, seeing it through to the end.

You haven't heard Duberry's name all game. You're pleased. It's a good sign. There's less scope for anxiety.

Your Sunday dinner sits unmoved in your stomach. Digestion will not begin until after the final whistle.

Duberry hoofs it over the halfway line.

Duberry slices his clearance.

'Duberry . . . scrappy, very scrappy . . .' says the commentator, just as the final whistle goes and a smile creeps across your face. Leeds have won. Three more points.

Blackburn (0) 1 Leeds (0) 2
Martyn; Mills, Ferdinand, Duberry, Harte; Kelly, Dacourt (Wilcox 64), Batty, Kewell; Viduka, Fowler
Scorer: Kewell 2

| 1 | Liverpool | 14 | 25–11 | 32 |
| 2 | Arsenal | 15 | 33–17 | 29 |

3	Leeds	15	18–9	28
4	Newcastle	15	25–18	27
5	Chelsea	16	19–12	24
6	Villa	16	21–8	24
7	Spurs	16	25–23	24
8	Fulham	15	17–13	22
9	Man U	15	31–27	21

Immediately after the Blackburn game it's the FA Cup third-round draw. Leeds don't come out of the hat early. Every home team drawn out and it could be Leeds next. Leeds avoid a few difficult ties. Leicester come out of the hat. Number 21. That means Leeds are number 20. You wait. 'Cardiff City . . . will play . . . number 20. Leeds United. Cardiff City will play Leeds United.' Your first thoughts: a bunch of thugs, the Millennium Stadium and that bizarre run of games in the '50s when Leeds–Cardiff came out of the hat three years on the trot, all third round, all at Elland Road, all Leeds 1 Cardiff 2.

'INNOCENT PARTY' FOWLER STILL DOGGED BY CONTROVERSY
Yorkshire Evening Post (13.12.01)

A newsflash on Radio Five: Robbie Fowler and another man were arrested in Hunslet, Leeds last night. This was not what Leeds United want to hear. Two years of Leeds's name being dragged through the tabloids should have been coming to an end.

The Sun covers it with four pages of banner headlines: 'MADNESS.' 'WILL THEY EVER LEARN?' 'SOCCER PARTY SENSATION.' 'COPS HOLD FOWLER.' 'Leeds stand accused of an amazing lack of judgement after letting their stars go on a city-centre booze-up which ended in Robbie Fowler's arrest,' say The Sun.

The story unfolds: Fowler and his mate's taxi stopped for petrol leaving Leeds. As Fowler slept, a freelance photographer appeared. There was an altercation. A camera and a mobile phone were damaged. The petrol station attendant called the police. Fowler woke up and hitched a lift with some passing Leeds fans. The police caught up with them. Both Fowler and his mate were arrested, then released.

Leeds United said it was nothing. They would not be talking to the player.

The press – on the other hand – had a story.

Why, they asked, were several Leeds United players out in the city centre dressed in army fatigues and war paint? One: as the jury in the Bowyer–Woodgate trial were considering their verdict? Two: during a war in which British forces were putting their lives at risk? And three: at all?

They had been warned by David O'Leary to be good, said the press. They had security guards to protect them from the public (or vice versa) and a coach to ferry them from bar to bar. But still?

LEEDS UNITED v LEICESTER CITY Premiership
Sunday, 16 December 2001

MORE REASONS TO HATE LEICESTER
1 Robbie Savage (again).
2 They have the LE postcode when Leeds is a far more important city.

After the win at Blackburn, there are three league games in seven days at Elland Road: Leicester, Everton and Newcastle. Seven points would do: nine, if possible. Johnson and Matteo are back in the team. Fowler should have worked his way into things. This is going to be a good Christmas.

Dave can't make it to the match so you ask your father-in-law if he wants to come. He'd love to. Even though he says he knows that Leicester (his team) are going to lose.

Dave Bassett is back at Elland Road. Leicester's new manager. Here for a draw, men behind the ball, then fire it up for Brian Deane to hold it up. Predictably predictable. The game starts well. Johnson hits the bar after 40 seconds. Eight minutes later Viduka does a tasty back flick and Kewell drives it in off the post. The early goal. Now Leicester just can't put 11 men behind the ball and will have to come out at Leeds.

With a minute to go to half-time you decide to take your father-in-law to the bar for a drink: give him the full Elland Road experience. He is having a good time. He watches all the football on TV he can, but he always prefers it live. He thinks it's wonderful: the power, the passion, the movement. There's so much going on, every player up to something, clashes, shirt-pulling, false runs. It doesn't matter who wins or who scores, it's the live game that's thrilling him. And you realise how you take it for granted, how you've become used to it. This is real football.

Leeds start the second half well. Kelly looks good in midfield. Ever since he suggested he might need to leave the club to get first-team football so he could go to the World Cup, he hasn't missed a game. He puts the ball across to Viduka who slots it in. Two–nil.

It's over. And everybody knows it's over: the players, the fans, O'Leary. The tempo can go down now. Take it easy. There's three games in a week. No need to tire ourselves out. Rio said it in the programme. These three home games are vital. We need to do well to keep up the pressure on Liverpool. O'Leary too: he wants us to win six games on the trot. Six not too difficult games. Well, this is win two. You think about the league table. Three points will take us back above Newcastle and Arsenal. And if Liverpool don't win, then Leeds will be right back in it. Hopes of being top by the New Year . . . as Brian Deane taps in an easy goal at the other end. And suddenly it's a different game. From cruising, Leeds are nervy. It infects the crowd. The fans whistle for full-time, which doesn't come before the ball is lofted up to Scowcroft, who buries it. Two–two. And the atmosphere shifts from Christmas party to anger. Just like the players, the fans have been cruising. No singing. No real engagement in the game. Expecting a win just by turning up. At the end, the big screen – carrying Sky – shows O'Leary scowling. But this is nothing compared to the week he is about to have.

Leeds (1) 2 Leicester (0) 2

Martyn; Mills, Ferdinand, Matteo, Harte; Kelly, Batty, Johnson (Bakke 17), Kewell; Fowler, Viduka.

Scorers: Kewell, Viduka

1	Liverpool	16	25–15	33
2	Arsenal	16	34–18	30
3	Newcastle	16	27–19	30
4	Leeds	16	20–11	29
5	Chelsea	17	23–12	27
6	Man U	17	37–27	27

THUG AND LIAR WALK FREE
The Times (15.12.01)

On 12 January 2000 there was a fight in Leeds city centre. There's nothing unusual in that. Ask the bouncers. Ask the police. Ask casualty. There are always fights. Packs chasing packs. Affray, ABH, GBH, manslaughter, murder.

Ask anyone who's been out drinking in Leeds. Have they been told that once they are outside this or that pub they are going to get a kicking? Have they run away from gangs of strangers looking for any excuse for a fight? Probably. But have they ever been caught? Probably not. You slip out of a fire exit. You get away. You put on a burst of speed for a few seconds and escape. But on 12 January 2000 Sarfraz Najeib got caught.

The press told the story once the second trial was over. The press were told the story by the court and the court were told the story by witnesses, defendants and victims. And *they* told it from their memories, their perspectives, their agenda.

One thing is unarguable: on 12 January 2000 Sarfraz Najeib got beaten, stamped on and kicked to within an inch of his life.

This is how it came out. This is the story if you followed the first case in the papers. The Leeds United players have a few days off. Jonathan Woodgate – only 19, but already an England international – books a couple of hotel rooms for his mates at the Marriott Hotel, Leeds. His mates have come down from Middlesbrough for a night out. They get stuck in, drinking Moscow Mules and Bacardi Breezer cocktails and pretty soon they're pissed. Especially Jamie Hewison. He's going for it. He's already had a couple of warnings from the bouncers at The Square on the Lane; they were only let in because one of them was Jonathan Woodgate. They move on. DV8, a lap-dancing club. Yates's. The Observatory. This is going to be one hell of a night.

Meanwhile Shahzad and Sarfraz Najeib and their mates arrive at The Majestyk. Not to drink. They don't drink. They want to listen to some music and there's no stereo at home.

After an evening of playing computer games, three more lads arrive at The Majestyk. Two England Under-21 internationals and one of the most gifted footballers in the UK: Lee Bowyer, Michael Bridges and Harry Kewell, all three first-teamers at Leeds United. Woodgate and his mates reach The Majestyk too. At first they are refused entry because Hewison is pissed, but Jonathan Woodgate says he'll vouch for him and they are let in free, straight to the VIP lounge.

Finally, another young man arrives. He's just finished playing for the Leeds reserves. Michael Duberry.

All the players are there. The evening is ready to unfold.

Hewison is causing trouble in the club, trying to start fights, lunging at a group of drinkers with a bottle. His mate – Neil Caveney – stops him. But, eventually, Hewison gets kicked out through the side door. He walks to the front of the club just as Shahzad and Sarfraz Najeib are leaving. They see this pissed-up man and taunt him. Or maybe not. Maybe they say nothing.

Hewison lunges at Sarfraz Najeib. Sarfraz hits out in self-defence.

Someone – not one of the named men – says, 'Do you want some, Paki?'

Then Sarfraz is chased through City Square across the front of the Queen's Hotel, past The Observatory and down Mill Hill to where his car is.

But he's unlucky. Whoever's chasing catches up. He's tripped and pushed against a wall. He's on the floor down a dark side street in the middle of the night, a semi-circle of men taking it in turns to kick him.

Shahzad Najeib watches. He can't reach his brother to help. He's been punched and beaten back. He heard Sarfraz scream when he was tripped. Now he can see the men kicking him. And he can hear every kick even though he's 30 yards away. Then he sees someone jump to stamp two-footed on his brother. He sees the jolt of his body and thinks he must be dead.

Finally he sees someone stoop to bite Sarfraz's face.

The attackers gone, Shahzad Najeib goes to his brother. Blood is leaking from his mouth and head. When the paramedics come they lift Sarfraz's body to reveal a huge pool of blood where his body lay.

At the hospital Shahzad sees his brother close up. His head is swollen to an unbelievable size. He looks inhuman. Shahzad calls his parents to tell them, but when they pick up the phone he can't speak. How can you speak in circumstances like that? Eventually he calls his aunt, who calls his parents.

Mr and Mrs Najeib arrive at the hospital. They look at their son, lying in a coma, his body and head covered in bruises and cuts. Shahzad watches them sobbing together.

The next day Sarfraz comes out of his coma. The first thing he does is cry out for his mother.

When the news of Bowyer and Woodgate's arrests came out, you thought they must have got the wrong men. You also thought that even if they had done it nobody would be able to get enough evidence to make it stick. It'll fade away, you told yourself, this will never come to trial. Leeds United were going places and this was a minor irritation. For you Bowyer and Woodgate were paramount. Leeds could not afford to lose them. You also thought: put the money of the club behind them. Defend them! Are Leeds United going to be big time or not?

Talking to some people you were more circumspect: If they are guilty then of course they should be punished, you said. People can't be allowed to get away with things like that. But you were thinking that they *must* get off. At all costs they must get off.

And you knew they hadn't done it anyway.

Ananova, the virtual newscaster, reported the first trial without the agenda of the print media. They sent you two or three emails a day, spelling it out, keeping it simple: a list of who said what. Witness after witness.

Evidence.

The first was a CCTV film. Images of what could have been Bowyer and Woodgate on their way to Mill Hill, then an embrace at the end of it.

Then Sarfraz Najeib's brother, Shahzad. He says he saw a group of men kicking the shit out of his brother. And they wouldn't let him get near to help him out.

Then a student friend of Najeib describes seven or eight men chasing his friend. And then a scream. He breaks down in tears and the judge has to adjourn.

A woman says she saw Woodgate and Bowyer running down a street near the scene of the attack.

Then a bouncer says Sarfraz Najeib was taking the piss out of Hewison. That's how it all started, he says.

A Leeds fan saw Woodgate kick out at an Asian lad. The Leeds fan expresses his fears about getting involved. He doesn't care about Woodgate and Bowyer. He cares about his children, who are getting grief at school because of his involvement with the trial.

Then a bar worker who says he saw Woodgate jump on Najeib with both feet, and Bowyer – he says – with his face near Najeib's as if he was whispering to him. Under cross-examination he admits he didn't know the pair until he saw them in a newspaper article *after* the night of the attack. His evidence is dismissed.

Then a Home Office forensic scientist who says that the chances of the blood found on the cuff of Bowyer's Prada jacket not belonging to Shahzad

Najeib is one-in-a-billion. He says it indicates very strongly that Bowyer came into direct contact with Shahzad.

Then a dentist who identifies 12 teeth marks on Sarfraz Najeib's face as those of Paul Clifford.

Then a Home Office forensic chemist who casts doubt over the shoes Bowyer and Woodgate put forward as the ones they were wearing on the night.

There is more.

Bowyer and Woodgate deny being involved.

A second forensic scientist says it is possible that Bowyer fell where Shahzad fell a few moments earlier and that it was there he picked up the blood of the older Najeib brother. It's a possibility that cannot be ruled out.

Bowyer is asked to wear the trousers and shoes he claimed he wore on the night of the attack. But Bowyer is not wearing underpants. The trial is briefly adjourned.

Bowyer apologises for the lies he told to the police about the night of the attack. 'I am not very clever,' he says. 'I am not very good with words.'

Then Michael Duberry takes the stand. He says that Jonathan Woodgate told him he'd been in a fight with a gang of Asians. Originally Duberry said nothing of the sort, but he wants to change his story. He claims that once the case had gone to court the solicitor at Leeds United told him to continue lying, to stick to his story. He says he didn't want to get Woodgate into trouble, but that he didn't want to get into trouble himself. 'I might not be liked at Leeds United,' he says, 'but in saving myself that's what I had to do.'

There is more to-ing and fro-ing. Some witnesses come back to be re-examined.

Then the closing speeches begin.

Bowyer's counsel talks about Lee Bowyer's dream of playing in a World Cup final and scoring the winning goal for England. 'I invite you, ladies and gentlemen, to help him achieve that dream for himself and for England,' he says. The prosecution QC disapproves. He counsels the jury to consider the evidence and to be true to their oaths.

The closing speeches go on, then the jury are sent to do their duty.

But after 21 hours of deliberations the trial is halted, the jury discharged. An article in the *Sunday Mirror* has, the judge says, created a serious risk of prejudice. In it, the father of Sarfraz Najeib suggests the attack was racially motivated. But the judge does not blame Mr Najeib. He gave his views to the *Sunday Mirror*, not knowing they would be published before the jury had finished its deliberations. The *Sunday Mirror*, however, looks set to face charges.

The judge says the trial must be re-held. Several weeks and eight million pounds have been wasted.

The court case affected the players differently. Lee Bowyer flourished. Leeds fans will never forget. Playing against the top teams in Europe – Barcelona, Real Madrid, Lazio – sometimes being flown from Hull Crown Court by helicopter – he played the best football of his life, from penalty box to penalty box, tackling, scoring, passing; like a man possessed, like a man who thought every game was his last. He had something special with the fans. A one-to-one. That's how it felt. Every time he celebrated a goal – such as the one that floored the mighty AC Milan or the two that turned the game round against Anderlecht – he ran, not to his team-mates, but to the fans to celebrate. He was sensational. Lee Bowyer ended up among the leading scorers in the UEFA Champions League, the world's most prestigious club tournament. The cries of 'Bowyer for Strangeways' and 'Bowyer's going down' from fans throughout the country just seemed to fuel his unbelievable form. Sometimes at the end of a game he would linger on the pitch and take his adulation from the fans that little bit longer and each time the fans felt this could be the last time they saw him. And they were gutted.

Jonathan Woodgate – on the other hand – went to pieces. He lost form. He looked like a broken man. A ghost. After the trial the press demonstrated the physical changes with before-and-after photographs, like a makeover in reverse. They went to town on the transformation that moral decline can bring: 'Gaunt, sunken-eyed and pale-faced,' said the *Daily Mail*, 'he has become like a walking skeleton, more like rattling bones in the corner of a laboratory than a highly toned, highly paid athlete . . .'

But Jonathan Woodgate and Lee Bowyer – and the Najeib family – have to go through it all again. Autumn 2001 and the same evidence is mulled over by 12 new men and women jurors. The national press don't follow it like they did the first time. They have been waiting for fresh news. The verdicts. And the sentences.

The news breaks: 'The Leeds United defender Jonathan Woodgate has been found guilty of affray, part of a gang of drunken men who chased and beat a young man into a coma.' But he is not guilty of GBH with intent. Not guilty of the beating itself. He is given 100 hours' community service. The judge in summing up says that he had already suffered for his involvement. Perhaps this is why he did not get a custodial sentence: he could have got three years for his crime. But he must pay his court costs – over one million pounds.

Lee Bowyer is found not guilty of both charges. But, because of the lies he told to the police during the investigation, the judge says, he must pay his court costs too. One million pounds.

One of Woodgate's Middlesbrough friends gets 100 hours' community service too. His other friend – the one who left teeth marks – gets six years.

When you heard the verdicts and sentences, your first reaction was to tell people. When something big happens you have a need to discuss it. You did try to remain calm. You were overjoyed, but had to be tasteful. Your colleagues shook their heads.

'That's terrible.'

'That's disgusting.'

'That poor boy. How's he going to feel now?'

They were talking about Sarfraz Najeib, not Jonathan Woodgate or Lee Bowyer.

They watched your eyes when they said these things. Then they were off. They didn't want to talk about it. Not with you.

You phoned Martyn that night. He was delighted. Like you, he'd been watching a man called Suresh Grover on Channel Four news going on about how heartless Leeds United were, how during the trial the prosecution hadn't been allowed to press for it being a racist attack, how the jury weren't told certain evidence.

'Who the fuck is he, anyway? It's not about race. He's just using the trial as a vehicle for his agenda!'

The press – busy balancing its dual role of making money and reporting the truth – was outraged by the sentences: 'THUG AND LIAR WALK FREE'; 'FREEDOM FOR THE FOOTBALL CAVEMEN'; 'SACK THESE FOOTBALL YOBS'.

There were literally hundreds of pages of newsprint that weekend and into the next week. The press gorged themselves on it. Reading them, you felt more and more angry. We have to trust English justice, you thought. If there's not enough evidence to put people away then you can't put them away. And all this stuff about racism. Didn't they hear the judge? It was clearly not a racist attack!

But the *Daily Mail* calls it 'THE LEEDS RACISM SCANDAL'. And the *Sunday Mirror*'s Richard Stott says he is worried that Leeds United's behaviour is 'likely to inflame racial tension in an area where it is high already'. *The Sun* appeals 'for calm among Asian communities of northern cities this weekend'.

But it wasn't racist! you're thinking. And the attack on Leeds! As if Leeds United were to blame? The players were in front of the court. The press might have dubbed it 'The Leeds United Trial', but it was a trial of individuals!

'The Leeds football trial is quite simply a litany of disgrace,' says the

Sunday Mail, 'Leeds have forgotten pledges to sack the players if found guilty.'

Again you are outraged. Leeds said that Bowyer and Woodgate would be sacked if they were found guilty of the more serious charge: GBH. Not affray. And the fucking press know it. They're just twisting things, laying into Leeds United. Nothing makes better press than laying into someone. Get their readers' cocks hard under their breakfast tables. That's what this is all about. Give your readers emotion on a Sunday morning so they feel like they're living. And that goes for the broadsheets as well. All their pious moralising, feeding their enlightened readers the lines they want, focusing on racism, the vagaries of the British legal system. Give them a few intellectual quandaries to discuss at their dinner parties. They need something to flex their ossified university educations on. Remember how sharp they used to be coming out of those undergraduate classes? After only a few glasses of wine they can discuss the disgrace with vehemence. The state of the courts. The racism.

And another reason for outrage in the press. These two men let off when they were clearly involved in this racist attack have form! They're known thugs! One is a raging racist. Lee Bowyer, who racially abused McDonald's staff in 1996, throwing chairs at them when he was refused a burger for breakfast. The *News of the World* reports: 'Zizam Hannan was left with a head gash needing five stitches . . . Bowyer was then caught on the security camera hurling two chairs across the room.' And in the *Sun*'s 'Bowyer File': 'Lee Bowyer's millionaire lifestyle masks a shocking history of boozing, violence and even drug abuse.' 'CANNABIS . . . RAMPAGE . . . UPROAR . . .' it screams.

As for Woodgate: he's been picked up more than once by the police for headbutting, fighting, starting on students. And there's more: there are allegations from his local pub that he liked to burn £20 notes and approach girls just saying 'Hello, I'm Jonathan Woodgate,' expecting that to do the trick.

You can defend that too: the English legal system doesn't allow previous convictions to influence a jury. Each crime must be tried separately. That's the law. You have faith in the law. But you can't defend what happened to Michael Duberry. After he changed his story Leeds United got hundreds of threatening phone calls, several death threats. He got a security firm in, some panic alarms. But masked men appeared at his house. And he had to be protected from a fan invading the pitch at a friendly game in Dublin. So he went away for a while, to Dubai. He was scared. He fought hard not to give evidence at the second trial, worried his life was under threat.

After reading every paper you could get your hands on about the trial,

ABOVE: Fans gather at the Billy Bremner statue.

BELOW: The police separate Leeds and Manchester United fans.

ABOVE: Chris, Matthew and Brian in The Britannia, at Chelsea.

BELOW: The approach to the stadium at Elland Road.

Fans board the bus to Elland Road.

Fans hang up flags at Troyes.

Leeds Fan. Me at 12.

ABOVE: Fans gather at The Waggon and Horses before going to Elland Road.

RIGHT: (as above)

ABOVE: Wetherspoons pub at Leeds station.

BELOW: The Scarborough pub.

ABOVE: Spencer's.

BELOW: The Billy Bremner statue – a popular meeting place.

the hundreds of pages of outrage and anti-Leeds bile, you round the weekend off watching *Panorama*. You have always liked *Panorama*. And the journalist who's reporting it: Fergal Keane. You've read books by him and heard his reports on Radio Four's *From Our Own Correspondent*. He's good. He'll give it to you straight, none of the press bias.

He narrates a reconstruction of the attack, its ferocity made clear. One gang chases another through the streets of Leeds, streets you've been drunk on, been chased on, chanted football songs on. They catch one of the group, kick him, stamp on him. And you feel sick. A part of your mind is still thinking: this is a stitch-up, this is more anti-Leeds propaganda. But as the attack goes on you feel more and more doubtful. Uneasy. It is a savage beating. A reconstruction, sure. But this is how it is when someone gets a kicking. You've seen it happen. Again, on those streets.

A few minutes into the programme you feel ashamed. Ashamed you were so defensive. Ashamed you saw everything from the point of view of holding onto Bowyer and Woodgate at all costs. Ashamed that – whoever did it – you didn't see it from the point of view of a young man kicked almost to death. You saw Sarfraz Najeib as an obstacle, not a person.

What if it was Bowyer and Woodgate who were fully involved? Would you want them to play for Leeds United again? What if Leeds did slip two or three places in the league as a result of losing them? So what?

Panorama show pictures of Sarfraz Najeib after the attack. He looks disgusting. To get deeper inside it, you try and imagine someone you love lying there, looking like that. Your wife. What if she was lying there and you were at her bedside and she had had her head and body kicked after a terrifying chase by half a dozen men across City Square? How abstract would you feel then? How would your reflections that it's innocent-until-proven-guilty sound then? How would your euphoria that they had 'got away with it' on the phone to Martyn have sounded if it had been Rebecca lying there?

Panorama lists the problems Sarfraz Najeib has had to deal with since the attack: seven days in LGI for treatment to a broken leg. A fractured cheekbone, a broken nose, cuts to his eyebrows, a head wound that needed 12 stitches. Months of corrective surgery. Fragments of bone removed from his nose because they were making it difficult for him to breathe. The imprint of a heel on his face, now faded. Teethmarks on his cheek. He still has trouble standing on his injured ankle. And trouble going out. He feels paranoid. He suffers post-concussional syndrome which makes it hard for him to sleep. He is still on anti-depressants. And his father says that his smile has gone.

You try again to imagine these things happening to the person you most love – like this man loves his son – and again it's your wife lying there.

You get hold of a copy of the *Mirror* the next day. 'THEY USED ME LIKE A HUMAN FOOTBALL' is the headline. Then that swollen-face picture again, like an image of an Israeli bomb victim or someone being lifted out of an earthquake building. You read the accounts of Sarfraz's brother. And his father. How they feel about Sarfraz's beating. How they think he feels, how he's a changed person, a shattered person.

Then you read Sarfraz Najeib's story. They went to the club to listen to music. They didn't drink alcohol because they are Muslims. They saw Woodgate in the club. Then again outside, play-fighting with his mates. They did nothing to provoke the attack, just walked past with their heads down. But someone said something to Shahzad. Then someone else said, 'Do you want some, Paki?' They walked on. But one of the lads hit Sarfraz on the back of the head. He turned round and hit the man in self-defence. Then his friends and his brother were running. Sarfraz ran too, a little behind. He ran 400 yards across City Square and down Mill Hill where he was tripped, fell and lost consciousness . . .

Outside the court Lee Bowyer said some thank-yous. To everyone who stood by him. The chairman. The manager. And most of all, he said, the fans. The fans of Leeds United. He wouldn't forget, he said. He'd never forget the support he's had.

Which is why you were fucked off – like you thought everybody else should be fucked off – when you heard the news that Leeds had put him on the transfer list. Woodgate had accepted his punishment from the club: eight weeks' wages, fronting the community programme – specialising in passing on his wisdom about the evils of alcohol – and having to move away from Middlesbrough and his mates. Duberry accepted his punishment. But not Lee Bowyer. Leeds told Bowyer they were going to fine him four weeks' wages. He had – by his own admission – broken the club rules: he'd been drunk in a public place.

But Lee Bowyer said he wasn't going to pay. Leeds slapped him on the transfer list. Bowyer said he was being victimised. And you thought, What a twat! All that bollocks about being grateful to Leeds United for sticking by him. He'd never forget? He already had.

LEEDS UNITED v EVERTON Premiership
Wednesday, 19 December 2001

REASONS TO HATE EVERTON

1 Eight of their fans chased me through Leeds the night we played them in the FA Cup third round, 1985.
2 I resented it when they were part of the so-called big four. (Although it is comforting that they are not mentioned in that context now.)

After a week of the media tearing into Leeds United, its players, its manager, its chairman – and most of the papers reminding its readers what bad people Leeds United fans are – Everton come to Elland Road. This is a time for unity, a time for the fans to come together and to sing from the same hymn sheet. Most of them do:

> *Lee Bow-yer!*
> *Lee Bow-yer!*
> *Lee Bow-yer!*

Everyone knows that Lee Bowyer has refused to accept the club's internal disciplinary actions regarding the night of the attack on Sarfraz Najeib and that now he's on the transfer list.

> *Lee Bow-yer!*
> *Lee Bow-yer!*
> *Lee Bow-yer!*

Until now you have supported Bowyer. You have sung his name at countless games over the last few years. You have stuck by his right to be innocent until proven guilty. And – since he wasn't found guilty – you were ready to welcome him back. Although you feel very uneasy about the whole thing. He has admitted he was there. He has admitted he was pissed. He should take the punishment and shut up. Pay the club back for its unbending support in the face of a media storm.

Lee Bow-yer!
Lee Bow-yer!
Lee Bow-yer!

But you are in the minority. Nine out of ten are backing Bowyer, not the club.

You feel disgusted. A part of you would like to walk out of the stadium and leave this lot behind for good.

Stand up for Lee Bowyer
Stand up for Lee Bowyer
Stand up for Lee Bowyer.

Most people stand. You stay sat down. There are mutterings around you. In the East Stand a friend of yours is shouted at by one, then two, then a mob, until he is forced to stand, just so he doesn't get a smack when he heads off to the toilet at half-time.

Stand up for Lee Bowyer.

You stand up. You tell yourself it's so you can see the game and, again, you wish you weren't there. You could be at home with your wife. You could be walking along the canal where you live. Anything but this. And you don't give a shit if Everton score with this next attack. A part of you hopes they do.

A few minutes in – a football game happening somewhere out there – a banner is unfurled in the Family Stand: 'LOSE BOWYER MEANS LOSING THE TITLE – IT'S YOUR CHOICE . . .' The banner faces the West Stand and Peter Ridsdale – the man imposing this penalty on Lee Bowyer. People are taking Bowyer's side against Ridsdale. At one stage during the game, an image of Ridsdale comes up on the big screen. He is settling into his seat in the directors' box. Some fans boo. You feel disgusted. They are booing Peter Ridsdale. After everything this man has tried to do for the club.

The match goes on, the ball moving to and fro. You try to engage with it, but it's not easy. You're not here. You're thinking again about Sarfraz Najeib and his broken body and mind.

Leeds are better than Everton, even though the fans are directing their support solely at a player who is not even on the bench, let alone the pitch. You'd have thought it would undermine the players' game. But when the first goal goes in the entire team goes over to the West Stand and salutes the TV gantry where – so the press say the next day – Lee Bowyer is watching the match. That goal was for him. And you realise that you are out of touch with everyone: the fans standing up for Lee Bowyer, the players saluting their team-mate on the gantry.

Still, Leeds are winning. And when the second goal goes in – Robbie Fowler's first for the club – you are as animated as everybody else, punching the air. This *is what it's all about, isn't it? And Leeds need the three points desperately.*

Fowler looks overjoyed. The big screen shows a close-up of his face. And the Kop sings: 'Super, super Rob . . . super Robbie Fowler.' Fowler salutes the Kop. At last, something positive. Fowler hits the post. Fowler runs Everton ragged. Everyone is united at least in this. Except the Everton supporters who sing something back about Fowler being a smackhead. The Leeds fans retort: 'Same old Fowler – always scoring.' There is laughter. Everyone is in a good mood. Then another song breaks out: 'Pay up – and play for Leeds.'

Another song for Bowyer, coming from the same voices that were right behind him a few minutes before. It is as if the game is being played on the terraces. Or in people's heads.

When Fowler scores his second and Leeds are 3–0 up, coasting to a sound victory, the songs move away from the pitch and turn on those who have been slagging Leeds off all week. First, the Daily Mirror:

> *You can stick the* Daily Mirror *up your arse.*
> *You can stick the* Daily Mirror *up your arse.*
> *You can stick the* Daily Mirror,
> *Stick the* Daily Mirror,
> *Stick the* Daily Mirror *up your arse.*

Next, the BBC's premier news analysis programme: 'You can stick Panorama *up your arse . . .' You laugh. It's funny. Sort of. You feel part of the crowd again. If they started singing for Lee Bowyer again you'd probably join in and wouldn't for a minute feel like a hypocrite.*

Late in the game a plane comes in low over Elland Road. And, like every low-flying plane you and everyone else has seen in the last few weeks, you fear the worst.

'That's just what we need at 3–0 up,' says Martyn, 'a fucking terrorist attack.' Instead, Everton score twice, taking the edge off a night that has provided some catharsis for a football club and its fans that have had a lot to think about recently.

Leeds (2) 3 Everton (0) 2
Martyn; Mills, Ferdinand, Matteo, Harte; Kelly, Johnson, Batty (Bakke 81), Kewell; Fowler, Viduka (Keane 89).
Scorers: Viduka, Fowler 2

1 Liverpool	14	25–11	32
2 Leeds	16	21–11	31
3 Newcastle	16	28–19	30

4 Arsenal	16	34–20	29
5 Villa	17	23–19	27
6 Chelsea	16	19–12	24

The following morning Lee Bowyer accepts his punishment: a fine of four weeks' wages. Rumours were that Chelsea and another London club were already sniffing around. But Bowyer is a Leeds player. He paid £88,000 and asked the club if the money could go to inner-city communities and a local children's hospital.

LEEDS UNITED v NEWCASTLE UNITED Premiership
Saturday, 22 December 2001

'DUE TO FOOTBALL – Cooper's Bar will be closed from 10 a.m. to 7 p.m.,' says the sign on the door. It's no surprise, really. Last season Cooper's got smashed up in a fight between Leeds and Newcastle, a cavalry of 50 Leeds charging up from Wetherspoons to win the day.

You try Wetherspoons. Closed too. The Saturday before Christmas, 3,000 top-of-the-league Geordies hitting town and everyone in party mood having finished with work for the Christmas break: it's probably a wise move.

Groups of men – notable for their winter wardrobe of chunky Stone Island jumpers, bulky jackets with a dash of Burberry – stand talking into mobile phones.

'It's shut! We'll see you in . . . Spencer's . . . The Scarborough . . . Yates's . . .'

Leeds is packed with last-minute Christmas shoppers. The few flakes of snow drifting down between the tall buildings in City Square give the city an air of calm. But down every side street out of the corner of your eye – like half-materialised ghosts – are the police. Out in force. On foot. On horses. Vans idling. Three check the arrivals board at the station and move off to meet the 11.45 a.m. from Newcastle. One marked VIDEO OFFICER carries his camera on his shoulder.

The train in, a mass of people appear. Low-key, they could be Leeds or Newcastle, merging with the shoppers, the silly Christmas hats, the plastic bags full of presents. Argos. Mothercare. Harvey Nicks. At the Leeds United city-centre store there is a queue at the tills. The shop displays are pushing bed wear (nighties, pyjamas, duvet covers), Leeds tops (on offer from today until Christmas Eve at only half-price) and a book for every Leeds fan's tastes: Eddie Gray's, David Batty's, Lucas Radebe's, a fans' diary by Richard Sutcliffe and – out in time for Christmas stockings – David O'Leary's *Leeds United on Trial*.

The Hogshead pub on the other side of Briggate is filling up. Groups of Leeds fans huddle round tables. A few Geordies, their black and white tops visible round their hips under thick jumpers and jackets, are talking to the Leeds fans, laughing, buying each other drinks. The Saturday before Christmas and all is well: two sets of football supporters enjoying the pre-match banter.

But walking to the ground three Geordies emerge, shouting 'We are top of the league, We are top of the league . . .' and other songs to wind up the Leeds fans. We'll see who's singing that at five o'clock, you think. But you can't say it. It would be bad luck. But whoever does win today's game will be top for Christmas.

Jon is unhappy. He's always had a special thing about Newcastle. He lived there once. These fans have given the game an edge for him. And then there's Alan Shearer. Jon doesn't so much hate other teams as individual players. He hates Shearer more than you do. He doesn't care if it's a draw today, so long as Shearer doesn't score and he doesn't have to watch him wheeling past with his arm in the air. He hates the way Shearer does that.

REASONS TO HATE NEWCASTLE

1 The lad on the next street – when you were a kid – who used to support Newcastle.
2 The bricks and bottles their fans threw at you in 1984.
3 They are threatening to take our Champions League place.
4 Alan Shearer.

You're surprised to see Lee Bowyer warming up before kick-off. He waves and smiles to the Kop. You knew he'd paid his club fine, but you didn't expect to see him play. You applaud like the rest of them as he steps towards the Kop to take a bow, but feel uneasy. Weren't you the one refusing to sing his name four days earlier? Where's all your pious morality now? And when he scores – equalising Bellamy's opener – you are on your feet again, singing: 'Lee Bow-yer! Lee Bow-yer! Lee Bow-yer!'

In the second half, Leeds score twice, having looked second best to Newcastle's first-half quick thinking and enthusiasm. Viduka. Then Harte, making up for the sluggish defending that let in Newcastle for their goal.

At 3–1 you think, One more goal and you'll try and start a chant of 'We are top of the league', put the Geordies in their place. They might play fancy football, but it's Leeds who are putting the ball in the back of the net. And that – essentially – is what football is all about. It's not the team that plays it fancy that wins: it's the team that puts the ball in the back of the net.

Elliot scores. Three–two.

Shearer scores. Three–three.

Solano scores, skinning Harte again. The last minute. Three– four.

And the Newcastle fans fill the stadium with their song – half of them stripped to the waist, their shirts above their heads: 'We are top of the league! We are top of the league!' They have won at Arsenal. Now they have won at Leeds. They will lead the way this Christmas.

And Jon will not be happy. He will have been right in front of Shearer when he wheeled past, celebrating Newcastle's third goal.

Leeds (1) 3 Newcastle (1) 4

Martyn; Mills, Kelly, Ferdinand, Harte; Bowyer, Batty, Johnson, Kewell (Bakke 47); Fowler, Viduka.

Scorers: Bowyer, Harte, Viduka

1	Newcastle	18	34–23	36
2	Arsenal	18	37–22	33
3	Liverpool	17	26–17	33
4	Leeds	18	26–17	32
5	Man U	18	43–28	30

On the way back to Leeds Jon asks you – aware that you took a firm position on Bowyer at the Everton game – if you chanted his name when he scored.

'Yes,' you say. 'Did you?'

'Yes,' he says. 'Everybody did.'

You skip watching *The Premiership*. You can't deny it was a great game. And Newcastle won because they were good, not because Leeds were shit. Except Harte. You don't watch it because you can't face seeing an interview with Alan Shearer. It's the way he talks about himself: Alan Shearer this, Alan Shearer that, like he's talking about someone else, like he's a brand name.

At 3 a.m. you wake up. You can't shake a dream: Alan Shearer telling you you've left the tumble dryer on, that the whole house is about to go up in flames. And behind him on the panels: NTL, ITV, Carling logos.

You check downstairs. The dryer is off. Unplugged.

SICKENER: THUG BOWYER GLOATS AS HE SCORES ON HIS RETURN
Sunday Mirror (23.12.01)

'"Lee Bow-YER, Lee Bow-YER" the crowd shrieked in frenzy . . . Bowyer milked it, running to all parts of the ground, gleefully applauding, raising his mittened hands in salute . . . It was not so much joy that appeared on Bowyer's face, but a kind of gloating arrogance.' There is a picture of Bowyer, his face screwed up after scoring his goal.

The press were still at it. But now he had played his comeback game the story would run out of legs. That would be it. For now.

Everything about being a Leeds fan can be crystallised into Lee Bowyer. Here is the man whose name I have chanted more than any other in the last three years. The man who netted against Anderlecht, Barcelona and Milan. The man who – the first time I took my wife to the football – ran right up in front of me in the Kop and celebrated there, with me, and I lost it, screaming, shouting, and she stepped back for a second wondering what had come over me before joining in herself. I love Lee Bowyer. I love it when he's in the team because he's 100 per cent. He won't let you down. He'll run from penalty area to penalty area for 95 minutes. He'll applaud the fans after the game even if we've lost. He is a fucking superstar and I love him.

But I've seen him, those expressions he makes with his face. The rage. And there's the idea that he could have been involved in that beating, racism, overspillings of anger. So what do I do? Do I have to make a decision? Do I have to say I love him or I loathe him? Or can I say both? Can I say I love him on the pitch but I think he's quite possibly a bit of a cunt off it? Which is the stronger – my immediate reaction when he scores a goal or my ideas of what is good and what is bad that I have gathered around me over the years?

Out with a couple of friends that night, we talked about the football. One a Brighton fan. One Man U. The Man U fan said he was glad Bowyer had got off. He thinks he's a good player. He'll be good for England. He asked what I thought.

I said I was sick of it. I was sick of reading about Leeds United being the arsehole of the world. In the past I'd felt pleased to be associated with Leeds United and all the bad news that seems to follow the club around, I said. But this has turned me off all that.

Neither of them had watched the *Panorama* programme. I told them about it. I explained how seeing the reconstruction had terrified me, the fuzzy images of five men kicking the shit out of another. And the interviews with Sarfraz Najeib's father and brother. They made it more human for me, I said. When I heard that Bowyer and Woodgate might have been involved in something like that I didn't think about it from the victim's point of view. How it feels to get kicked half to death. But hearing Shahzad Najeib say how he felt seeing his brother being attacked, unable to get to him at first, helpless, then getting to him and thinking he was dead – how would I feel about it if it had been my brother there and it was me unable to help? And how would I feel if I was called out in the middle of the night to see my son smashed to pieces on a hospital bed?

I told them that I'd been to the Everton match and had not been able to raise myself to sing for the player. All I'd felt was uncomfortable. With the fans, the players, the club. It was all wrong, I said. I didn't feel anything for any of them. I didn't want to be there.

They were surprised. They knew me as a big Leeds fan, always talking about it, always up about it. Why was I so down? I could be down on Bowyer and Woodgate. Fair enough, they said. But why was I down on the club and the fans?

I wanted to justify what I'd said. So often you feel something and can't justify it, but this time I had to. So I told them about the men who sit near me. Always giving me the chat. Moaning about me going to the toilet during the match. Taking the piss out of me and other people around us. And the time there was that trouble in the stand. These lads were arguing with another Leeds fan, something about slagging off this player or that. Something and nothing. There was nearly a fight, but one of the lads managed to calm the others down. Leave it, he said. It's not worth it. That sort of thing. When they left their seats at the end of the game I was behind them. Once they were under the stand they turned and formed a semi-circle at the foot of the steps. The lad they'd been arguing with came down the steps, a hundred people pushing him down, no opportunity for him to turn back. He barely saw them before they grabbed him by the coat, pulled him out of the way of the rest of us, threw him to the floor and started kicking. That's what fucks me off, I said. That's the sort of thing that makes me sick of it.

BOLTON WANDERERS v LEEDS UNITED Premiership
Wednesday, 26 December 2001

MORE REASONS TO HATE BOLTON
1 They've won at Old Trafford and we haven't done that for decades.
2 They drew at Leeds earlier this year.

*You know that Leeds are kicking off at Bolton at midday. If you mentioned it –
here on Boxing Day with your wife's family – they'd put the radio on for you. The
game would be part of the day. You're part of the family, after all. The idea,
however, does not appeal. If Leeds were sure to win it would be great. You could
celebrate, laugh and joke, enthuse. But the way Leeds are playing just now,
anything could happen. Listening to Leeds lose sat with the entire family could be
difficult. Difficult and depressing. You'll play it close to your chest, listen furtively
to Leeds United Clubcall on your mobile upstairs.*

*You phone Clubcall 15 minutes in. Leeds are winning 2–0. Fowler scored both
goals. You announce the score downstairs. Your father-in-law puts Radio Five on:
the Arsenal–Chelsea commentary. The Christmas tree lights come on at the same
time. He brings you a beer. You sit by the tree grinning. You have the newspaper
on your knee, monitoring the league table. Everyone is happy that you're happy.*

*The second half is starting, it's still 2–0. You remember the last three games:
2–0 up Leeds drew 2–2, 3–0 up Leeds won 3–2, 3–1 up Leeds lost 4–3. And
Bolton are attacking. You've had a couple of beers. Lunchtime drinking always
makes you jumpy. You wish it was over and you could change the league table,
add three points and move Leeds up.*

*The smell of reheated turkey brings you back to your senses. Now you have
the worry that lunch will be served before the game ends. At 2–0 there's still
everything to lose. You'll have to suggest you turn the radio off if the meal is
served.*

'Rebecca?'

Your wife's mother is calling her. There's still 20 minutes to go.

'Rebecca can you help me serve?'

'Let's go to . . . Upton Park.'

*You sit in the living-room. Alone with your wife's grandmother. She looks
uneasy. She gives you a tight smile across the room and it occurs to you that you*

are ruining Christmas. But all you have to do is concentrate on the last 15 minutes, then you can be Mr Christmas. You'll redeem yourself. You'll suggest games, bring up conversation pieces. You'll be the life and soul.

'Let's go to the Reebok . . .'

Oh fuck! This is it. This is 2–1. Three points blown. Why does this always happen?

Penalty! To Leeds! Fowler for his hat-trick . . . misses.

Furious, you turn off the radio and sit down to eat. To hell with them! Fuck them! You have to get on with real life. There are four people tiptoeing around you – and you're spoiling everything.

You eat.

After the main course you slip upstairs. To the toilet, you tell them. There's no reception on your mobile to get Clubcall. It must be full-time now. All you need to know is the score. Mercifully when you go back downstairs your father-in-law has the radio on. Leeds have won 3–0. Fowler again. His hat-trick. You raise your glass and wish everyone a Merry Christmas.

Bolton (0) 0 Leeds (2) 3
Martyn; Kelly, Woodgate, Ferdinand, Matteo (Harte 45); Bowyer, Batty, Bakke (Wilcox 6); Smith, Viduka, Fowler.
   Scorers: Fowler 3

1	Newcastle	19	37–23	39
2	Arsenal	19	39–23	36
3	Liverpool	18	28–18	36
4	Leeds	19	29–17	35
5	Man U	19	45–28	33

SOUTHAMPTON v LEEDS UNITED Premiership
Saturday, 29 December 2001

ANOTHER REASON TO HATE SOUTHAMPTON
1 You have a vague memory they beat Leeds in a semi-final before you really got into Leeds United.

In the Midlands still, it's Radio Five. You listen until 4.45 p.m. Few mentions of Leeds at Southampton. Destined, the reporter says, to be an unfestive 0–0 draw.

Not ideal, you think. But at least it's not a defeat. You'd settle for a draw.
'They've broken the deadlock at St Mary's . . .'
Shit! This is it, you think. The last minute. We've lost. We've bloody lost at
Southampton. We're not even going to get in the Champions League at this rate,
let alone win the league. You can't make sense of the words from St Mary's at
first. The reporter is saying something about the Southampton defence. Why
doesn't he just say the score? He says . . . 'Viduka' . . . that could be good . . .
Then 'Bowyer' . . . and 'scores'. Bowyer has scored.

You are on your feet, punching the air. Through the sliding doors your wife is
watching you. She is sitting with her grandmother, who is asleep and doesn't see
your aggressive posturing.

The final whistle. Southampton 0 Leeds 1.
How do you feel about Lee Bowyer now?
You love him. You love Lee Bowyer, unequivocally.
The reporter winds up his match report: 'The headlines once again belong to
Lee Bowyer . . .'

Southampton (0) 0 Leeds (0) 1
Martyn; Kelly, Woodgate, Ferdinand, Harte; Mills, Batty, Smith, Bowyer;
Fowler (Wilcox 90), Viduka.
   Scorer: Bowyer

1	Arsenal	20	41–24	39
2	Newcastle	20	38–25	39
3	Leeds	20	30–17	38
4	Liverpool	19	29–19	37
5	Man U	20	48-30	36

O'LEARY REVELATIONS TURN STOMACH
The Guardian (17.12.01)

I bought David O'Leary's book *Leeds United on Trial* just a week after the
end of the court case. Some of the stuff in the last chapter was still fresh
news, in the papers the day before.

   His line is pretty sound: he's furious with the players for being out
drinking and running around Leeds city centre, they had brought the name
of Leeds United into disrepute; he's disgusted at the attack on Sarfraz

Najeib and the impact it has had on his family; he's behind Duberry and the difficult position he found himself in; he respects the principle that a man is innocent until proven guilty; and he details the abuse and threats he got for playing Bowyer and Woodgate, letters claiming a so-called holy war had been declared on him and his wife. He addresses the issues clearly and with attitude. Sometimes it reads like it could have been written by the Leeds United press office, sometimes an angry and frustrated voice comes though: O'Leary's.

Added to that are pages and pages of the usual boring football autobiography prose: this game, that game; this player, the other player. The odd swipe at people who have crossed his path. And moving sections about his father and his good friend Gérard Houllier. A book – like many football books – that fades in and out of being interesting and boring.

But then who has ever managed to write a decent book about football?

He must have expected the storm of criticism that would come with his publication of a book called *Leeds United on Trial*. He was profiting from the misfortune of the Najeib family, said the press, backed up by the Najeib family spokesteam. 'We are disgusted by this and it is another example of the way Leeds have been totally insensitive to the Najeib family,' said the Najeib family spokesman, Suresh Grover – the man from the Channel Four news. 'O'Leary is making money from this incident because he knows there is a huge amount of interest in it.'

O'Leary defends himself. He didn't have control over the title, he says. The book was supposed to come out after the first trial had died down. He didn't make money from the serialisation.

And so for the first time I felt uneasy about O'Leary the man. O'Leary the manager, I have no problem with. He's served up the best Leeds United team I've seen. I am forever in his debt. But the book – and his recent defensive attitude (off the pitch) – irritated me. From being the most loved manager in the country he's suddenly the most loathed. Fans of other clubs tell me how much they hate him. People on *606* call just to have a go at him. I can sort of see why.

Why did he write the book? Why was it called *Leeds United on Trial* right after the trial about a man who nearly got kicked to death? Why did he say there was one chapter about the trial when there were three? Why did he say he got no money from the serialisation when it would have been tied into the book deal?

Half-truths.

Why doesn't he talk straight any more?

LEEDS UNITED v WEST HAM UNITED Premiership
Tuesday, 1 January 2002

MORE REASONS TO HATE WEST HAM

1 They should have sold Lampard to us. Not Chelsea.

2 They have won the FA Cup twice since we last won it 30 years ago.

A frozen New Year's Day and you make your way to Elland Road driving over patches of black ice. After the three dodgy home games following the court case, Leeds have picked up six points from two away games. Added to that, Liverpool have slipped up drawing 1–1 with Bolton at Anfield, Chelsea have lost 4–2 at home to Southampton, Man U are playing Newcastle tomorrow and Arsenal's game has been frozen off, so today – if we win – we go back to the top of the league.

Mark can't make it up from Cambridgeshire, so you take your wife. She has an unbeaten record watching Leeds. You've taken her four times: 4–1, 4–0, 2–1 and 4–0. An enviable record.

Eight minutes into the game the woman-in-front turns round and grabs your wife by the hands and says 'You must be our lucky mascot!' Mark Viduka has scored twice already.

You had been nervous about playing West Ham. They are good. Unbeaten in six, they drew with Liverpool a few days earlier. But, although they pass and move nicely, they have little to offer up front.

Bowyer is in the team and so is Woodgate. His first home game since the verdict and he already looks fit. His touch is still there and – apart from one weak header – he looks the part alongside Rio.

After the second goal goes in the crowd turns on David James, the West Ham keeper. He's wearing his hair bushy-yellow these days: 'Gower, what's the score? Gower, Gower, what's the score?' Rebecca laughs. She thinks the Kop is witty.

Towards the end of the first half Bowyer comes up towards the Kop for a corner. The Kop sings his name. As Harte lines the ball up by the corner flag, Bowyer turns to the Kop, smiles and signals that the Kop should keep it up. The singing of 8,000 people doubles in volume. It's no wonder Lee Bowyer thinks he's a superman.

The second half starts like the first, with a goal. Robbie Fowler runs onto the ball, James comes out too far and – with the flick of his boot – Fowler lobs it over him. It's the kind of goal good teams score. Sometimes you forget Leeds are a good team with good players. Sometimes you have to pinch yourself.

On the radio on the way home you ask Rebecca what she thought of Leeds. Her last game was two years ago. What's changed?

She says Leeds pass the ball well. They're patient. They don't give it away. She says we dominated the midfield and that's why we managed to stifle West Ham, who did, she admits, pass and move better than Leeds at times. Leeds were the better team because they looked like scoring at the end of all that passing. She sounds like a well-tuned football pundit and you wonder why it took you 20 years to understand the importance of patient passing and winning the game in midfield.

She has kept up her unbeaten record: 5 games, 5 wins, 17 goals for, 2 against. She should have your season ticket.

Leeds (2) 3 West Ham (0) 0

Martyn; Mills, Woodgate, Ferdinand, Harte; Smith, Kelly, Batty, Bowyer (Wilcox 87); Fowler, Viduka.

Scorers: Viduka 2, Fowler

1 Leeds	21	33–17	41
2 Arsenal	20	41–24	39
3 Newcastle	20	38–25	39
4 Liverpool	20	30–20	38
5 Man U	20	48–30	36

CARDIFF CITY v LEEDS UNITED FA Cup
(Third Round)
Sunday, 6 January 2002

In the 1950s Leeds played Cardiff City in the FA Cup third round three years on the trot. Each game ended Leeds 1 Cardiff 2. But that was 50 years ago. This is 2002 and football is different now: Leeds are top of the hugely successful Premiership, Cardiff over 50 places below.

You wake at 4 a.m. You've had a dream that Leeds are out of the cup. They've lost 4–3 to Cardiff.

REASONS TO HATE CARDIFF CITY

1 Their fans are animals.
2 Sam Hammam – the Cardiff chairman – says Cardiff are a bigger team
than Leeds.

*You tried to get a ticket to Cardiff. You hoped the game would be moved to the
Millennium Stadium, but it stayed at Ninian Park. You will have to listen on the
radio again. Predictably, in the first minutes hard tackles are going in, this time
from Cardiff, not Leeds. Cardiff want to blunt Leeds United by taking out a key
player. In the eighth minute Rio Ferdinand goes down after a savage tackle.
Cardiff have done their homework: they know that if they injure Rio, Leeds will
be half the team they could be. Rio goes off: Duberry comes on. He plays
alongside his old friend Jonathan Woodgate. This is their first game together since
the end of the trial. One newspaper reports the next day that the new centre-back
partnership for Leeds 'barely acknowledged each other during the game'.*

*You are outraged at the foul on Rio. Was anyone even booked for that? It was
so obviously part of Cardiff's game plan. Their player should be at least sent off.
In fact, the manager should be sent off as well. It was premeditated. Foul play.
Cheating.*

*And the Cardiff fans are in on it too. The commentators describe missiles,
coins and bottles coming onto the pitch. Harte's been hit. And Martyn.*

*Then Viduka scores and you immediately relax. It's going to be okay, you
realise. You had forgotten Leeds are playing a shit team. We might have injured
players and have to resort to First Division defenders, but we're playing Second
Division opposition. It's going to be okay. You allow yourself a smile and say
something encouraging to your wife. Their fans can stop their child's play now.
It's over for them.*

*When Cardiff score you feel that sickness in the pit of your stomach, the panic
that things are not going the way they are meant to. There is supposed to be an
unbridgeable gap between the Premiership and the Second Division. Leeds should
beat Cardiff. Cardiff should not even be allowed to score. This is against the order
of things. You wish it was over. You would accept a draw now. You'd like to hear the
final whistle, take Cardiff apart at Elland Road. Beat them there. That would do.*

You're rattled.

*You hear the Cardiff fans singing 'You're not singing any more . . .' There's no
noise from the Leeds fans. They're rattled too. And so are the players.*

*When Alan Smith is sent off your wife glances at you. You smile through
gritted teeth at her. This is as much as you can manage in the circumstances. You
can see she's thinking about going into another room. But your smile was
encouragement enough for her. Stay, you are saying. It doesn't matter. It's only a
game of football!*

And a comforting voice in your head is saying, So what? It's only the FA Cup. It would be good to be knocked out of it. Leeds are top of the league. It would be to our advantage if Leeds went out.

But you don't believe the voice. It's a lie, a defence mechanism. You used to have it fine-tuned, back in the old days. It's just a bit rusty now. You haven't needed to find excuses, reasons and counter-reasons, techniques to cope with defeat. It used to be your specialist subject back when for the first nine years you supported Leeds they didn't get past the fourth round of the FA Cup. And because you used to love the cup, every time Leeds got knocked out you were devastated for days. The dream of the final. The excitement of the draw, round after round. The idea that one day Leeds could play in the final and you would be there.

The second half is agony. It makes you feel sick. You imagine you actually could vomit. But you are fixed to it, tied in. Every time Cardiff come forward you close your eyes. Rebecca has stopped looking up at you. She wants to express her solidarity. She wants to communicate that even if Cardiff do score she will be there for you. She will still love you. She will help you get over it.

When Sam Hammam comes on the pitch you are furious. He is walking past the Leeds fans to stand behind one of the goals. He must be stopped. It shouldn't be allowed. But you bottle it up, keep it quiet. You mustn't speak. You're too nervous. It could bring bad luck if you speak now.

And when Cardiff score the winner, for the first time in years you don't know how to react. Normally you have a slant on it. A take. You get that feeling you used to get when Leeds went out every year in the third round: the you-have-to-face-all-your-friends-at-school-the-next-day feeling, even though you're 34 and no one at work cares about football.

The final whistle goes.

Your first thoughts – first ways of coping with this catastrophe – are to decide what you'll say to people when they say 'Huh, huh. What about Leeds yesterday?'

'Cardiff cheated!' you'll say. 'They fouled. Their chairman incited a riot. It's all wrong. It's all wrong . . .'

But the result would barely get a mention, so you wouldn't need your excuses.

Cardiff City (1) 2 Leeds (1) 1
Martyn; Mills, Woodgate, Ferdinand (Duberry 10), Harte; Kelly, Bowyer, Batty; Smith, Viduka, Fowler
Scorer: Viduka

STUNNED O'LEARY RELIVES TURKISH HORROR
Metro (8.1.02)

Before the match you checked Ceefax for news of trouble. You'd expected it. Cardiff have a reputation. So do Leeds. There might, you thought, have been trouble the night before. Or in bars during the hours before the game. It's inevitable. But the first reported trouble is during the first half of the game: inside the stadium, missiles being thrown. And when the referee is hit there is a break for him to receive treatment. Leeds fans are lifted over the fences to safety. It sounds like a scene from Hillsborough. When the pitch invasion starts you look at your wife, all-knowing.

'There's going to be trouble now,' you say.

You saw it in the '80s. You took part in it. Invade the pitch, celebrate, then a sudden turning – something animal, like a flock of birds turning with one collective will – and running at the opposition's fans to goad them, to see what they would do.

The commentator describes the pitch invasion like it's an extension of the match: the Cardiff fans move towards the Leeds goal . . . there's a man down in the penalty area . . . he's receiving treatment. It sounds absurd.

There are thousands of Cardiff fans goading the Leeds end now. The police stand between the two sets of fans in full riot gear, dogs and batons lashing out, an advertising board hurled into the Leeds fans.

The commentator is saying that these are the worst scenes seen on a football ground for years, then hands over to Radio Five's man on the pitch who says he has tried to find Cardiff fans to interview, but they are all so appallingly drunk they can't speak. And Sam Hammam is on the pitch again, running up and down with a Welsh flag.

On 606 the first two callers are Leeds fans. One says she was hit three times by coins during the game. The other says the man behind her was hit with a bottle.

'It was terrifying,' she says. 'The Leeds players were too scared to take corners.'

You feel outraged. The result can't stand! You will not accept it! It doesn't count!

'It wasn't easy for the players,' says another Leeds fan on *606*. Nor was it easy for the fans who had the misfortune to be in Istanbul. The memories of that.

Cardiff fans come on. It wasn't so bad, they say. It was just exuberance.

They have lower standards, you think. They are used to week-in-week-out barbarism.

The Leeds fans were throwing things too, says another Cardiff fan.

'RETURN TO HOOLIGAN DARK DAYS. STUNNED O'LEARY RELIVES TURKISH HORROR.' This is a story with potential. Images fill the shelves of WH Smith: hundreds goading the Leeds fans, police swinging batons at a group of animated Cardiff fans, screwed up faces, people being stretchered off the pitch, two fans picking up an advertising hoarding, the referee having his head injury tended to.

The Sun carries the same image as the *Mirror*: men with twisted faces goading the Leeds fans: 'WAR ZONE.' It lists Cardiff's 'CUP SHAME':

The Leeds team bus was attacked on the way to the stadium.

A linesman was hit by a missile.

The referee was injured and needed treatment.

Ian Harte was hit.

Danny Mills was hit.

Nigel Martyn – trying to avoid missiles – was eventually hit and will say in an interview the next week: 'There were coins, sweets, lighters, and bottles . . . every time I went to get the ball from behind the goal I had to be careful because there was so much stuff being thrown at me.'

The press go on. The players had been afraid to go near the edge of the pitch to take throw-ins, to attack or to defend. The match was influenced by the fans. It is an outrage. David O'Leary says 'We were getting into an Istanbul situation out there . . .' This was what Leeds players had to put up with. How can they be expected to play with those memories? The football means nothing. Cardiff should be banned, Leeds reinstated.

But was it all Cardiff? Some of the papers report missiles being thrown at Sam Hammam as he walked past them. Hammam confirms it. 'Leeds fans are certainly not blameless,' he says, 'and certainly not some sort of holy people.' Your immediate reaction is to think 'Good, he deserved it. Walking out there, goading the Leeds fans, stirring up xenophobia in the Cardiff fans. He's not even Welsh. He's a madman. Maybe if he'd been pole-axed he'd have kept his mouth shut and not ended up inciting a riot by standing in front of his fans and running around with a fucking great Wales flag!'

Some Welsh Minister or other – interviewed on Radio Five that morning – says it wasn't so bad. Not a riot. He adds that the Leeds players bottled it. What about Galatasaray? Does he remember that? Does he think the Leeds players don't have a good reason to 'bottle it'? How would he feel if two Welsh fans had died and some Leeds politician said the Welsh players were chicken for being reminded of something like that? He's a fucking MP!

You realise you still have to come to terms with the defeat.

Over the day – as therapy – you slag off the Welsh Minister to every person you meet. People are quietly sympathetic.

The evening papers pick up the story where the morning press and the tired radio coverage is slipping. Sam Hammam is the new focus in most of the papers. There are dozens of stories about what he did during and after the game: confrontations, goading, acts of violence. His life history. His mad antics at Wimbledon. His suspect Welsh nationalism, his pitch walk, his flag-waving, his fight with O'Leary, his dealings with a Radio Five reporter. He is the one who is responsible for playing extracts from the Monty Python 'Professional Yorkshiremen' sketch, a string of Welsh songs and for parading around with a Welsh flag. He has been stirring Cardiff up with his nationalism-cum-xenophobia for months. He has a bad history. He is the national hate figure of the week. Or a fascinating character of fascinating contradictions. It depends which paper you read.

And another story: it emerges that outside the ground – having been pelted with coins, bottles of piss and other Welsh detritus – the Leeds fans had to avoid a hail of half bricks. One woman was hit in the face. Then – funnelled to the coaches by the police, safe from the Cardiff fans – one man fell and was attacked by a policeman and his dog. This man is no regular Leeds thug. He is the treasurer of the Leeds United supporters club. His story is the new news slant now that Sam Hammam has been fully demonised by the press. Pictures of him on his sofa at home wearing his yellow Leeds shorts to show off the huge bruises on his thighs, the puncture marks and gashes, where the dog bit. There are photos of the police assault too: a grey-haired 50-year-old man struggling on a tipped-over fence, trying to get to his feet, dazed, a dog apparently trying to rip his arm off. His story: he tried to get on his bus, but found his way blocked by the police and the dog; he ran down the side of the bus to get away from the dog; he fell; then he was attacked. Even the police in Cardiff were against Leeds.

And you get the feeling the whole world hates Leeds United. You feel like you've been manipulated. The press and the radio have been stirring you up all week, moving the story from the pitch invasion to the antics of Hammam to the attacked Leeds fan. There are so many angles and the press is squeezing their balls dry over this one. So by the end of the week you are exasperated, and exhausted. It's been an emotional roller-coaster. And it rings a bell: this is how the press have been pumping the Bowyer–Woodgate trial for weeks.

NEWCASTLE UNITED v LEEDS UNITED Premiership
Saturday, 12 January 2002

MORE REASONS TO HATE NEWCASTLE
1 They beat us last month.
2 They are in our Champions League spot.

You know Leeds will lose today: it's Newcastle again. And Rio is injured. (Replaced by Duberry.) There's no point in listening to the radio. You could have a nice day instead. Take the car out. Meet some friends in Harrogate. You want your wife to enjoy her life: an alternative to her sitting in one room as you sit clenched with anxiety in another listening to football.

You will not think about it from 3 p.m. to 5 p.m. At 4.55 you turn on Radio Five: '. . . Smith after 28 seconds,' says the commentator, but then . . . 'that Duberry own goal... then Dyer . . . then Bellamy . . .' You switch it off. You feel like shit. You will not watch The Premiership. *You will not buy a Sunday paper.*

Newcastle (2) 3 Leeds (1) 1
Martyn; Mills, Woodgate, Duberry, Matteo; Kelly, Batty, Bowyer, Johnson (Wilcox); Smith, Viduka
  Scorer: Smith

1	Man U	22	54–32	42
2	Newcastle	22	42–29	42
3	Leeds	22	34–20	41

MILLS BOMB TICKING
Observer (20.1.02)

After weeks of Leeds being the pariah club and another weekend of articles picking us out as the dirtiest team in the universe, with bans hanging over Smith, Mills and Bowyer for bringing the game into disrepute, and the hangover of the trial, and the press sticking some of the blame for Cardiff on Leeds fans, you are sick of it. Everywhere you turn, someone is having a go at Leeds United: its players, its manager, its fans, everybody.

Even people who don't like football think that Leeds United are bad news.

It came to a head in a meeting last week. You sat with a mate who supports Bradford City. The bloke next to him sounded like he was from the north-east. Your mate picked up on it, never one to miss an opportunity.

'From Newcastle?'

'That's right.'

'You follow Newcastle United?'

'Season ticket holder,' says the Geordie.

'Ahhhhh. This is Tom,' says your mate. 'He's a Leeds fan.'

'Alright,' he says.

Your mate sits back. His work is done.

'We played your lot at the weekend,' says the Geordie.

'Yes,' you say.

'Dirty lot!' he says. 'And that Mills. He's an animal. I thought you lot were supposed to play good football.'

You try not to react. This is a meeting. It would be rude to turn his table over and kick his chair from under him.

'Bad, was it?' you say.

'Bad? It was brutal . . .' He goes on.

It used to make you proud. Leeds were dirty on the pitch and off it. You loved the reputation. Leeds stood out. But now you're sick of it. You're off the club as it is. You've been cool since the end of the trial. You've lost the point.

Why do you go?

135

LEEDS UNITED v ARSENAL Premiership
Sunday, 20 January 2002

You leave the house to get the train. Another morning of press and radio speculation. Leeds v Arsenal: war on the pitch, scores to settle, that sort of thing. And it's true. The game gets nastier every time it's played. However much the players and managers say there's no animosity between them, you know it's bollocks.

You walk to the station: three weeks since the last home game. You've been working like a dog and looking after your wife who is still not well, not thinking about Leeds United. But there's something in the way you're walking today. You're bouncing. The anxiety that you've felt all morning – you realise – wasn't about the pressure you've felt yourself under. It's about the football.

You'd forgotten!

Fuck all the press coverage! Fuck all the whingers in meetings and on the radio! This is the football! This is you going to catch a train to watch Leeds United! You are a Leeds fan on his way to Elland Road: a few pints, the match, then a few pints more. You've forgotten that – however perfect they might be – your wife, your house and your job are not the sum of who you are. To get the full picture you need them, but you also need Leeds United.

You are half-running to the station, even though the train is not due for 20 minutes. You're excited! You need this. You need to be able to walk out of the house once a fortnight, go and have a few drinks, stand up on the Kop and shout. It's what you are.

MORE REASONS TO HATE ARSENAL
1 Arsène Wenger
2 Martin Keown

At Elland Road the rest of the crowd is up for it too. No flat atmosphere today. Leeds score early: Robbie Fowler. And with Ferdinand back, the Leeds defence looks sound. The whole team's good. So is the bench. This could be the turning point, you think. Lots of players back; the full squad. One–nil up against Arsenal.

But it's clear that Arsenal are a good team too, though they are not at their best. The game is cagey. Arsenal are playing it tight because for them it is a six-pointer. Leeds are a rival for the championship. They come closer and closer. They should be at 1–1, maybe even winning. But you are pleased with Leeds. We have held out. We can defend.

Then Pires scores. The big screen – courtesy of Sky TV – shows Wenger leaping from the dug-out. You feel overwhelmed with rage, but you hold it inside yourself.

At the end of the game you feel a little flat. You'd have liked a win. Still, you've had your day and all the problems in your head seem less important now.

Leeds (1) 1 Arsenal (1) 1

Martyn; Mills, Woodgate, Ferdinand, Matteo; Bowyer, Batty, Johnson, Wilcox; Viduka, Fowler.

Scorer: Fowler

1	Man U	23	56–33	45
2	Newcastle	23	42–29	43
3	Leeds	23	35–21	42
4	Arsenal	22	43–26	41
5	Liverpool	23	32–24	40
6	Chelsea	23	40–33	37

LET'S ALL LAUGH AT MAN U - NUMBER TEN
Man U 0 Liverpool 1

On the one hand it's funny that Man U have lost at last. They'd won eight games on the trot and it was starting to look inevitable that they'd be 20 points clear of the rest at the end of the season. And that they lost to Liverpool is funny too. That's the worst for them. They'd rather lose to Leeds than to Liverpool.

Your wife was round at a friend's house. And her boyfriend – Man U – was going on about how he couldn't wait for the match. Like the Man U fans on *606* a few days before, he thought it was going to be 4– or 5–0. Man U are at the top of their form: Liverpool the bottom of theirs. That old Man U arrogance was back again.

So it is funny that Man U lost.

But you'd have preferred a draw.

There is *something* from the game that has put a smile on your face: Liverpool scored with five minutes to go. The Stretford End would have loved that. You imagine thousands of Man U fans leaving the ground, gutted, still hearing the taunts of the Liverpool fans coming from the away end even when they're out on the street.

LET'S ALL LAUGH AT MAN U – NUMBER ELEVEN
Middlesbrough 2 Man U 0

Normal service resumed: Man U lose to a shit team. Boro. Two late goals. It's funny – worth a laugh again. But not a belly laugh. It was the FA Cup. You'd have preferred Man U to stay in the cup all season, build a fixture pile-up, lose in the final, exhausted. But it's worth a smile all the same, if not just for the fact that Ferguson's old number two – Steve McClaren – has put one over on him.

CHELSEA v LEEDS UNITED Premiership
Wednesday, 30 January 2002

You are waiting at the side of the road. A silver Sierra draws up. Inside, two skinheads in Chelsea tops. You get in.

Brian – the driver – has been watching Chelsea for over 30 years, his son, Chris, since he was three. They drive down from Milnthorpe, Cumbria to London at least once a month. They're taking you to Stamford Bridge. Chelsea v Leeds.

Brian is 45 and covered in Chelsea tattoos, HATE on one fist, no LOVE on the other. But everybody loves Brian. Your wife's great-aunt used to have him round for tea all the time. It was at her funeral that you devised this trip.

The journey to London passes quickly. Brian tells stories about his 30 years as a Chelsea fan and his son watches him from the back seat, taking it all in, laughing, asking his dad questions. They're both looking forward to the game. They like playing Leeds and the way the Leeds fans are always up for it. The first time Brian went to Elland Road he went on the Gelderd End. He was just a kid. The Leeds fans were wearing war paint. And he overheard one say: 'Shall we stab him here or wait until he's on his own?' Brian walked the other way. 'Leeds fans are barmy,' he says.

And you've heard the stories about famous battles at Chelsea – 500 Chelsea fans waiting at Fulham Broadway tube station armed with scaffolding. The Leeds fans piling back onto the tube trains to escape the onslaught. Or the time Chelsea showed off their new electronic scoreboard, in the early '80s, and a posse of Leeds fans smashed it up with bricks.

But there'd never been that much trouble with Leeds down at Chelsea. It was coming up to Leeds that used to scare Brian. Never easy, he says. It was only when he got into the ground he'd feel safe. With the rest of the Chelsea fans. But when the 90 minutes was nearly up his heart would start pounding. He had to get away from the ground. And it wasn't so easy for him. He couldn't go with the rest of the Chelsea support back to the station. He had to make it on his own. He was a northern Chelsea fan. He had to find his car or get to the bus station. Back to Cumbria.

He'd seen fans who walked on their own being picked off before, ambushed. A big group of fans might be involved in a pitch battle, hundreds of them, but no one would really get hurt. It was the fan on his own who was going to get hurt. And once he left the ground they'd be looking for people like him, small packs of Leeds fans trawling the back streets and the car parks. Sometimes he'd join the march with the rest of the Chelsea fans to the station for safety, then double back to his car at Elland Road.

These days Brian quite enjoys going up to Leeds. It's a different story now. He likes to walk up to Elland Road in his Chelsea shirt. He might get the occasional odd look, but nothing else. He takes his sons. They wear Chelsea tops too. He reckons there's still trouble around. All this coin throwing recently is a sign it's still there under the surface. But if you wear colours, he says, it shows you're not interested. It's the ones dressed smartly that you have to look out for. If you just walk to the ground and don't draw attention to yourself you'll be okay. Especially with a 9 year old and an 11 year old.

At the motorway services the three of you walk past several looks of concern before a man emptying bins asks, 'Who you lot playing today?'

'Leeds,' says Brian.

The man scowls.

And you realise that everyone thinks you're a Chelsea fan too: in the shop, in the toilets, in the café. You stand slightly at a distance from Brian and Chris. What if some Leeds fans came in and saw you with them? What would they think?

Back on the road, Brian says he's never gone looking for trouble. Not even in the past when it was all the rage. But when it starts up around you, you have to defend yourself, don't you? He's done a bit of that. He's been involved in running battles, city-centre riots, that sort of thing. He got arrested once for fighting Man U fans on Preston station. It wasn't his fault. His mate pushed him into it. And he was so pissed he could barely stand. He got hit, went down and woke up in the back of a police van. That was the sum of it. No charges. Another time he went into a DIY store with some mates and they threw paint all over the place. Made a right mess. And he put his foot through a plate-glass window once too. He was part of a riot, smashing up a town centre. He thinks it was Shrewsbury. But he got his foot stuck in the hole he'd made in the glass – 3 ft off the ground – and two of his mates had to lift him free.

When he was younger – way back – he did some construction work at Stamford Bridge. Putting up segregation fences.

Coming off at the end of the M1 Brian is getting fidgety, biting his nails, rubbing his hands together when the car stops at lights. He points out a petrol station.

'That's where I always stop for petrol on the way home,' he says.

It's not just the coffee, the Coke and the family pack of Maltesers that's getting him excited. He's in his pre-match routine now. He's excited. Down the A5 to Paddington. Park up. Get to a pub. He's like a kid before Christmas. This is what he likes to do in his spare time.

Pedestrians trying to cross the road look into the car and see two Chelsea skinheads in their 'Fly Emirates' and 'Autowindscreen' shirts and don't walk in front of us like they would any normal car. They wait for us to pass.

When you were just a little boy you used to have a fantasy about Chelsea. Your first dad left home when you were three. It was never easy to engage with him after that, so in the fantasy he used to get beaten up by a gang of Chelsea fans. You would see it happen and chase them off, catching them one by one, kicking the shit out of them, a string of ambulances picking them up off the streets of Leeds. Revenge. Then you'd go down to London at night, break into Stamford Bridge and burn it down. You used to go through that one every day for years. Variations on assault, beating up, maiming, killing Chelsea fans. Always ending at Stamford Bridge with a can of petrol and a box of matches. Then the lap of honour at Elland Road when everyone knew you'd done it.

On the tube Brian is singing Chelsea songs under his breath. 'Oh, Denis Wise . . . Scored a fucking great goal . . . In the San Siro . . .' You sing along, replacing Denis Wise with Dom Matteo. Your version rhymes better. But you don't pick Brian up on that. Brian asks you to sing the Leeds song about Chelsea for Chris. You're happy to oblige: 'When I was just a little boy . . .' Chris's face drops. He doesn't like that one. And you immediately wish you hadn't sung it. You head for a pub and order some drinks. You're meeting Matthew there. He's come up from Brighton to see the game.

At the next table a group of three well-dressed men are looking over. They don't like the look of us. One catches the eye of another and scowls. You look back at their gold bracelets, their thick-gelled hair and their blue January sunglasses and scowl back.

'Most people think we're scum, don't they?' says Brian.

Brian gives you a tour of the all-new Stamford Bridge. He's very proud of the bars, the hotels and the penthouse flats. Chelsea this, Chelsea that. Even the rubbish bins are branded white on blue Chelsea FC. Brian loves it here. He loves Chelsea. He takes you into the Chelsea Megastore: three floors of it, packed with people wanting to buy, buy, buy.

Official Club Sweets: a choice of Jelly Babies or Wine Gums.

Toothbrushes. Three colours.

Mini-skirts. Three colours again. And a discreet CFC on the hip.

Chelsea chocolate.

A whole floor devoted to BEDROOM ACCESSORIES & CHILDREN'S WEAR.

The Official Club Air Freshener.

Door plates. (Names still available: Callum, Joshua and Lauren.)

Wrapping paper. Gift tags.

And if anyone is worried that they are being cynically exploited to buy things marked up 500 per cent because they say Chelsea on them, their minds are put at rest by the statement of intent on the back of the 20 or 30 shop assistants: 'REMEMBER: EVERY PENNY YOU SPEND WITH CHELSEA GOES DIRECTLY TO YOUR CLUB.'

Outside the shop Channel Chelsea are busy talking to the fans. The interviewer is Bubble from *Big Brother*, baseball cap on backwards. Chelsea fans greet him like an old mate, pulling him away from the camera to shake his hand.

'Tough game?' says Bubble to one Chelsea fan.

'Easy win,' says the fan back to him.

Then Bubble picks out a couple of Leeds fans.

'You lot hate us,' he says.

They're camera shy, smiling, with nothing to say.

'Why do you hate us?' he presses them.

Still nothing.

'Don't you hate us, then?' he says.

'No,' says the Leeds fan.

'Well, we hate you,' says Bubble. Everyone gathered round is laughing and the Leeds fans disappear off camera.

Now Bubble's talking to Brian. Brian's telling him how he comes down from a village called Milnthorpe every week to watch Chelsea.

'Where's that?' says Bubble.

'The village?' says Brian.

'Yeah,' says Bubble.

'Cumbria,' says Brain.

'Where's that?' says Bubble.

'We all hate Leeds and Leeds and Leeds . . .' is coming out of the door of The Britannia at full blast. Brian lets you go in first: 500 Chelsea fans packed into a narrow pub, no room to move, the queues at the bar indistinguishable from the rest of the drinkers.

Some are banging on tables. Some are standing on tables. And even though they're singing about Chelsea, the atmosphere is fantastic. There's still 90 minutes to go before the game and it's like a celebration of a cup-final victory. Songs are coming from one part of the pub, answered by a group of six stood on a couple of tables in another part.

Everyone is hot and pink-faced. All grinning.

'Sometimes I wish this atmosphere would transfer to the ground,' says Brian, still caught for a moment in the cockney accent he's singing along to the songs with.

Another round of 'Ten Men went to Mow', all of them belting it out like it was the national anthem. Then more 'We all hate Leeds and Leeds and Leeds . . .' which is bearable. One fan tries to start up a chant of 'Always Look out for Turks Wielding Knives', but it doesn't take off.

> Forever and ever
> We'll follow our team.
> We are the Chelsea
> We rule supreme.
> We'll never be mastered
> By you northern bastards . . .

We could be in Leeds, except for the substitution of two words. I look to see if Brian is singing along. He is. He's an honorary southerner when he's got his blue shirt on.

As kick-off approaches the songs get worse. Less about loving Chelsea, more about hating Spurs.

> We'll be running round the Tottenham with our willies hanging
> out . . .
> Singing: 'I've got a foreskin, haven't you?'
> I've got a foreskin, haven't you?
> Singing: 'I've got a foreskin,
> I've got a foreskin,
> I've got a foreskin, haven't you?'

Everyone has a film of sweat on his face and neck. The pinkest faces belong to three skinheads stood on a table, leading the singing. Fat. Red-eyed. Gorged on beer. Taunting the Chelsea fans right behind us: 'One game a season. You're only one game a season . . .' Thinking there are no Leeds fans present, they're turning on each other. 'One song . . . You've only got one song . . .' The lads behind us belt out a round of 'Who the fucking hell are you?' There are nasty glances between the two groups. Gestures. Then the skinheads start another song:

> Oh when the blues
> Go marching in,
> Oh when the blues go marching in . . .

And everyone joins in. Rattling it out that bit louder, relieved they're all together again.

Then a solitary figure is standing on a table. One of the skinheads. He quietens everybody with a calming gesture to lead a song: he sings a line and everybody else has to echo it. Like American soldiers on a training exercise. That's the idea. It's something about a girl he's taken home.

'Hare lip,' he sings.

'HARE LIP,' repeats the packed pub.

'Broken nose.'

'BROKEN NOSE.'

'VD.'

'VD.'

It goes on. She's not the best of the bunch, he seems to be saying, but he's going to take her home and shag her anyway. A girl at a nearby table – the only girl in the place – looks away as the two men sat with her join in the singing.

In the stadium we are on the front row, a few yards from the glowering Leeds fans. There are spare places in the Leeds end and you ask Brian if he minds – a few minutes into the game – if you pop over and sit with them. That's okay, he says. Of course it is. But the places fill up, so you're stuck in the Chelsea end.

You want to join in with the singing, but you can't with most of the songs. When they sing 'We all hate Leeds and Leeds and Leeds', you join in, substituting 'love' for 'hate'.

Then Chelsea score. You stay sat down. A few days before, two friends warned you to at least stand up if Chelsea scored, make yourself less conspicuous because the Chelsea end will be full of animals. But you can't. The best you can do is stare straight ahead and say nothing. It's almost unbearable. If you speak to Brian or his son now – however much you like them – you will say something bad.

The Leeds fans are quiet, singing nothing. Stood staring just like you.

Then Chelsea score again.

At half-time you go under the stand and queue for the toilet. Someone says, 'One more goal and I'll enjoy the second half.' He's standing with hundreds of others, watching the two goals over and over on the TV screens, each with a plastic bottle of Bud in his hand. You feel distraught.

In the second half you are more aware of the Chelsea fans around you. One is doing your head in. He's joining in with the 'We all fucking hate Leeds' songs a bit too loudly for your liking. And 'Can We Play You Every Week?' Your anger boiling, you say to Brian that he should stop you if you try to follow the man to the toilets. You would never do it, of course, but you'd like to crack his head against the concrete toilet wall a couple of times.

'Silverware, Oh silverware. You ain't got no silverware.'

The Chelsea fans are having a good singsong now. You are deep inside yourself. You want to kill them all, burn their precious Stamford Bridge down just like you always meant to.

On the way out of the ground, you stick your leg out into the crowds half a dozen times to trip Chelsea fans. They apologise. You swing out again. A couple of kicks. Two or three people stumble as they make their way for a victory drink, thinking it's funny how Leeds rolled over for them tonight. They thought it would be harder than that. They thought Leeds were supposed to be good.

Chelsea (2) 2 Leeds (0) 0
Martyn; Kelly, Woodgate (Harte 45), Ferdinand, Matteo; Bowyer, Batty, Johnson (Keane 38), Wilcox; Viduka, Fowler (Kewell 64)

1	Man U	25	60–34	48
2	Arsenal	24	49–29	47
3	Newcastle	24	45–30	46

4	Liverpool	24	34–24	46
5	Leeds	25	35–23	42
6	Chelsea	24	42–23	40

Weeks later – when you've got over the defeat – you talk to Matthew on the phone. You didn't have a chance to talk to him properly after the game. You want to know what he thought of it.

He thought the pub was amazing. He'd never seen anything like it. But he wasn't scared. It made him realise that some people live and die for football. And he enjoyed the game, although he could see you didn't. But he thought you did well to keep a lid on it. You were worried he'd think you'd been unpleasant. No, he thought you were nice. You did well, seeing as you were sitting amongst the Chelsea fans. He thought it was funny you were singing along to all the Chelsea songs, substituting words to make them into Leeds songs.

In the car on the way back north you sulk, sleep, then finally open up and talk. Brian has driven for 8 of the last 20 hours. And he's run out of Maltesers.

LEEDS UNITED v LIVERPOOL Premiership
Sunday, 3 February 2002

MORE REASONS TO HATE LIVERPOOL
1 You fear them.
2 You hate them instinctively. You don't need reasons.

Every time you play Liverpool you look at the red of their shirts and expect defeat. Like it's natural. Like that's how it should be. It's a hangover from when you were a kid. But it's not like that now, you tell yourself. We drew at Anfield late last year. You don't need to expect a rout any more.

But today there will be a rout.

Rio's own goal does not bode well. Rio is the rock. If he's scoring for the other side you can only expect the worst. Then – after half-time – Heskey gets two in three minutes. Three–nil. As his second hits the back of the net, hundreds of Leeds fans are on their feet, storming out. You watch the trails of them leaving to go under the stands, the Liverpool fans too ecstatic to sing 'We can see you sneaking out'. There are still 27 minutes of the game to go.

IF YOU'RE PROUD TO BE A LEEDS FAN

It is only at 3–0 down that the Kop gets behind Leeds. You're the same. You've been as muted during the game as everybody else. Why don't we get behind them like we used to? Do we expect them to turn everyone over? Do we have a divine right to win all the time, not to let goals in? It's not like we're Liverpool. Now, however, the Kop is singing: 'We are Leeds' and 'Marching on Together'. Defiant. We're Leeds fans and it doesn't matter if it's 3–0 or 10–0.

And something clicks.

A memory: you used to come to the football because you were a Leeds fan. It used to be about expecting the worst, but standing up and singing with the rest of them because you loved Leeds. Leeds were shit, but it didn't matter, because you were Leeds. Now you come to the match and if Leeds don't win you feel like you want to be somewhere else. In the garden. Sipping coffee in Starbucks. What's happened to you?

The best times were when Leeds were rubbish, you think. Whether it was 0–3 or 5–2 you'd be singing. Because going to the football was about going to the football. Not about winning. Not about being top of the league.

Now it's 3–0 you can feel it. You're a Leeds fan and however much the scousers are singing it doesn't matter. You'll stay to the end and applaud the players off. You feel more of a Leeds fan than you have all season. This is what it's about. It's about standing up and getting behind your team.

By the end of the game (the score 4–0) a third – maybe more – of the Leeds fans have gone home. That leaves 26,000. About the number of people who used to come when Leeds were rubbish. A thinning-out. Those left in the Kop applaud the players off. Fowler applauds the Leeds fans, then walks sheepishly towards the tunnel, turning to the Liverpool fans. He applauds them too and they rise in adoration.

Leeds (0) 0 Liverpool (1) 4
Martyn; Kelly, Matteo, Ferdinand, Harte; Bowyer, Batty, Dacourt (Wilcox 57), Kewell (Keane 75); Viduka, Fowler.

1	Man U	26	64–35	51
2	Newcastle	25	48–32	49
3	Liverpool	26	38–42	49
4	Arsenal	25	50–30	48
5	Chelsea	25	45–25	43
6	Leeds	25	35–27	42

MIDDLESBROUGH v LEEDS UNITED Premiership
Saturday, 9 February 2002

You've never liked playing Boro. Even when you were a kid, the games were full of hatred, players being set off, scuffles in car parks, the odd person at school supporting neither Leeds nor Liverpool, but Boro! And it was clear Boro hated Leeds. They hated that Leeds were still in Yorkshire, whereas they'd been turfed out. They hated Leeds's success: Middlesbrough have never won anything. Then at college your best mate was a Boro fan. Mick. It's never easy when your friend supports another team. Once both Leeds and Boro were in the same division you hated them. You didn't tell him, but you wanted them relegated.

The worst moment was Leeds's first game as champions: August 1992, Boro away. A 4–1 defeat. Mick went. It was one of the best games he'd been to, he said. That was it for you: ill-will towards Boro came before anything.

Then you met a girl from the area. Emma. Her dad supported Boro. So did she. That was enough for you to hate Boro even more. People you cared about, cared about Boro. You were vulnerable now. One defeat and half of Teesside would be on your back.

REASONS TO HATE MIDDLESBROUGH
1 First game defending the title in 1992–93. Boro 4 Leeds 1.
2 You know too many people who support Boro.

You get away from the travel agent, to stand in Dixons on Briggate at 4.42 p.m. It's Boro 1 Leeds 2. The six or seven men stood there (two with attendant girlfriends) have clenched fists. There can only be a couple of minutes to go. This is a result that could turn the season round. Since New Year's Day it's been terrible: haemorrhaging goals, bad morale, a string of defeats. A win and all that would change. A win and we'd be back up there. In with a chance.

Meanwhile your wife is still in Going Places booking a trip to Bruges for next week. Five days away. You would have asked the woman keying in your holiday if she could get lufc.co.uk on her terminal, but you didn't dare. So here you are at Dixons.

Scoreflash: Boro 2 Leeds 2 and your heart drops in your chest. Two men peel away from the scrum around the TV. One of the girlfriends follows. Under his breath a man mutters 'For fuck's sake!'

And to make it worse Liverpool are winning. Six–nil! And Newcastle are winning too. This is terrible. Your dreams of another season in the Champions League are fading. You want it so badly. Teams from Italy and Spain. The music. The silver stars all around the stadium. Another trip to Madrid.

You think of Mick and Emma. They'll laugh when they see the score. They'll know you're thinking of them. They'll enjoy that.

Then there's an image of Lee Bowyer shaking hands with the scorer of the equaliser, Dean Windass. And the final score. Two–two. You leave with the rest of them, trooping through the door of Dixons out onto Briggate.

Middlesbrough (0) 2 Leeds (1) 2
Martyn; Kelly, Ferdinand, Matteo, Harte; Bakke, Batty, Dacourt (Wilcox 85), Kewell; Fowler, Viduka.
    Scorers: Bakke, Fowler

1	Man U	27	66–35	54
2	Liverpool	27	44–24	52
3	Newcastle	26	51–33	52
4	Arsenal	26	51–30	51
5	Chelsea	26	46–26	44
6	Leeds	26	37–29	43

PSV EINDHOVEN v LEEDS UNITED, UEFA Cup (Fourth Round, first leg)
Thursday, 28 February 2002

You wake up at 2 a.m. Amid the howling of the wind and the rain lashing against the roof of your Bruges hotel, you can hear someone shouting. At first you can't make out what's going on. You feel that middle-of-the-night terror. Then you recognise the tune. You sit upright. 'Oh, Ha-rry Kewell.' Did you hear that right? Are you dreaming? You strain your ears.

Harry-Harry-Harry-Harry Kewell
Harry-Harry-Harry-Harry Kewell

PSV EINDHOVEN V LEEDS UNITED UEFA CUP

Harry-Harry-Harry-Harry Kewell
Oh, Ha-rry Kewell . . .

You're not dreaming. This is Bruges, Belgium. Ten miles inland from Ostend, the night before Leeds play in Holland. And someone in the storm is singing the Harry Kewell song.

You can see the sign on the ticket office door from across the road: 'SOLD OUT.' Your stomach drops. You're surprised. It's a big stadium and only the UEFA Cup after all. You'd have thought there'd be no problem getting tickets off the club. It's not like it's the Champions League. There were loads of spaces at Real Madrid last year. Still, you think, there's always going to be touts . . .

Except all the way around the stadium there are stewards. Six hours before kick-off and not a tout in sight. You decide to go back down to the station, a few of the bars. There'll be touts there. Tickets galore. You're not worried. Wherever there's demand there's supply. And there's plenty of demand, dozens of Leeds fans walking up and down between the station and the stadium.

Rebecca thinks it's funny the way the Leeds fans are walking up and down: 'Like they're promenading,' she says. 'It's the way they eye each other, checking out who's who. You're doing it too,' she says. 'Stop it!' She says she can spot who are Leeds fans. But she's not sure how she knows.

You follow the loud music to a concealed square. Hanging from one of the pubs there's a huge banner: 'PSV VERSUS LEEDS UNITED – FAN SQUARE.' It's a three-sided square, bars on one side, houses on another; and a building site. It's tight and the roads leading up to it are narrow. Just the place to put a few hundred Leeds fans for a few hours before the game. In the centre of the square they've set up three bars and a blow-up football pitch. Two flags are up already: 'BELFAST WHITES' and 'LEEDS UNITED SCOTTISH WHITES'. At 2 p.m. there are more police and stewards than Leeds fans.

You still feel gutted. And a bit panicky. You haven't got a ticket in your back pocket like you thought you would have by now. It was meant to be easy: train ride, get ticket, a few pints, a meal, then the match. But you're still looking around for a tout and there's no one. No one pulling a string of tickets from their pocket. No one asking 'Tickets?' Just dozens of men like you casting about in the growing crowd, catching your eye like you might be the tout who's going to make their day.

Rebecca wants to move on. She doesn't like Fan Square. She says it's claustrophobic. Even when it was empty it was horrible, all cut off from the

149

rest of the city. She says it's just a side street next to a building site, not a square at all. It's like a stage set for the Leeds fans. That's why she's happier in Eindhoven's Main Square, with Leeds and PSV fans being friendly together because they *are* friendly, not because they've been cajoled into being friendly. And in the Main Square she doesn't feel ashamed to be English. She thought she would. She says she feels welcomed to Eindhoven, not tolerated.

After the concession of a couple of kitchenware shops and a bagel café you get back to Eindhoven's Fan Square. The crowd is building now. Leeds fans talking to PSV fans. Laughing. A few plastic glasses scattered on the floor. Discarded chips. Cans. Rebecca is amused by the Burberry everywhere: baseball caps, shirts, collars, the panel on front of someone's sweatshirt. And it's not all Burberry – some of it's Aquascutum. Very expensive, she says. She wants to know why lots of Leeds fans are wearing it. It reminds her of armour: helmets, breastplates, that sort of thing. What's it all about? She's seen women around Eindhoven wearing it too: umbrellas, handbags, scarves, blankets on the back seats of cars.

Eindhoven is a big, flat, concrete city. No character. It must have been bombed in the war. Or only have developed recently. The locals are going about their business: men in suits, street cleaners, evangelists. Some of the locals catch your eye. They want to know if you're one of them. Or one of their visitors. Their city is not normal today.

There are dozens of PSV fans walking around, either in PSV tops and scarves or with discreet PSV badges. Two are wearing PSV ponchos.

'It wasn't like this in Madrid or Troyes,' you tell your wife, wanting her to think there's something special going to happen today. 'You never see home fans trawling the streets like this.'

But there are Leeds fans everywhere too: stood talking to mates on mobile phones, looking at the Leeds United Travelling Fans' Guide to Eindhoven, carrying plastic bags stuffed with cans of Heineken, staring from restaurant windows, ordering at bars. At the station, dozens of Leeds fans queue at the Ticket Service booth. Do they sell tickets for the football here? Finding out – just like we did – that they don't, they make their way up to the stadium to be disappointed again.

Back in the Main Square some Leeds fans are having a kick-about. A single police officer watches, leaning up against the side of his armoured van. Two policewomen on horses chat as three children – one in a Leeds top – talk to the horses. A man, dressed from head to foot in white, rolls his moped up to some Leeds fans and tries to convert them – with the aid of a loudspeaker – to Jesus. Girls walk up and down the café promenade smiling to each other as a small group of Leeds fans sing: 'Hey-ey, Baby, I wanna know-ooooo, If you'll be my girl . . .' The girls smile again. Everyone is having a good time.

The hundreds of Dutch and English drinkers watch the kick-about, men balancing pints at arm's length as they play the ball to members of the public to see if they play it back. They applaud all those who do. A man in a suit with a briefcase. A grinning boy. Two girls. A man with silver hair: Peter Ridsdale, out inspecting the troops. He looks well, has a deep tan. He knocks a crisp ball back to the drinkers and receives a standing ovation.

Coming back from the stadium, an hour to kick-off and still no tickets, the Leeds United bus rolls by in the heavy traffic. Rebecca takes a picture of Robbie Keane, Harry Kewell, Alan Smith, each sat behind the other. She waves and Robbie Keane waves back. You hope the wave will help her get over the disappointment of us not having tickets. After the build-up of the day – the travelling, being with hundreds of Leeds fans in the Main Square, anticipating being one of a thousand Leeds fans up against tens of thousands of Dutch fans – she was excited. This is her first away game. She likes it. She likes being in the minority.

But seeing the players just makes it worse. They – like most of the fans – are going to be in there, under floodlights that are already on. We are not. We're going to be sat on a train back to Bruges.

In a bar off Fan Square people are talking about tickets. You ask several people. Nothing doing. Several people ask you. Maybe you look like a tout, standing in bars, catching people's eyes. Outside the bar Rebecca is talking to a lad. A Leeds fan. He lives in Rotterdam, he says. He's tried to get tickets for weeks. You can't get them in Holland unless you have a PSV card. What's he going to do? He'll stay in the bar, drink with the other Leeds fans without tickets. Half an hour to kick-off and the square is still packed. You console yourself that at least you're not the only one who failed to get a ticket. But you still feel stupid.

Outside the bar two lots of opposing fans stand 6 ft apart shouting songs at each other. The police watch, tapping 3 ft sticks on the backs of their boots. They are ready. Invisible to most of the crowd, they have moved in. The armoured vans that were covering the streets some distance away are closer now, next to the bars, every exit covered. We are surrounded. Horses and dogs remain at a slight distance.

Rebecca is disgusted that so many people are so drunk. 'They should give us their tickets,' she says. 'They're too pissed to notice a game of football.' You remind her that in Madrid and Troyes you were like that too, and you still enjoyed the game. It's all part of coming away to watch Leeds: travel, get pissed, watch the game. If you can get a ticket.

Some shouting starts on the far side of the square and two dozen police race off. But nothing is happening. The police come back round to go straight into a bar, single file. No one is removed or dragged into vans. The only incident is a pissed-up PSV fan abusing a policeman sitting in the driving seat of one of the armoured vans. The policeman opens the door suddenly, knocking the PSV fan back, eyeing him until he walks away.

Some of the fans, clearly without tickets, set on drinking through the match, kick-off only a few minutes away, are singing: 'We're all going on a European whore, a European whore, a European whore . . .' They say they're going back to Amsterdam after a couple more drinks. There's a train at eight o'clock. Some of their mates stayed there rather than come as far as Eindhoven anyway.

The woman whose house overlooks the square has drawn her blind.

REASONS TO HATE PSV EINDHOVEN
1 They beat us 5–3 in 1995.
2 Van Bommel – PSV's top player – was offered the choice between a move to Leeds or Man U. He says he'd prefer Man U.

Your train pulls out of Eindhoven station. The lights are bright above the PSV stadium. It must be nearly half-time. You try to look through the backs of the stands to see some action. But there's nothing to be seen. You pretend to Rebecca that you don't mind too much. It was enough to be there during the day, with all the Leeds fans in the squares, enjoying the European away-day atmosphere. You've always enjoyed that part of these trips more than the matches, you say. But you can't conceal it from yourself. You're gutted you didn't get in. And you feel stupid: coming all this way . . .

You find out the score the next morning in the paper. Nil–nil. Leeds held on in the first half and ran the game in the second. Maybe there's hope for the quarter-finals. You check the attendance: 31,000. You'd thought their stadium would hold 60,000. You should have done your homework.

PSV (0) 0 Leeds (0) 0
Martyn; Mills, Ferdinand, Matteo, Harte; Kelly, Bowyer, Bakke, Kewell; Fowler, Viduka.

LEEDS UNITED v CHARLTON ATHLETIC Premiership
Sunday, 24 February 2002

You haven't been in this pub since you were 18. But James wanted to go to the most Leeds United pub you knew. It's James's first game since 1972. Thirty years. So you take him to The Scarborough. You said it would be full of nutters. The hardcore. One of the reasons you never went there was because you were scared of the maniacs in there. The ones who used to be there in the '80s, anyway.

Inside, working your way to the bar, you bump into a big lad. You fear the worst. But he says sorry and lets you through, smiling.

You'd wanted to show James the dark side of Leeds United. The real thing: thuggery, racism, misogyny, homophobia. Now you're embarrassed that The Scarborough is so tame. You apologise.

But James is happy. He thinks it's like a tribal gathering, people in their uniforms – expensive jeans, trainers and jackets – observing the ritual of wearing the same battledress, going to the same bars, standing in the same circles in the same bit of the pub, armies gathering before a war, stoking themselves up with alcohol. He is relaxed. Yes, he's seen a few people who look a bit dodgy, the type that could turn nasty with a few pints inside them. But on the whole it's a good atmosphere here, nice to join in the pre-match drinking.

You wait to get a late bus to Elland Road, so he can hear the singing from the last fans racing from the pub to the ground. No surrender to the IRA. Munich songs. That sort of thing. Old-time classics you never get on the Kop any more. But the bus is quiet. Nice people out for a nice afternoon.

You'd told James he'd see some unpleasantness. Not fights – just aggression and drunkenness. But it's the opposite. The sun is shining and everyone's relaxed after a couple of pints.

'This is nice,' says James, nodding his approval.

ANOTHER REASON TO HATE CHARLTON
1 There are only two reasons to hate Charlton.

Leeds are good in the first half, making plays towards the Charlton goal. Three strikers on: Viduka, Keane and Fowler. Bold stuff from O'Leary. But suddenly it's half-time and Leeds haven't scored.

What does James think of it so far?

He's enjoying the match, but Elland Road is a bit of a shock. The last time he came it was all standing. Then, the crowd had its own momentum, you could go where you liked, he says. Now it's all seats it's lost something. He's noticed a huge steward presence, but few police. He likes the way the stewards move up and down the aisles like they're being choreographed. And he's surprised by the huge TV screens with their adverts, the Lurpak stand, row on row of advertising hoardings. And the man in the middle of the pitch with the microphone. James has heard about him from people at his gym: the failed local DJ that everybody hates. And why is the volume of his voice turned up so high so that James can't hear his own thoughts?

The people-behind-you talk all through the second half. Viduka is shit. Kewell is shit. Both are lazy Australian bastards. And Fowler? What's up with him? He's shit too. And one of them has heard Bowyer is going to Arsenal. It was definite. Everybody knew it. He didn't want to live in the north. He was a London lad. He'd always meant to go to a big London club as soon as he could. Who was there on the bench? We need a new player on. Harpal Singh? The Paki? Yeah. They'd rather do without. Rather draw 0–0 than have a 'Paki' in a Leeds shirt.

At least there's some racism for James, you think, feeling pathetic and wondering what the hell you could have been thinking having him come to the football just to see all the bad stuff. What's the matter with you? You're supposed to be a Leeds fan and you bring him here to show him the dark and unpleasant side of it. You want him to witness the blackest songs, to see the worst of people. Why? Are you trying to show him it because you think it's bad? Or are you trying to show him that you are cool because you hang around at the football? Maybe you want him to think that you are a bit like this and you want to see how he reacts? Maybe you think he'll be as excited by tension and the threat of violence as you are. Maybe you love that threat? It's not that that's putting you off football.

James is annoyed by the people behind you for slagging off the players, Viduka especially. These are men who couldn't run 50 yards without having a coronary, he says, and they slag off someone who looks perfectly good. And even if Viduka is having a bad game, they should get behind him. Support him. Isn't that the point? Aren't we supposed to support them, rather than turn up and expect them to win?

The team is booed off at the end. You don't boo. You and half the Kop are applauding, James too. The players applaud back. They played okay. They just couldn't score.

After the game James is talking about the fans. He's heard men speak about winning, losing, loving players, hating players, shouting, laughing. All extreme emotions. He doesn't think men do a lot of that normally.

And he says he likes the way you join in all the songs before he's even heard them start. And the way you get behind the team even though he can tell you're disappointed.

You ask James what's the main thing he'll remember about his day at the football.

'Rio Ferdinand,' he says, smiling.

Leeds (0) Charlton (0) 0

Martyn; Kelly, Ferdinand, Matteo, Harte; Keane, Bakke, Dacourt (Batty 45), Kewell; Fowler, Viduka.

1	Man U	28	67–35	57
2	Newcastle	27	52–33	55
3	Arsenal	27	55–31	54
4	Liverpool	28	55–31	53
5	Chelsea	26	46–26	44
6	Leeds	27	37–29	44

LEEDS UNITED v PSV EINDHOVEN UEFA Cup
(Fourth Round, second leg)
Thursday, 28 February 2002

There's an odd atmosphere in Leeds, strange men walking the streets, chanting in voices too loud for 4.30 p.m. on a wet Thursday. Shoppers stand in doorways to watch, or weave out of the way of these strange men, who behave like comedy characters, moving more slowly than everybody else. They stop people: a bus driver – even though the lights are green – to ask where the 'stadium field' is. A woman making her way home. One of the strange men tries to hug her, but she slips quickly away from his clumsy grasp. Through the window of a shop, two policemen are guiding three of these strange men away from the girls who work there. The girls watch from behind the till, laughing nervously. In bars there are small groups of these strange men in clusters of six, eight and ten. They are wearing red and white striped tops, silly hats. And some have flags draped over their shoulders. One is slumped in front of McDonald's as his friends order food. He cannot lift his head when they call out to him.

In Wetherspoons and Cooper's in the station there are still a few of these strange men left, but they are outnumbered now by more familiar faces: men in baseball caps, tan jackets, Burberry.

Police vans and officers on foot trawl the streets. They are watching, but not interfering. There are no riot police. Not visibly. Just the regular troops. No long sticks. No armoured vans.

ANOTHER REASON TO HATE PSV
1 They wouldn't let you in their stadium.

The Kop is quiet a few minutes in. The game began with singing from both ends, but the PSV fans are so unrelenting, singing uninterrupted for quarter of an hour, that the Leeds singing has dried up. But there's still a good atmosphere: as individuals the fans are up for it, on the edge of their seats. They want Leeds to win this: they don't just expect it. And the players are up for it too, in the first half, committed. Mills, Bowyer, Smith – called in the press 'Leeds's sinning triumvirate' – give the Leeds team more bite now they're back from their bans. The Dutch play well: pass, move, pass, move. But they have nothing up front. They don't look likely to score. It's a good game. Sort of. A cup game. If Leeds lose this, the season is in tatters. If Leeds win, there's a trip to Rotterdam and a good chance of a third European semi-final in three years.

This is the first time you've been in the West Stand for 15 years. The view is brilliant. You can see the game unfold, the shape of the teams. Leeds players you thought were weak are in fact quite good, using space, trying to get the ball to a team-mate. And you can read the game before it happens here. The players know each other's games. Only Harte looks dodgy. Caught out of position. No pace. Is it an off day, or is he always like this? You only usually see players running to and from the Kop, no idea of how fast they are.

In a quiet period, the game flat, people watch something happening in the south stand. Police and stewards moving to the scene. A scuffle. It's hard to see who's attacking who, and why. Maybe a Dutch fan in the wrong stand? One man emerges from the melee holding a child – a one- or two-year-old boy – with his right arm, up against his chest. With his other arm he's punching people, fighting off the police. The child is wearing a bright yellow Leeds top. The crowd around the man boo as he – and the little boy – are dragged out of the stand and ushered towards the exit. The man is still punching people, still balancing his son on his hip. Other people join in the fight, objecting to his eviction. But he is bundled out by the stewards and the police, appearing at the last minute to fall down the stone steps.

There is no singing in the West Stand and little applause. It's passive support.

The one fan making animated gestures, getting out of his seat and shouting, who would be unremarkable in the Kop, looks as if he's behaving like a lunatic. People comment on him, shake their heads.

The half-time whistle goes. Leeds have played well. It's true PSV are not up to the standard of most of the teams that came to play Leeds in Europe last year, but it's still 0–0 after 135 minutes between the two teams. It's all to play for.

Both teams are more committed in the second half. It feels now like there's something to play for. PSV get behind the Leeds defence several times as the half goes on. And certain Leeds players – Kewell and Bowyer in particular – are giving the ball away. Kewell's body language is not good. He throws the ball against the ground twice in one minute, frustrated that his team-mates aren't ready for his quick throw-ins.

But the Leeds fans are singing more now. 'Sing your Hearts out for the Lads', 'We are Leeds', 'Marching on Together'. The PSV fans counter with 'You Only Sing when you're Winning'.

This brings back memories of the last time Leeds played PSV. Under Wilko. Leeds played gung-ho football, the Dutch sliced Leeds up. It finished Leeds 3 PSV 5. And the Dutch fans sang most of their songs in English: 'You're Supposed to be at Home', 'You're not Singing Any More', that sort of thing. You remember feeling furious at their cheek. And humiliated at the same time.

As PSV get more and more of a grip on the game someone screams 'CHANGE IT O'LEARY.' O'Leary doesn't turn round. He has been standing up throughout the game, moving from foot to foot, occasionally placing one foot forward to shout something at a player. But you agree. Why hasn't he brought Keane on? Is he waiting for extra time that might never happen? As PSV push on, there is more and more grumbling in the West Stand. Players are singled out. You wish you were in the Kop. At least you could sing there. At least you could do something.

There is a minute to go when PSV break through. The ball hits the bar and bounces back into play. Two Leeds players challenge one PSV player, so it looks as if Leeds will clear it. Then the ball is in the back of the net, the PSV bench is dancing with joy and three out of four people around you are leaving their seats, making their way under the stands.

You shout 'Come on Leeds.' It's natural to when Leeds let one in. The Kop is shouting it too. But here in the West Stand people are streaming out. Someone behind you says 'Come on Leeds? Does he expect two goals in a minute?' You want to turn round and say that you have to get behind your team whatever the circumstances. But he's right. Leeds won't score two in a minute. Maybe you were stupid to try and get behind them seeing as it's so hopeless.

Meanwhile the PSV fans are singing 'Always Look on the Bright Side of Life'. At the end, the Leeds players slope off. You applaud. Some people look at you. What the hell are you doing clapping? Are you Dutch? You can't be clapping the

Leeds players. Whoever you are, you don't fit in here in the West Stand. Those left in the Kop clap too. Some of the players clap back.

Outside you overhear conversations about how Leeds are going to do next season. How things will be better then.

Leeds United (0) 0 PSV Eindhoven (0) 1
Martyn; Mills, Ferdinand, Matteo, Harte; Bowyer, Bakke, Dacourt, Kewell; Smith, Viduka.

EVERTON v LEEDS UNITED Premiership
Sunday, 3 March 2002

ANOTHER REASON TO HATE EVERTON
1 They knocked us out of the FA Cup live on national TV in 1985.

Another Sunday. Another Leeds game on Radio Five. And the commentator goes straight for the jugular. Everton might be rubbish, they're saying, but what about Leeds? Now they've dropped out of the championship race there's speculation that half the players want to leave: Viduka, Kewell, Dacourt. All off to the continent. And added to that . . . what about O'Leary saying he wishes Bowyer and Woodgate had been sent to prison? The commentator and the expert – today it's Dave Bassett – go on discussing the fall of Leeds United. Team spirit is appalling, they say, something must be terribly wrong.

In the background you can hear 'Marching on Together'. Leeds's travelling support – as always – are up for it. Whatever is going wrong, you can rely on them.

Team news. Rio is out. He's hurt his back. And you can't help but worry – three centre-backs are out: Radebe, Woodgate and Rio. That leaves Matteo and Duberry. At least you can rely on Matteo, you think. And back on Merseyside too. He's going to be a key figure today.

Leeds start the game well, closing in on the goal, making chances. And the fans are still going: 'We are Leeds', 'Marching on Together', 'Glory, Glory Leeds United', 'We all Love Leeds and Leeds and Leeds'.

The commentators don't mention it, but it's 75 per cent Leeds on the pitch and 100 per cent Leeds in the stands. One of Leeds United's strengths at times like these has always been their fans.

'Out of the UEFA Cup . . . out of the FA Cup . . . down to sixth in the league,' says the commentator. 'It's been a bad year for Leeds United.'

But Leeds are playing well today.

You go downstairs and immediately there's shouting from the fans and the commentator's voice is raised. You rush back upstairs and hear '. . . second bookable offence . . . that's a red card . . .' You try to make sense of the commentary. Who's been sent off? '. . . down to ten men . . . Dominic Matteo is off.'

Now we're missing four centre-backs as Bakke slots in alongside Duberry and that feeling that this season is a catastrophe comes over you again. There is always something else, always something to make things more difficult.

At half-time you listen to interviews about other games, other sports, sat with your eyes closed, thinking, Why am I torturing myself on another Sunday listening to this? Why don't I go and help Rebecca in the garden? It's light outside. This is the first weekend of March. You could flick Ceefax on in an hour and it would all be so much easier.

Leeds start the second half well. Bakke is playing like a natural centre-back, another Leeds player finding that he's better at centre-back than his usual position. In the background the Leeds fans roar on. You wish the commentator would mention it, say something good about Leeds United.

On the pitch Smith is charging in. He's been booked already. But still he gets stuck in with late tackles. And you think it's just a matter of time before he's off too. Batty runs his studs across the chest of Gemmell – according to the commentator – and there is outrage in the home stands.

But every Leeds fan knows this is what Leeds do when they're down to ten men. They've had some practice. Like Villa at home when we unsettled them so much that they lost the will to play. It's ugly, but it works. In the circumstances David O'Leary must be happy.

Leeds are earning their point.

Leeds fans sing 'Going Down, Going Down, Going Down', a familiar song for Everton fans over the last few years. But Everton are still in the game, coming closer and closer, misplacing the final ball, firing wide.

Alan Smith goes in hard again. Another bookable offence, but no response from the referee.

'He's terrified of reducing Leeds to nine,' says the commentator.

'And he's sent Smith off already this season,' says Bassett. 'At Cardiff.'

The Leeds fans sing: 'Oh Eddie, Eddie, Eddie, Eddie, Eddie, Eddie, Eddie Gray . . .' They are making a point about Brian Kidd.

'We are Leeds, we are Leeds, we are Leeds . . .'

'Marching on together . . .'

'We all love Leeds and Leeds and Leeds . . .'

Relentless singing as Ginola comes on, threatens to score and fires a couple of free kicks wide.

Then Radzinski goes down in the area again. Batty again. No penalty again. Nil–nil. Again.

Everton (0) 0 Leeds (0) 0
Martyn; Kelly, Duberry, Matteo, Harte; Smith, Bakke, Batty, Kewell; Fowler, Viduka.

1	Man U	29	69–37	58
2	Arsenal	29	57–31	57
3	Liverpool	29	47–25	56
4	Newcastle	28	52–35	55
5	Leeds	28	37–29	45
6	Chelsea	27	47–28	44

O'LEARY REMOVES KIDD GLOVES
www.lufc.com (4.3.02)

After the game Peter Ridsdale goes over to the Leeds fans. He wants them to stop chanting nasty things about Brian Kidd. You didn't hear anything about Kidd on the radio, just 90 minutes of unequivocal support from several thousand loyal fans.

But there's anger at the club. O'Leary is upset. 'I was disgusted with the fans,' he says. 'As long as David O'Leary is at the club Brian Kidd will be at the club.'

The players come out in Kidd's support too. There are pictures of Rio Ferdinand, Nigel Martyn and Alan Smith at the specially arranged nothing-to-do-with-the-management press conference. They have don't-fuck-with-us expressions on their faces. They are behind Kidd, so the fans had better shut up.

You imagine the players slagging off the fans on the coach journey home from Everton, forgetting the support they've had, forgetting who pays their fucking wages, forgetting how the fans have been behind them even when they have had to put up with some of the worst behaviour from football players ever seen. Fans have had a lot more than abuse to put up with on their travels watching Leeds United. It makes you furious.

The club fire out a series of press releases and stories on lufc.com before the next game with Ipswich. O'Leary is first up. He wants the fans to show

160

their true support, says the website. 'This is now a test to see how good our fans are.' You remember the noise coming from the Leeds fans at Everton. He must have missed that, because he's talking about how good Sunderland and Newcastle fans are. 'It's no good for two minutes or five minutes,' O'Leary is quoted, 'it's about that passion throughout the game.' You feel angry. Didn't he hear the fans at Everton? Hasn't he been at the games in Europe home and away where Leeds have lifted the team? Who the fuck is he to slag the fans off?

The next website story is posted onto lufc.com. David O'Leary – it reports – has decided to take control of training again. 'Brian's sessions are interesting,' he says, 'but if he is one per cent from being the complete coach, it is that he could be a bit more confrontational with the players. He lets them get away with things that I don't think he should.'

So the fans have a point then?

Mixed messages from Leeds United Football Club.

You feel angry. Who to hate? Kidd? The players? O'Leary? Yourself?

Peter Ridsdale's department produce an altogether better press release. Although he warns fans that there will be grave repercussions if they carry on slagging Kidd off, he reasons his way through it. He's not so hot-headed as O'Leary. He's careful not to insult the fans. Ridsdale needs the fans. Their money. O'Leary will be elsewhere in three or four years – he can afford to be a blind egotist.

Ridsdale explains that it won't help the team for the fans to be having a go at one of the coaching staff. It'll undermine them. Even though it's been a disappointing 2002, the fans have to keep up their wonderful support. Remember what we have achieved over the last few years. Stick with us.

LEEDS UNITED v IPSWICH TOWN Premiership
Wednesday, 6 March 2002

ANOTHER REASON TO HATE IPSWICH
1 You are not there, not at Elland Road.

You turn on the radio at 9.20 p.m . And immediately . . . an update from Elland Road. It feels odd to hear the commentators talking about Leeds playing at home, odd to hear the familiar noise from the stadium coming over the radio. Again.

Originally scheduled for the Tuesday, they changed the date of the game to

Wednesday. Expecting the game to be on the Tuesday, you'd worked out exactly when to work and when not. You were working Wednesday evening, not Tuesday evening. Then they made the change.

All right, it was changed because (1) Everton away had been changed to the Sunday because (2) Leeds had to play PSV on the Thursday because (3) Champions League don't want the UEFA cup corrupting the Champions League brand on a Wednesday and because (4) the TV like to cover the UEFA Cup. But, all the same, you're sick of it. Sick of changed dates. Sick of playing on Sundays, Saturday mornings, Thursdays, Mondays. Sick of TV's messing football about. You used to like it when it was every Saturday at 3 p.m. You knew where you were then. But it's no use complaining: TV controls football now. You're just a fan.

The good news is it's 2–0. Harte has just added to Fowler's opener. You can hear the crowds cheering. You feel happy and sad. Happy Leeds are winning. Sad it's the first win for nine weeks and you're not there.

Leeds (0) 2 Ipswich (0) 0
Martyn; Kelly, Duberry, Matteo, Harte; Smith, Bakke, Batty, Kewell; Fowler, Viduka.

Scorers: Fowler, Harte

1	Man U	30	73–37	61
2	Arsenal	29	57–31	57
3	Liverpool	30	50–25	59
4	Newcastle	29	52–38	55
5	Leeds	29	39–29	48
6	Chelsea	28	50–30	47

After the game the radio reporter says that when Ian Harte scored he ran over to Brian Kidd and hugged him. You wonder how the fans reacted to that. You remember when the players ran over to Bowyer when he was refusing to pay his fine, how it made you feel. After all the criticism aimed at Leeds fans by the club, now this, the players making clear gestures aimed against the fans.

It makes you feel hatred for the players. Maybe you're just displacing your anger because you've missed a game, but you're thinking again about the players and how they are insulting to the fans by showing solidarity with Kidd. As if the Leeds fans aren't Leeds fans at all, but the opposition's fans. And those same questions are in your head again. Who pays their wages? Where were they five years ago? Where will they be in five years? They hold their press conferences and make their post-goal gestures! Have they forgotten where the fans come into the equation? Don't the fans count for anything any more?

Martyn says everyone was in that mood at the match. At least the few people he overheard. Waiting for Dave in Wetherspoons he overheard a conversation between two lads. They weren't happy with O'Leary slagging off the fans, saying fans in the north-east were the better fans, that Leeds fans didn't sing. And he was the one who started it all! That book was when it all started to go wrong. Nobody trusts him any more, firing off his opinions all the time. Slagging off players. Now the fans. One minute he's saying that he'll back Kidd all the way, the next he's saying he's going to take Kidd's place in training. What the fuck's all that about? What's the matter with him?

Martyn adds that when they announced the attendance: 'Leeds United thanks you for your support,' a fan shouted: 'I should fucking well think so.'

But there was no anti-Kidd singing, says Martyn. Lots of support for Eddie Gray, but nothing directly aimed at Kidd. Until the Harte goal and Harte runs over to Kidd.

'Fuck you, Kidd!' shouts someone.

And some abuse for Harte.

'Not a happy place,' says Martyn. 'We might have won, but it wasn't a good night.'

You feel better. You thought you were having such bad thoughts that you weren't a proper Leeds fan any more. But Martyn feels it. And so does everyone around him.

LEEDS UNITED v BLACKBURN ROVERS Premiership
Sunday, 17 March 2002

Two days before the Blackburn home game – on a 'special replacement bus service' between Dewsbury and Leeds – you see a chalk board outside a pub: 'Watch LEEDS v BLACKBURN Live – SUNDAY 2 p.m.'

It takes a couple of seconds for it to sink in.

Sunday? But it's on Saturday! You know the game is on Saturday because you've specifically booked an Apex fare for the 1740 Leeds–London train straight after the match. On Saturday! You're down in London all Sunday, for two friends' birthday parties. And your ticket to come back is fixed for the evening.

The pub must have got it wrong. The game is definitely on Saturday.

'It's on Sunday,' says Martyn.

'Bastards!' you say.

'Sky Digital picked it a few weeks ago.'

'Bastards!' you say. And you mean it. You are sick of the way they fuck about with the games.

'Dates and times may be altered at short notice,' the club say.

'There was nothing on the website,' you say.

'There was – a few weeks ago,' Martyn says.

Well, you didn't see it. And you're furious. You had to miss the last match because they changed it and you'd set something up for work. Now you're missing two on the trot. When was the last time you missed two on the trot? Have you ever? This is not just about missing games. It's about how much of a Leeds fan you are. Are you still a real Leeds fan? You've missed two matches. That's it. Your credibility has expired.

Fuck them! you think. Fuck the lot of them! You'll go to London. You've got your train ticket. And another thing! That's the last time you get a season ticket. That's three games you're missing in the league this season. They piss about with fixtures, change them after you've carefully choreographed your life around their meaningless fixture list.

'What are you going to do?' says Martyn.

On the train on the way to London you feel terrible as it goes past Elland Road. You feel like pulling the emergency cord. It is an emergency, sort of. In the past if this had happened you'd have missed the parties, found a way of getting out of the work commitment. If it took pissing off friends and colleagues you'd do it. Leeds United came first.

Not any more.

And that question is hanging there again: are you still a proper Leeds fan? You've missed how many games this season? Zurich in the UEFA Cup, even though you had a ticket. And now Ipswich and Blackburn. And you can't go to the last game of the season, against Boro. Four games? You've only been away three times. And one of those times you were stuck outside without a ticket.

Of course, you're still a Leeds fan. You are happy when they win, sad when they lose. But there's something going on. Something's changing . . .

You arrive at the party late. Everyone else is there. Drinking. Laughing. Rebecca is talking to five or six people. You get a pint and pick off solitary men. This is how you are at parties. Go straight in and talk about football. You are nervous. They've all been partying for hours. You talk to a Villa fan, an Oxford fan, a Reading fan. This is what you do. Certainly at the beginning of parties. Football. How are this team doing? What's going on with that team? That sort of thing. It's who you are. What would you talk about if you didn't have Leeds? You'd stand there like a lemon, then maybe make a run for it. The one thing you are good at is that you can talk football. Could you talk so authoritatively if you weren't a fully paid-up season ticket holder? Would people even want to know you? They might find a better Leeds fan to talk to.

You are drinking quicker and quicker, getting angrier and angrier, slagging off O'Leary for slagging off the fans, slagging off the players for sticking with their team-mates against the fans. People are surprised. They don't think O'Leary's so bad. They think now Woodgate's served his sentence he should be left to get on with it. They even think Bowyer should not have had to pay a fine – he was innocent, wasn't he? And you are listening to yourself trying to backtrack, suddenly aware you are more anti-Leeds than anyone in the room.

And there's something else, something funny's going on. Three or four people have asked you straight out if you're getting a season ticket next year. Maybe it's the obvious question, but it's odd so many people should ask in one evening. Then one of them spills the beans. Rebecca's been getting them to ask you. She wants positive proof. She wants witnesses. You said to her once you found out about Blackburn being on Sunday: 'That's it! I'm not getting a season ticket.' She wants confirmation.

ANOTHER REASON TO HATE BLACKBURN
1 It gave you so much pleasure when they got relegated after spending all that money. Their return has taken the edge off that.

The next day Rebecca phones her friend Peter, the Ipswich fan. You hassle her until she hands the phone over.
  'What was the Leeds score?' you ask him.
  He looks it up on Ceefax.
  'Three–one,' he says. 'Fowler twice and Kewell.'
  And you feel happy. Then sad. Then happy. Then confused.
  'Bastards!' you say. 'Why do they always win when I'm not there?'
  At work the next day a colleague comes up to you. 'Leeds did well yesterday,' she says.
  You nod, say nothing.
  'Were you there?' she says.
  Tongue-tied, red-faced, you say no. No, you weren't there.
  And you feel ashamed.

Leeds (2) 3 Blackburn (0) 1
Martyn; Mills, Woodgate, Ferdinand, Harte; Smith, Dacourt, Batty, Kewell; Fowler, Viduka.
Scorers: Fowler 2, Kewell

1	Man U	31	78–40	64
2	Arsenal	30	60–32	63
3	Liverpool	29	52–26	62
4	Newcastle	30	54–40	56
5	Chelsea	30	58–30	53
6	Leeds	30	42–30	51

LEICESTER CITY v LEEDS UNITED Premiership
Saturday, 23 March 2002

MORE REASONS TO HATE LEICESTER
1 Years of defeats to them – even though they are an inferior team to Leeds – have left a scar on you.
2 Now they're going down you might miss them.

'Why have you got the telly on?' Your wife wants to know why you have both the TV and the radio on.

'Because I can't get Radio Leeds and Radio Five are doing the rugby. I need to have Ceefax on too.'

It's that one time of the year when – outrageously – rugby takes priority over football. And to make it worse it's not even rugby league, but rugby union! Although you are vaguely interested in England beating Wales, you would much rather hear the football. Any football. Reports from around the grounds are short, mere sentences, so eager are they to get back to Twickenham.

'LEICESTER 0 – 0 LEEDS' sits there each time the screen scrolls round. You are doing some paperwork, but still have to look up every time you see the screen flicker: once every 30 seconds, over 200 times during the match. Then: 'LEICESTER 0 – 1 LEEDS, Viduka 18'.

'Let's go to Filbert Street . . .' you hear on the radio, but Ceefax registered the goal first. A Fowler shot that Viduka swept up on the rebound. 'Leicester,' the commentator says, 'can feel hard done by.' Fuck that! you think. You don't care if Leicester go out of business: Leeds need the three points. Today Chelsea and

Newcastle aren't playing. This is an opportunity to resurrect the season. The Champions League – all the razzmatazz, better players, money for the club, a sponsor for the White Elephant Stadium on the M1 – is not as impossible as you thought it was a couple of weeks ago. The screen flickers again. 'LEICESTER 0–2 LEEDS, Viduka 18, Fowler 32'.

Half-time feels good. Although – because of the rugby – you know nothing about the game, except that it's hard luck on Leicester. And Man U are losing. Which is good because – although Leeds won't catch them – we play them next week and anything that might undermine their barnstorming confidence is good. The idea that we could beat Man U drifts across your mind. But you mustn't think it.

In the second half there are no visits to Filbert Street. But you know from Ceefax that Leeds are winning 2–0 and Man U are still losing. It's a good day, a calm way to experience the Leeds game. Just numbers on a screen. You can make the rest up: a solid defensive performance, Leeds playing it safe, snuffing out the impotent attacks Leicester occasionally hoof up the pitch. Leicester are history. They have been a thorn in the Leeds – and your own – side for years. And now they are gone. Nearly gone. It feels good.

For the first time in weeks you are interested in the league table. Interested enough to write the new version out before it comes up on Ceefax. Leeds are two points behind Newcastle, who hold the magical fourth place – the Champions League berth.

All week you have heard radio reports, seen newspaper stories, read websites: Bowyer for Arsenal, Dacourt for Lazio, Kewell for Liverpool, Viduka for Real Madrid. Doom and gloom. The breaking up of the once-promising Leeds United side. But maybe not, you are thinking. Maybe – if we get fourth place – it'll all look very different.

Leicester (0) 0 Leeds (2) 2
Martyn; Mills, Woodgate, Matteo, Harte; Smith, Batty, Dacourt (Johnson 15), Kewell; Fowler, Viduka.
   Scorers: Viduka, Fowler

1	Liverpool	32	53–26	65
2	Man U	32	78–41	64
3	Arsenal	30	60–32	63
4	Newcastle	30	54–40	56
5	Leeds	31	44–30	54
6	Chelsea	31	58–31	53

LET'S ALL LAUGH AT MAN U – NUMBER TWELVE
Man U 0 Middlesbrough 1

As with the Leicester game, there was little to go on. Just the knowledge Boksic had scored and the Man U comeback machine wasn't working. And Ceefax. Throughout the game, especially as injury time in the second half approached, you expected an equaliser and an 'unlikely' winner. But then you saw Boksic on screen during *Final Score*. It was over. Man U had lost again and were now struggling to keep up with Arsenal. The next day they'd slip to third, behind Liverpool, who did Leeds the kindness of beating Chelsea.

You bought a Sunday paper for the first time in weeks. You were sick of reading bad things about Leeds: the court case, racism, defeats, the fans, everything. But a Leeds win and a Man U defeat is a rare combination. It was worth the £1.20. 'ODDS ON ANOTHER GUNNERS DOUBLE' it read. Although you hate to see Arsenal do well, you know how that headline will make Man U fans feel. What a shame Arsenal couldn't win the Champions League too, and really stuff it down Man U's throat. The report goes on to say 'The inescapable conclusion was that United were not playing well . . .' Good. Nice to know anyway, but with Man U heading to Elland Road next week, even better. 'Beckham became involved in a running argument with a linesman . . . and ended up being shown the yellow card . . .' Very good. You have warm memories of the year they self-destructed, players being sent off every week. The last time Arsenal sneaked the league.

And best of all: 'If Arsenal keep winning and the [Man U–Arsenal] fixture is put back until the end of the season they could be in the happy position of picking up the Premiership trophy at Old Trafford.' What a wonderful thought! you think. Who is this writer? He really understands football. You feel so uplifted you half think of writing him a letter of congratulation.

And you think of next week. Everything is moving towards next week. The season's trials and tribulations will be forgotten next Saturday. It can't come quickly enough. And there's no way – no way! – any date change is going to make you miss this one. You don't even care it's kicking off at noon: you won't need beer, this one is about pure adrenaline.

LEEDS UNITED v MANCHESTER UNITED Premiership
Saturday, 30 March 2002

You wake up at 5.30 a.m. You can't sleep. Your stomach is turning and you have butterflies. As you walk to the toilet you retch. You're nervous. But this is not the morning of your wedding or the day you have to address an audience of 1,800. This is Leeds versus Man U.

You go back to bed and try to read, but it is impossible. You can't concentrate. You get up. It's 6.30 in the morning. Your legs are like jelly. Your heart is beating so loudly you can hear it. You hang around the house and drink coffee, which just makes things worse.

At 7.30 a.m. you can't stand it any more. It's useless hanging around at home. You might as well go now. You can't feel any worse there than you do here.

In Ilkley, Martyn gets up with his daughter, Josie. She's been waking up early because it's been light in the mornings recently. He wouldn't have been able to sleep anyway. He tries to play with his daughter, watch TV programmes with her, but his mind is somewhere else. He feels bad that he can't give his daughter 100 per cent today, but there's nothing he can do about it. He's been feeling like this all week. Man U at home.

In houses throughout Leeds – and beyond – there are people lying awake. None of them will be able to go back to sleep. They all might as well go into Leeds, even though kick-off is not until noon.

On the train there are no Leeds fans. Todmorden is closer to Manchester than Leeds. But people are reading the sports pages. This game – says the press – is important. On the radio they said that Man U have to win this one or their championship is over.

At Halifax two men in their 50s with grey, unkempt hair get on. They are wearing Leeds United gear: white shirts, Strongbow, ragged '70s scarves. These are men who are used to sitting on trains on the way to Leeds matches. The older of the two men wears a baseball cap decorated with a dozen pin badges: Leeds–Roma, Leeds–1860 Munich, others you can't see. His friend goes through the paper. Greavsie's column. Greavsie thinks Robbie Fowler's on a roll. He's going to damage Manchester United today. And you can tell by their nervous chatter, the serious looks on their faces, that Leeds United are the most important thing in these men's lives and this game is the most important game of the season. Two other insomniacs.

You try to read your paper too, but you are still feeling sick and anxious. Your breathing is too shallow. You remember all the games against Man U over the years. The three wins at Elland Road in four years in the '90s. The game where Leeds were one up and the seconds slowed into minutes, minutes into hours, as Man U tried to equalise and at the end of the game, having shouted and screamed and felt every kick, you cheered so loud at the final whistle that you thought you were starting a heart attack and stood completely still, watching the stadium empty, people trailing out under the stands, thinking that if you made a move you'd feel that pain again, that you might die.

As the train draws into Leeds you are feeling more and more anxious. Your chest is fluttering, your legs and arms, all the muscles in your body tight and knotted. You stretch them like you're warming up for the game yourself. It's like you have some part to play. Different from other games. Like you have responsibilities today. Like you can't just sit there passive, not just a spectator, standing for the entire 90 minutes, joining in every chant going. There's no other way against Man U. Shit game or not, that's how it is. And afterwards – win or lose – you'll feel both exhausted and depressed.

And you wonder what makes you think you're going off the football. This feeling you've had for weeks. Are you really going off it? The way you are now it feels like the most important thing in the world.

At 9.20 a.m. Leeds station is packed with police, some in yellow, some in black riot gear, helmets swinging at their sides like they're going bowling. Outside the front of the station, three police vans and one car. One of the riot police has a megaphone. They congregate at the side of the station next to Burger King. Small groups of young men stand monitoring the police build-up, waiting for something to happen.

More police vans arrive. And horses. There are six vans now. Eight horses. The atmosphere in the station is not normal. Even though – at ten – it is busy with shoppers arriving; parties of girls for hen nights, dresses in polythene; men for stag nights, suits in suit holders. There is a deathly silence. Shoppers. Easter egg buyers. Friends meeting friends. You can barely make out the sound of their footsteps, only the three of the police vans' engines idling. And dogs barking somewhere.

Some of the young men – wearing expensive jumpers and jackets – try to walk through the police line. They want to get to Boar Lane, they are saying. The police turn them back. Others watch, sucking on cigarettes, talking on mobile phones.

More vans arrive, two packed with police, who step out and take off their yellow jackets to reveal uniforms black head to foot, helmets on, visors up, fitting heavy belts around their waists. Each belt is weighed down with gadgets: long wires, a stick, handcuffs, a radio. A man goes round and collects their yellow jackets – like a football coach collecting tracksuit tops before kick-off – and dumps them all in the back of a van.

Two R2 Elland Road buses have drawn up, blocking taxis from getting to the front of the station. The dogs are barking again. The buses draw up to the side exit. More Leeds fans have gathered. Cars are moved on and people are turned back. The command vehicle – another police van, but fitted with floodlights – arrives, edging up onto a kerb. There are now ten vans, all of them full of police.

The first Man U fans arrive and wait to show tickets to the police. Three Leeds fans are immediately over there.

'All right scum?' one says.

The Leeds fans are ushered away. The dogs' barking has become more insistent. You can make out three or four different barks.

There is a steady trickle of Man U fans. The two Manchester trains – one via Huddersfield, one via Halifax – must have come in. And there are more people watching. Men in Rockport and Hackett tops. Short hair. Well dressed. Such calm expressions on their faces they look beautiful. Behind the black glass of the vans you can see shapes moving.

One man sticks out. He's wearing a blue jumper. Polo neck. A Henri Lloyd label. He talks into a mobile phone, smiling. He has perfect teeth. He lines up with his mates against the glass front of Paperchase. The girl inside Paperchase has retreated behind her counter after having her face right up against the glass. The man in the blue jumper is handed a can of Miller. They all have cans of Miller. They are young. As they chat into mobile phones the three plain-clothes police officers talk into mobile phones too.

Now more Man U are arriving, wearing hooped tops, baseball caps. Few are young. Most of them are over 30. Some of the police have climbed out of their vans and are standing round the back, out of sight of the Leeds fans. Other police move the Leeds fans back. They have plugged the gap between the buses and the side entrance. There are at least 50 police covering the small gaps either side of the buses. The Man U fans climb on quietly, barely looking up.

'What are you waiting here for?' a policeman asks a lad, another policeman standing back slightly.

'My mate.'

'You'll have to move on.'

'I said I'd meet him here.'

'Has he got a phone?' the policeman points at the lad's mobile.
'No.'
'Are you going to the match?'
The second policeman steps forward. 'Can I see your ticket?'
'Who do you support?' The first policeman again.
'United,' the lad says.
The three of them laugh. There is a slight pause.
They move him on, advise him to go straight to the ground, not to hang around outside the stadium. 'You know the nature of this match,' says the first policeman.
They approach another lad.
'Make your way back.'
'How far?' says the lad.
'What?'
'How far do you want me to move back?'
The policeman smiles. 'Over there. Where those others are.'
On the buses 40 or 50 Man U fans sit quietly. They look bored. As if they are halfway through a six-hour coach journey, not sat in a station car park surrounded by police and men who are acting like a pack of lions waiting for a chance to get at them.
At the barriers inside the station the police pull out certain young men. They let some go by without a glance, but stop others. You think there must be some sort of dress code that they know. You try to identify who they stop and who they don't. It's the men in hooped tops and with tight sweatshirts over hardly visible shirt collars. Not the lads in jumpers with Stone Island, Hackett logos. Amongst them – ignored – are people wearing football strips: Liverpool, Newcastle, Burnley. The police persuade one group of lads to get on the bus. More hooped tops arrive, and one lad who looks just like one of the actors off *Cold Feet*. The one who was on *The Fast Show*. There's something about the length of his sideburns that singles him out as not being from Leeds.
Back outside the two R2 buses are full. Another has drawn up and is waiting further back. There are now dozens of men stood watching, all along the front of the station and down the feeder road that goes to City Square. They are wearing Burberry baseball caps, shirts, collars, jackets. One has a Burberry shirt and baseball cap – he has gone too far. The rest look perfect. Some are marching up and down looking mean. Most have cans of lager. The men who were drinking Miller are now drinking Stella, stood so close to a police van the police should be able to smell the lager on their breath.
The police bikes make off. The fans in the buses are more animated

now: you can just hear chanting over the sound of the idling vans, although you could have mistaken it for dogs barking. The buses move out. No one chases after them. No one throws missiles. No one shouts. They just watch. Inside the buses you can make out 'We all hate Leeds and Leeds and Leeds . . . all hate Leeds and Leeds and Leeds . . .' You spot one Man U fan, a mouth opening and closing on his pale 35-year-old face, his hair receding. He is an ugly man. The face of Manchester United.

The walk to Elland Road is quiet.

'Nobody walks to the game any more,' says Jon.

He's right. It used to be packed. It was exciting, streams of people descending on Elland Road from every direction. Now the M621 is like a car park both ways for the hour leading up to the game. In three years' time nobody will walk to the White Elephant Stadium.

Once you pass through the park that runs alongside the end of the M621 there are a few more people. There are empty cans of lager scattered everywhere, a queue at the chip shop, and outside The Waggon and Horses hundreds of drinkers squinting in the sun.

MORE REASONS TO HATE MAN U

1 Are there any reasons not to?

The match starts. The home crowd is up for it. The Kop will stand for 90 minutes, belting out song after song; even if we go two or three down it wouldn't matter. The fans are committed.

Beckham comes in for the usual abuse:

> *Posh Spice is a slapper*
> *She wears a big fat jewel*
> *And when she's shagging Beckham*
> *She thinks of Harry Kewell.*

But it's half-hearted. There is none of the venom of previous years. No 'Hope your kid dies of cancer', not much 'Posh Spice takes it up the arse'. No 'Munich '58' from the Leeds fans. No 'Always look out for Turks wielding knives' from the Man U fans. No Turkish Delights thrown at Leeds fans. And no banner saying 'ISTANBUL REDS'. It's tame. Relatively. The Leeds fans are singing 'We are Leeds', 'Marching on Together', all positive behind-the-team stuff. Barely a 'Scum! Scum! Scum!' to be heard. The Man U fans are silent . . . until their first attack results in a goal from Scholes. One–nil. A high-pitched cheer travels across the pitch towards the Kop, as the celebrating Man U players gesture to the East

Stand. The East Stand gesture back.

The Man U fans sing a couple of songs, then go quiet again. They are like slot-machine puppets. You slot the money in – or a goal in this case – and they leap about, make some noise. Then flop back into their seats. The Leeds fans are outsinging them in seconds.

Then Bowyer – out for weeks with his ban and after all his troubles – makes a trademark run through the Man U midfield and lays it to Viduka, who scores. One–one. There is bedlam. And hope.

The Leeds fans turn their attention from celebrating to Gary Neville:

> If the Nevilles play for England . . . so can I
> If the Nevilles play for England . . . so can I
> If the Nevilles play for England
> Nevilles play for England
> Nevilles play for England . . . so can I!

And it's hard to disagree. (Sadly for Neville, he will miss the World Cup through injury. Bad luck.)

Martyn fumbles a shot. Solskjaer is there. Two–one. The Man U fans sing his name a few times then go silent. As they quieten down – before the Leeds fans start singing again – Solskjaer scores again. Three–one.

In the second half Leeds work hard, building laborious attack after attack until Man U pick up the ball, move it down the pitch for Giggs to score. It's 4–1 to Man U. And although there's still 33 minutes on the clock, dozens of people leave the East Stand. They are not going for a piss. They are going home. They can't handle what they are seeing. It's too much to bear.

In the Kop people start voicing their opinions. 'WHAT ARE YOU FUCKING PLAYING AT?' 'WHAT THE FUCK'S GOING ON?' 'FUCKING CHANGE IT, YOU IRISH CUNT.'

The atmosphere has changed. This is not the same as losing 4–0 at home to Liverpool or being knocked out of the UEFA Cup. There is no irony, no self-deprecation in this defeat. This is anger that people can't control. This is very different.

The first chants of 'Who's that dying on the runway' start up. You are glad to notice that you haven't joined in.

The man in front of you shouts at the three younger men singing it.

'Shut it you brain-dead shits!' he says. 'Half our team nearly got killed in an air crash a few years ago!'

One of the boys – clearly pissed – his face red, shouts 'Fuck off!' and stares back at the pitch. His face is contorted like he might cry.

Then Harte scores. Four–two.

And Bowyer. Four–three.

And suddenly – Man U have been resting, punting the ball to and fro, biding their time for their important Champions League quarter final three days later – it's all Leeds. And Man U are rattled. They could have kept it going, won 6– or 7–1. But now they are reeling. One more goal and they'll drop the two points that could cost them the league. The Leeds fans know it. The Leeds players know it. Shots skim wide. And Leeds – in the end – are quite unlucky not to equalise.

Leeds United (1) 3 Manchester United (3) 4

Martyn; Mills, Woodgate, Matteo, Harte; Smith, Batty (Bakke 60), Johnson, Kewell (Bowyer 12); Fowler, Viduka.

Scorers: Viduka, Harte, Bowyer

1	Liverpool	33	55–26	68
2	Man U	33	82–34	67
3	Arsenal	31	63–32	66
4	Newcastle	31	60–42	59
5	Chelsea	32	60–32	56
6	Leeds	30	47–34	54

Next to Billy Bremner 50 lads are singing 'We are Leeds' repeatedly. This is unusual after a defeat. People are gathering. But not just to meet friends. They are waiting. The rest of the Leeds fans have gone home. Eventually the club close the gates of Elland Road and the police come on horseback to move people on. The lads keep up their chant. They know that inside Elland Road 3,000 Man U fans are waiting to be allowed to go home.

The police work the crowd well, funnelling us up towards the motorway bridge near The Waggon and Horses. Stage by stage they isolate car parks, roads and verges, and push Leeds fans further up the street.

Now the lads are the only ones left, stood facing the police. Their numbers are up, 300 or so wearing trademark jumpers and jackets. They sing 'We are Leeds', but are drowned out by a police helicopter. A police film crew sweep their camera across the men as they are moved further back by the dogs and horses.

After 20 minutes, 200 Leeds fans are left on the motorway bridge, watching the police empty the south stand half a mile away: hundreds of Man U fans are stood on Elland Road like sheep waiting for the sheepdog's next move. Further back, in front of the closed Waggon and Horses, two rows of eight police stand with their riot shields resting on the floor in front of them, helmets on, staring straight ahead.

The fans disperse. Some wander back into town. There is no stand-off.

In larger numbers they can be policed effectively. Nothing has happened. Yet.

Everything is quiet in the station, a few groups of lads walking to and fro, the police following at a respectful distance. Starbucks is full of Starbucks people: young families, couples, individuals staring at people walking past. It's a Saturday afternoon. The sun is shining. People are walking round carrying expensive-looking carrier bags. This is the new Leeds. Except that two groups of men have stopped in front of Starbucks and are staring each other out. The atmosphere chills. The police run in to stand between them. Nobody speaks. One family leaves a table of cappuccinos to drag their young daughter and dog off the station concourse, another family takes its lattes and muffins inside, behind the thick plate glass of the window.

The two groups of men are almost indistinguishable, standing with the same postures. One lot is eating at McDonald's. Man U fans. Thickset, shaved heads, smart shirts. The Leeds fans came down the concourse and spotted them then. The Leeds fans are also thickset and shaven-headed. They too wear smart shirts. No one throws a punch. The police stand among them, useless. Or powerless. There is only the sound of the Carphone Warehouse shutters rattling shut. Towards Wetherspoons a larger group of Leeds fans is amassing, watching. Everything is quiet.

Then one Leeds fan is shouting 'SCUM! SCUM! SCUM! SCUM!' at the top of his voice at a Man U fan who stands inches away, unmoved. The shouting echoes loud around the station. The police usher the Leeds fans away. They retreat, staring stony-faced at the police, and join the 20 or 30 men in front of Wetherspoons.

The police chat – almost affably – with the Man U fans who eat their burgers, scanning up and down the concourse. Three men lean against the barriers in front of the Tourist Information Office 20 yards away. One is particularly striking. He is tall, immaculately dressed, and his expression is one of wry amusement. Utterly fearless. Utter contempt for the Man U fans.

The Man U fans finish their burgers and are led through a door, to a passage to the other side of the station barriers where they can safely catch a train back to where they came from. Whether they want to or not. Immediately two of the three standing next to the Tourist Information Office are on their mobile phones. Police walk up and down the concourse, one with a radio bleeping every second like a heartbeat monitor.

The atmosphere lifts. Dogs, women and children reappear. The shutters come back up on the Carphone Warehouse and the people bearing cappuccinos and lattes come out of Starbucks to drink outside again.

And you notice in McDonald's, eating a burger with a friend, a man you've seen before, in Madrid and Eindhoven. He's 5 ft 9 in., with dark hair and clear, icy blue eyes. When you're looking at him in Wetherspoons and he casts his eyes around the pub, you always make sure to look away. You remember him from somewhere. School? College? Somewhere. Maybe he lived near you once? He's always around. Always nearby at times like these.

TOTTENHAM HOTSPUR v LEEDS UNITED Premiership
Monday, 1 April 2002

ANOTHER REASON TO HATE TOTTENHAM
1 They're a London team.

'Goal at White Hart Lane . . . It's Spurs 1 Leeds 0 . . . amazing there've been no Leeds goals, Fowler alone could have had three . . .' For the first time this year you think the season is dead. There is no way Leeds can catch Newcastle now. You feel defeated. Maybe the players feel like you do and that's why it looks like they've jacked it in. But there's still UEFA Cup qualification . . . 'not going too well . . . relentless goal mouth action . . . Casey Keller has had to be at his best today . . . with everything Fowler and Viduka are throwing at him . . .' And you think – perhaps Leeds can win this . . . 'goal at White Hart Lane . . . it's now Spurs 2 Leeds 0 . . . Teddy Sheringham . . .' And it is confirmed: the season is over.

Ceefax flickers: 'SPURS 2–1 LEEDS, Viduka 47.' But there will be no more reports from White Hart Lane except the half-past-the-hour visit and the final report. 'Two defeats over Easter for Leeds United . . . Newcastle are five points clear with two games in hand . . .' The season is dead and buried.

Spurs (2) 2 Leeds (0) 1
Martyn; Mills, Woodgate, Matteo, Harte; Smith, Bakke, Batty (Keane 66), Bowyer; Fowler, Viduka.
  Scorer: Viduka

| 1 | Arsenal | 32 | 66–32 | 69 |
| 2 | Liverpool | 33 | 55–26 | 68 |

3	Man U	32	82–44	67
4	Newcastle	31	60–42	59
5	Chelsea	33	60–32	57
6	Leeds	33	48–36	54

WOODGATE'S JAW BROKEN IN CLUB ATTACK
The Guardian (11.4.02)

Without a midweek game there is still enough news regarding Leeds United to keep the newspapers, radio, television news and sports programmes well occupied. After dithering about his future Olivier Dacourt seems to be on his way to Lazio. You already have your argument ready.

Although he was your player of the season last year, this year you have been disappointed. He has been in and out of the team with injury. You wonder how many full games he has actually played. He must have missed a third of the season. And then there's getting fitness back, two or three games until he's up to scratch. He's a disruption. It would be better to let Bakke or Johnson play week in week out. Consistency, that's what we need. And £16 million? You weigh it up. You'd take it. The player's heart has gone.

There always has to be a reason to let a player go. You have to have an answer. Or you'll feel like you did when the other Frenchman left.

It's always on Radio Five that you hear news first: Jonathan Woodgate found guilty of affray, Robbie Fowler arrested the previous night, Lee Bowyer put on the transfer list . . . and today: News is just breaking that Jonathan Woodgate was involved in an assault last night and has a broken jaw.

There isn't much information: just that he failed to turn up at court for an appeal against a driving offence because – his solicitor said – he was in hospital, under anaesthetic. The next day the papers are full of it. But there's no real news, nothing to add. The police know nothing about it either. There are no charges. But a swarm of radio and newspaper journalists who went out drinking in Middlesbrough the following night found a few landlords and a few drinkers to interview. The Daily Mail leads with reports that witnesses say they saw him being abused by Asian youths outside a pub. One witness claims that although they didn't see the attack, they were told it was a group of Asian lads who had a go at him. Other newspapers avoid that line.

Leeds United say they are prepared to give Jonathan Woodgate the benefit of the doubt until they know exactly what happened. As usual they are investigating exactly what went on. Then they report that he has been completely exonerated: it was just a case of 'horseplay' with his mates. They may discipline him internally, but as far as they are concerned that is the end of the story.

Jonathan Woodgate will be out of action for the rest of the season.

To complete the week of news stories, Suresh Grover – the man from the Channel Four news that night – announces that 'Proceedings were issued against Lee Bowyer for damages for assault, battery and conspiracy to pervert the course of justice arising out of the events of the evening of 11 January 2000.' He adds that the other men involved will be included in the proceedings in time. The civil case – the third case to do with 11 January 2000 – is launched.

LEEDS UNITED v SUNDERLAND Premiership
Saturday, 6 April 2002

ANOTHER REASON TO HATE SUNDERLAND
1 They took our unbeaten record earlier this season.

The minute's silence eight days after the Queen Mother's death is mostly observed. There are a few shouts, half a dozen mobile phones trilling. One in ten join in the national anthem, some singing an alternative version:

> *God save our gracious team*
> *Long live our noble team*
> *God save our team . . .*

There's a good atmosphere. Even though you could argue the season is over, no hope of Champions League, the singing is upbeat. And when Jody Craddock loops in an own goal over the helpless Sunderland goalkeeper the Kop belt out 'One Jody Craddock, There's only one Jody Craddock.'

Leeds are moving well, pushing Sunderland back, playing good football without Kewell and Rio. It is not an end-of-season game after all. Sunderland spring the odd attack, Phillips and McAteer testing the Woodgate–Matteo back two, trying to expose Leeds's weak Harte.

The game settles into a satisfying to-ing and fro-ing, Leeds having three out of every four attacks. Mark Viduka is his usual self. He misses a chance but the Kop are with him: 'Mark Vi-DU-ka! Mark Vi-DU-ka!'

And one man's voice – high-pitched – shouting 'SHIT!' between each 'Mark Vi-DU-ka'. Most people laugh, but one lad is looking round, furious. The man is spurred on. 'Fucking rubbish . . . fucking gatepost . . . fucking lump of wood . . .' And an argument breaks out.

'You didn't say that against Liverpool last year!' says the lad. That game Viduka scored a hat-trick. We won 4–3.

'That was one game!' says the man.

'Eighteen months ago!' says someone else.

In the second half Sunderland are on top. Most of the Kop aren't too bothered. They aren't watching anyway. They are watching a man at the front of the Kop, 45, wearing a blue baseball cap. He is trying to get the fans around him to sing. He's pissed. A second man in a baseball cap stands up to join him, but most people look on in silence as he gestures to the back of the Kop that the front of the Kop is full of wankers, on his feet for five minutes. One man takes offence. There is a row. A face-to-face eyeballing session.

A steward comes over to shut him up.

'Fuck off!' says the man.

The steward goes back to sit down. Some people laugh, but not everybody. People are calling out now. 'Sit down.' 'Shut your mouth, you twat.' He looks round. His face is tired. A head steward goes over. They have a discussion.

The man sits down and Keane breaks through. He's been offside a dozen times, but suddenly he's there and the flag is down and he slots it neatly into the net.

Keane does a double somersault and you feel intensely that he must not – as the rumours have it – be sold to Man. City. He has the keenness of Smith and the touch of Fowler. Or the touch Fowler used to have. And he tries. He has the potential to score 20 a season.

In the last few minutes and in injury time a third of the Leeds fans disappear. The Sunderland fans sing, 'We can see you sneaking out.' The Leeds fans retort 'We can see you going down.' And as the fans applaud the Leeds players off the pitch the stadium is only half full.

Leeds United (1) 2 Sunderland (0) 0
Martyn; Mills, Woodgate, Matteo; Harte, Smith, Batty, Bakke, Bowyer; Fowler (Keane 60), Viduka.
Scorers: Craddock o.g., Keane

1 Arsenal	33	68–33	72
2 Man U	34	83–44	70
3 Liverpool	33	55–26	68
4 Chelsea	34	63–32	60
5 Newcastle	32	61–43	60
6 Leeds	34	50–36	57

ASTON VILLA v LEEDS UNITED Premiership
Saturday, 13 April 2002

ANOTHER REASON TO HATE VILLA
1 Lee Hendrie

'Simon Mann has a goal at Villa Park . . . It's Aston Villa one . . .' He pauses. 'It's Aston Villa nil Leeds one . . .' Your heart has already missed a beat. They should train their commentators better; they shouldn't make mistakes like that. You feel confused. Imagine how Villa fans will be feeling now. They'd have been up out of their seats before he paused and made his correction. They'd have to deal with not being 1–0 up as well as being 1–0 down.

Your heart goes out to them.

You're listening to the Derby–Newcastle commentary on Radio Five. It's as vital that Newcastle fail as Leeds succeed. Which is why you celebrate Derby's first and second goals like they're Leeds goals. You compile an ongoing league table: Leeds winning, Newcastle losing:

4	Chelsea	35	63–32	61
5	Newcastle	33.5	61–45	61
6	Leeds	34.5	51–36	60

That's how it is right now, half an hour to go in Villa–Leeds and Derby–Newcastle. But you should never prepare a league table until the games are over. It's presumptuous. It always brings bad fortune. Newcastle score. Newcastle score again. It's Derby 2 Newcastle 2. You expect a Villa goal now. That is the tone of the afternoon. It seems inevitable that Villa will equalise. Radio Five have not been to Villa Park for ages. All you have is the Ceefax screen's 'ASTON VILLA 0 LEEDS 1'.

Then Newcastle score a third. This – you realise – is just as bad as Villa scoring. The commentator says that Lua Lua could have fired Newcastle into the Champions League.

But you don't give up. There's still time. You have the radio commentary. You have Ceefax and now you have BBC1's Final Score: reports from games, a screen split into four with latest scores, news flashes, updates. There's too much information. In the end Leeds have won and Newcastle have won and David O'Leary will be saying something like 'We can only concentrate on our own results.'

With sixth place sealed – West Ham unable to make up 13 points with their four games left – Leeds will secure the third UEFA Cup place next season if Arsenal and Chelsea win their FA Cup semi-finals. The logic is convoluted, but that's how it will be. You sit watching Chelsea–Fulham, Arsenal having already beaten Middlesbrough. You need Chelsea to win. It doesn't feel right wanting Chelsea to win. But when they score you accept it is good. Leeds are nearly there, nearly in Europe, nearly not having to spend the summer playing in Estonia and Bulgaria in the Inter Toto Cup, exhausting themselves before the season proper begins. But when Fulham attack, a part of your head is still urging them on. It's confusing.

At the final whistle you clench your fists. Chelsea are through to the cup final. Leeds United are in next season's UEFA Cup, even if Chelsea had to lend a hand.

Villa (0) 0 Leeds (1) 1

Martyn; Kelly, Mills, Matteo, Harte; Smith, Bowyer, Batty, Bakke; Keane, Viduka.

Scorer: Viduka

1	Arsenal	33	68–33	72
2	Liverpool	34	56–26	71
3	Man U	34	83–44	70
4	Newcastle	34	65–46	64
5	Chelsea	35	63–32	61
6	Leeds	35	51–36	60

LEEDS UNITED v FULHAM Premiership
Saturday, 20 April 2002

MORE REASONS TO HATE FULHAM
1 Let's face it: there aren't any. Well, until today . . .

When they read out the Leeds team the man behind you is delighted.

'YES! No Viduka! No Viduka!'

It's Fowler, Smith and Keane up front.

Martyn's pleased. He's wanted to see Leeds play without a big man up front. Especially today. Fulham have two tall centre-backs. They play offside. This could be a chance to get behind them, use Keane's pace to tear them apart.

No one has heard that Viduka was injured. Why isn't he playing? There's speculation around the Kop that he's in Turin going over the finer points of a contract to get himself back into the Champions League. But if Leeds win today and Newcastle lose there's still hope for Leeds to reach the Champions League. Chelsea have already lost this morning. This could be a good day.

But the match is dreadful. Leeds are hopeless. Fulham sit back. They must be surprised that Leeds, so high above them in the league, are so feckless. The highlight of the first half – the only thing worth remembering – comes after Batty's fourth dodgy tackle. The Fulham players are outraged he has not been booked. Their keeper, Van der Sar, runs the length of the pitch to object to the referee and is booked himself.

At half-time Martyn tells you that after the Man U game a few weeks ago he watched the highlights with his family.

Josie, his daughter, said: 'I like the team in red.'

'No darling,' said Martyn's wife, Damaris. 'Leeds are the team in white.'

'I like the team in red,' she said again.

Josie has stopped thinking that when Martyn goes to the football every other Saturday he is actually playing for Leeds. Now she has a mind of her own. Martyn looks worried.

The second half is worse than the first. It's the worst game of the season. And your last. You can't go to the Boro game. It could be your last game in the Kop if you decide to stick to your idea of not getting a season ticket, going to half a dozen away games and a dozen home games instead. You wanted something special today. But Leeds give the ball away so frequently that the man in front of you suggests there's something dodgy going on. When Malbranque scores for Fulham their fans celebrate like they've won the league. It is the goal that will keep them up in the Premiership.

Leeds without Viduka are useless, you think. You begin to realise your ill-thought-out desire to see him offloaded to Italy or Spain is extremely stupid.

In the last ten minutes the fans pour out of Elland Road. By the final whistle – when more boo than clap – four out of five seats are empty. Over the loudspeakers you hear that Newcastle have won and have as good as sealed the fourth Champions League spot. The one that was supposed to be Leeds's.

You leave the Kop expecting an emotional reaction. End of your season. A long summer ahead. But the only emotion you can muster is the desire to get back to the station in time to catch the next train home.

Leeds (0) 0 Fulham (0) 1

Martyn; Mills, Ferdinand, Matteo, Harte; Smith, Bowyer, Batty, Bakke; Keane, Fowler.

1 Arsenal	34	70–33	75
2 Liverpool	35	58–26	74
3 Man U	35	86–44	73
4 Newcastle	35	68–46	67
5 Chelsea	36	63–35	61
6 Leeds	36	51–37	60

DERBY COUNTY v LEEDS UNITED Premiership
Saturday, 27 April 2002

ANOTHER REASON TO HATE DERBY

1 They have been relegated. Their players will not be under pressure. They could beat us – their last home game in the Premiership.

The match means nothing. Except finishing fifth or sixth. You keep an eye on Ceefax. Bowyer scores early. Derby 0 Leeds 1. You should feel jubilant. And you would if you were there, but for you the season is over. Leeds are in the UEFA Cup, not the Champions League. Nothing can change.

And you don't want to listen to the radio. Newcastle sealing Leeds's Champions League place. Chelsea winning to keep Leeds at bay.

You try to remember the last time Leeds went into their penultimate game with nothing to play for. It feels bizarre. It shows – at least – that there's always been something good about Leeds in recent years. You remember season after season where the last ten games were meaningless and empty. Leeds are in Europe again. But you expected more. Although you accept that this is more than most football fans can dream of. So why do you feel so flat?

Derby County (0) 0 Leeds United (1) 1
Martyn; Mills, Ferdinand, Matteo, Harte; Smith, Bowyer, Batty, Bakke; Keane, Fowler.
    Scorer: Bowyer

1 Arsenal	35	72–33	78
2 Man U	36	87–44	76
3 Liverpool	36	58–27	74
4 Newcastle	37	73–49	71
5 Chelsea	37	65–35	64
6 Leeds	37	52–37	63

LET'S ALL LAUGH AT MAN U – NUMBER THIRTEEN
Bayer Leverkusen 1 Manchester United 1
(Man U lose on away goals.)

You are in the Lake District. A couple of days away with Rebecca. The TV at the B&B doesn't work properly. You had wanted to watch the second leg of Man U's Champions League semi-final against Bayer Leverkusen. But there's no reception. Just a few grainy images and a faint commentary. But you can make out the ghost of Alex Ferguson pacing up and down the side of the pitch. Is he jubilant or distraught? 'Leverkusen are close now . . .' says the commentator. 'One–one with five minutes to go.' Fantastic, you think. If it stays like this Man U will be out of the Champions League. And Alex Ferguson will not be going home to Glasgow to win his second European Cup.

But it's all Man U. You are desperate they don't score. Some days you feel that Man U losing is as important as Leeds winning. You disagree with the idea that there must be something wrong with you wanting other English teams to do badly in Europe. When Alan Green says he can't understand, it makes you think he can't be a real football fan. For you being a football fan is as much about hate as love. And hating a team geographically nearest to you – in your case Manchester United – runs parallel with your love of Leeds.

Man U come close. But it's not to be. 'Not this time,' says the commentator, 'not this time.'

Then you see the image of a white-haired man running across the pitch to his players. The Bayer Leverkusen manager. Like Bobby Stokoe or David Pleat. You can hear a stadium full of Germans cheering, just about see their players embracing. And you learn that the day before Arsenal won at Bolton, putting themselves almost out of Man U's reach in the league. 'A terrible 24 hours for Manchester United,' says the commentator.

DISAPPOINTED
Yorkshire Evening Post (2.5.02)

On 1 May 2002 the former soldier, Ali Umit Demir, was found guilty by a Turkish court of murdering the Leeds fans Christopher Loftus and Kevin Speight in April 2000. He was jailed for 15 years. Other men were found guilty of being involved in the fighting. They got a few days in prison each. The case had dragged on for two years after the murders. And Demir's sentence of 15 years – it transpired – could be reduced to as little as 5 years. There was much dissatisfaction back in Leeds.

I remember when I heard about it. I didn't know either of the men, but I felt it like every Leeds fan felt it. I'll never forget where I was.

We were in a hotel room in Granada, Spain: images on the TV of fighting between Leeds and Galatasaray supporters, men being chased along the streets, being beaten with sticks. Then a body covered in blood and someone bending over it, pinching its nose, attempting the kiss of life. Then someone I thought I recognised, fighting to get past a policeman to help the man on the ground. Then a man on a stretcher in the back of an ambulance.

Rebecca tried to translate the Spanish television voiceover. She thought two people were dead. But she couldn't be sure. I called her brother in Madrid. He confirmed it: two Leeds United supporters had been killed. The news cut to images from Leeds: a Bradford City fan laying flowers at the gates of Elland Road.

We went for a walk to clear our heads. Granada's famous Alhambra was open, no one else about. I wanted to explain to Rebecca how I felt. What was going on? Two Leeds fans were dead! Then suddenly I was crying. I wanted to say all sorts of things, but I was checking myself, thinking I'd sound stupid.

'They were Leeds, like me,' I said finally. 'They were Leeds supporters. I'm a Leeds supporter.' And I was worried about the man I'd seen on the screen. I knew who it was. My old boss. Was he one of the dead men?

Next day we found a shop selling English newspapers. In the tabloids there were photographs of Turkish fans running their fingers across their throats. They made me sick. *The Guardian* carried a picture of Lee Bowyer and Harry Kewell emerging into the Ali Sami Yen stadium, a line of police holding shields up to protect them from missiles. The players' faces were full of fear. There'd been death threats, Bowyer appeared to be cowering, reluctant to enter the field. I'd never seen him like that before.

'On Wednesday, 5 April 2000,' I read, 'two Leeds supporters were stabbed to death after a fight between rival Leeds United and Galatasaray fans. The victims were a man of 37 and a father of two, 40.'

My old boss wasn't one of the dead. I went to the cathedral in Granada to light candles for the two dead men. The candles flickered and I cried again, thinking, why am I crying? I didn't even know them. For the rest of the holiday I was confused to find myself constantly on the edge of tears.

A few months later I bumped into my old boss. I didn't bring up Turkey, that I'd seen him on the television. I just asked him if he was going to Madrid.

'I don't go away any more,' he said. 'My daughter was watching the TV when the first reports from Istanbul came through. She saw me. She went mental. She made me promise I'd never go away again.'

Exactly a year after Istanbul – it was raining at Elland Road. A dozen people stood waiting, taking cover under the eaves of the Leeds Megastore. A steward stood guard next to a covered plaque. The evening before the place was buzzing: 40,000 Leeds United supporters celebrating victory over Deportivo la Coruna in the quarter-final of the European Cup. Now the place was deserted. Until suddenly there were 200 people making their way across from one of the Leeds United hospitality tents, most dressed in black, umbrellas up. As they drew near I saw their faces: tense, emotional, tired. Three film crews appeared, booms swinging, cameras tracking the group as they gathered round the covered plaque. A tall man with silver hair emerged: Peter Ridsdale. He addressed the crowd, but couldn't be heard for the traffic on Elland Road. He didn't speak for long. From the back I made out just one phrase: ' . . . that it should never happen again . . .' He unveiled the plaque and encouraged a group of people forward. They read the inscription, their faces reflected in the brass: the families of the two dead men, probably their mothers and fathers, their partners, their children. They embraced, comforted each other, then turned to leave and others took their place before the plaque: men in their 30s and 40s – one of them your old boss, all of them pale-faced and staring, some crying, some placing flowers at the base of the wall.

Eventually the assembly made its way back to the hospitality tent. The rain had not let up. With everyone gone, you stepped forward and read the plaque:

> IN MEMORY OF CHRIS LOFTUS AND KEVIN SPEIGHT
> WHO DIED TRAGICALLY IN ISTANBUL
> APRIL 5th 2000
> THEY WILL NEVER BE FORGOTTEN

BLUNDER CLUB FIRES ANOTHER OWN GOAL
Yorkshire Post (3.5.02)

'When will they learn?' asked the *Yorkshire Post* the day after Leeds United's name was again dragged through the media. During the Leeds Player of the Year Awards at Elland Road, the comedian Stan Boardman was reported to have made racist jokes. He is reported to have told one Asian man to 'Go back to your curry house in Bradford – your elephant is waiting.'

The *Yorkshire Post* – indignant – listed two years of problems at Elland Road. The Bowyer–Woodgate court case, the arrest of Robbie Fowler the night the team went out drinking dressed in army fatigues, Woodgate's horseplay, O'Leary's book. And now this. 'With such a record of gaffes and poor judgements,' argued the paper, 'perhaps no one should be surprised that the club was so insensitive as to hire for one of its most glittering nights of the year a comedian who specialises in offending people.'

The *Yorkshire Evening Post* reports that Leeds United have apologised to all who were at the dinner and have written to Stan Boardman saying they will be reviewing his £4,000 fee and will not be inviting him back to Elland Road. *The Guardian* report another 'joke'. Referring to the Sarfraz Najeib court case Stan Boardman is alleged to have said: 'I hear they went to a club last night. When they came out one said to the other "I could murder an Indian tonight."'

LET'S ALL LAUGH AT MAN U – NUMBER FOURTEEN
Man U 0 Arsenal 1

'ARSENAL REJOICE IN THEATRE OF DREAMS.' Headlines and photos cover the news-stands. Arsenal are champions. And they won it at Old Trafford, the so-called 'theatre of dreams'.

Today you put yourself in the place of all the Man U fans you know. The one who said he doesn't go to their games any more because it's so boring that 'United' always win. The one who said he didn't care about the Premiership: second place and the Champions League would do him – it's all about Europe nowadays. The little kids walking around Leeds and Bradford and Halifax wearing Man U tops, naively thinking that winning is the way it would always be, not imagining 'their team' would come third and they might not feel so superior wearing their sponsored-by-Vodafone shirts this summer. You put yourself in their place and think that it's good they are learning a lesson about pride and how it always comes before a fall.

LEEDS UNITED v MIDDLESBROUGH Premiership
Saturday, 11 May 2002

MORE REASONS TO HATE MIDDLESBROUGH
1 Gary Pallister.
2 Tony McAndrew.
3 Poor Noel Whelan having to play for them.

You hear the final score of the final game of the season driving away from Wakefield at 5 p.m. Leeds 1 Middlesbrough 0. Alan Smith hammering the ball in to bring a difficult season to an end. You've missed Leeds's last home game of the season.

Today you had to work. Again. Work has robbed you of two home games this season. Leaving Wakefield you imagine what is happening at Elland Road now: the players' lap of honour. That's what you regret most. Not the game. Not the win. But the lap of honour. That's the thing that always brings a lump to your throat, the thing that makes you start to anticipate next season. You haven't missed a final home game since the early '80s, the players running past the South Stand, along the Lowfields, then as they get to the halfway line the clapping starting up in the Kop, you picking out individual player's faces, trying to catch their eye, imagining they are thanking you personally for the support you have given them that year. And trying to catch the eye of players you think you might never see again. Who would it be this year? Dacourt? Kewell? Bowyer? Viduka? Keane? No doubt O'Leary will be running up at the rear, standing sincerely in front of the Kop to take the applause. Then, when the lap of honour is over, everyone trailing out into the late afternoon sun, summer starting. Leeds finishing fifth. Chelsea having lost at home to Villa, so that Leeds can leapfrog Jimmy, who, ever since he left Leeds, still remains at an inferior club three seasons on.

Not such a bad season, after all. Fifth. An achievement after all the shit the club has been through. Or put itself through. No silverware again, but Leeds have qualified for Europe in their own right. And next season . . . Next season Leeds are going to do something special. Now the team is over all those difficulties.

Leeds United (0) 1 Middlesbrough (0) 0
Martyn; Kelly, Ferdinand, Matteo, Harte; Bowyer, Bakke, Johnson, Kewell; Smith, Keane.

Scorer: Smith

1 Arsenal	38	79–38	87
2 Liverpool	38	67–30	80
3 Man U	38	87–45	77
4 Newcastle	38	74–52	71
5 Leeds	38	53–37	64

LET'S ALL LAUGH AT MAN U – NUMBER FIFTEEN
Manchester United 0 Charlton 0

After the Leeds report, news from Anfield. Liverpool have hammered Ipswich and Manchester United have only drawn with Charlton, to finish third. They are the third-best team in England. They must join

Newcastle in playing a qualifier to get into the Champions League; their bitter rivals Arsenal – who have won the Double, leaving them with nothing – currently being presented with the Premiership trophy, parading that and the FA Cup round Highbury. Although you hate Arsenal and Liverpool – and Leeds are two places further down even than Man U – you are still laughing. Which will Man U fans be squirming about more? Arsenal winning everything or Liverpool finishing higher than them?

O'LEARY IS SACKED AFTER PLAYERS PUT BOOT IN
Yorkshire Post (28.6.02)

You thought it was over. England out of the World Cup. All the Leeds players on holiday. Even the Rio transfer speculation would have to wait until he got back from wherever the world's best defender likes to unwind. The fixtures were out but you had yet to transfer them to your wife's diary.

Then you heard it on the radio driving home. 'The Leeds United manager David O'Leary has left the club . . .'

The first thing your wife said was 'Shall I drive?'

And you thought: why?

The press the next day came up with reasons: he's spent £100 million and won nothing, he wrote that book, he defended himself about that book, he profited from that book, he slagged off the fans, the chairman, the players. No silverware. No Champions League football. And his column in the *Sunday People*: why Leeds shouldn't sell Rio Ferdinand. He has too much to say. That was the general opinion.

The press also report the rumour that Peter Ridsdale had rung round some of the senior players. Ridsdale's conclusion: the team had lost faith in David O'Leary.

But the search for reasons doesn't make the weekend papers. It's the search for a successor that interests everyone now. O'Leary will only be news when he goes for his next job – or when the updated paperback of his book comes out. And the autobiography you've heard might be on its way.

'Martin O'Neill will be the new manager at Leeds United,' report *The Sun*. According to them, Leeds and Celtic have already worked out a package – the day *before* O'Leary was called in for his 11 a.m. meeting.

'Leeds want Greg,' says the *Daily Star*. They're talking about John Gregory!

And then on Sunday – after managers from Gus Hiddink to the Middlesbrough boss are brought into it – the *News of the World* suggests Terry Venables. Peter Ridsdale is a big fan, it appears.

Another football news story for the machine to process.

But what about real people? People you know?

Martyn thinks that it's not such a bad move. Ever since the week between that West Ham game when we won 3–0 to go top of the league on New Year's Day and that game at Cardiff he thought something was up. Something behind the scenes. And Martyn's other mates aren't so bothered either. There'd been a turning against him once he started slagging the fans off after the Brian Kidd incident.

And Dave is glad. He hated O'Leary anyway.

Peter Ridsdale thanks David O'Leary for his four years of service, for all he's done for the club.

And you think: this the end of an era. The club have drawn a line under the most intense four years you can remember as a Leeds United fan: two European semi-finals, top of the league for long periods, never below fifth place at the end of a season; an air crash, the terrible events in Turkey, the trial, the retrial; Milan at home, Cardiff away; the best four years supporting Leeds. Now it's over.

And although a part of you is excited about the future, another part of you is sad about O'Leary's departure. You don't want to feel towards David O'Leary the way you felt towards Howard Wilkinson at the end of his time at Leeds. After all he did for the club. After all he did for you. Would any other manager have managed to take the team to within a whisker of the Champions League after having all that off-the-pitch stuff to deal with?

VENABLES LANDS UNITED JOB
Yorkshire Post (8.7.02)

Your first thoughts were 'Oh Jesus – Venables!' when you heard on the radio that the stock exchange had just been told that Terry Venables was the new manger at Leeds United. He didn't fit in with the usual stereotype of what a Leeds manager should be: dour, blunt, glowering at the camera. He's certainly no George Graham, Howard Wilkinson or Allan Clarke!

But then your mind started coming round to it. Everyone says he's a great coach. And a great communicator of ideas. He's great with the media too. Aren't those the main components of his job description? Maybe he would be OK. At least Leeds would probably win a cup.

But then, your mind had started coming round to Steve McLaren as manager. The press had puffed him up as the best young coach in England. You were convinced, or at least open to McLaren coming.

Perhaps your mind would have come round to whoever had got the job, because in the end, you have to be behind whoever was manager of Leeds United (at least until he fucked it up), just like you have to be behind the players. You're a Leeds fan, aren't you?

CONFESSIONS OF A LEEDS FAN – PART EIGHT
2001–02

It was not the season you expected. Being top of the league for so long was wonderful, even if the quality of football was never really as good as last year. It got your hopes up. But the court case and the book and the Christmas pub crawl and some of the stuff you've seen fans doing and Bowyer's betrayal? Some of it does your head in. Then there was the dip in form: a hangover from all the troubles the club has had over the last two years.

So you're disappointed, like most other Leeds fans. Relatively.

You have decided not to get a season ticket next season. Instead you will go to half the home games, six away and at least one European. You'll get more out of that. You'll have to be sharper next season. Not just turn up week after week. You'll have to get onto the ticket office the minute tickets go on sale. And the games will be better. You won't take it all for granted. And you won't feel that flat frustrated complacency that you've got sick of feeling at Elland Road. A complacency you've been part of.

Maybe you aren't the fan you were.

v. by Tony Harrison

'My father still reads the dictionary every day. He says your life
depends on your power to master words.'

Arthur Scargill, Sunday Times, 10 January 1982

Next millennium you'll have to search quite hard
to find my slab behind the family dead,
butcher, publican, and baker, now me, bard
adding poetry to their beef, beer and bread.

With Byron three graves on I'll not go short
of company, and Wordsworth's opposite.
That's two peers already, of a sort,
and we'll all be thrown together if the pit,

whose galleries once ran beneath this plot,
causes the distinguished dead to drop
into the rabblement of bone and rot,
shored slack, crushed shale, smashed prop.

Wordsworth built church organs, Byron tanned
luggage cowhide in the age of steam,
and knew their place of rest before the land
caves in on the lowest worked-out seam.

This graveyard on the brink of Beeston Hill's
the place I may well rest if there's a spot
under the rose roots and the daffodils
by which dad dignified the family plot.

'V.' BY TONY HARRISON

If buried ashes saw then I'd survey
the places I learned Latin, and learned Greek,
and left, the ground where Leeds United play
but disappoint their fans week after week,

which makes them lose their sense of self-esteem
and taking a short-cut home through these graves here
they reassert the glory of their team
by spraying words on tombstones, pissed on beer.

This graveyard stands above a worked-out pit.
Subsidence makes the obelisks all list.
One leaning left's marked FUCK, one right's marked SHIT
sprayed by some peeved supporter who was pissed.

Far-sighted for his family's future dead,
but for his wife, this banker's still alone
on his long obelisk, and doomed to head
a blackened dynasty of unclaimed stone,

now graffitied with a crude four-letter word.
His children and grand-children went away
and never came back home to be interred,
so left a lot of space for skins to spray.

The language of this graveyard ranges from
a bit of Latin for a former Mayor
or those who laid their lives down at the Somme,
the hymnal fragments and the gilded prayer,

how people 'fell asleep in the Good Lord',
brief chisellable bits from the good book
and rhymes whatever length they could afford,
to CUNT, PISS, SHIT and (mostly) FUCK!

Or, more expansively, there's LEEDS v.
the opponent of last week, this week, or next,
and a repertoire of blunt four-letter curses
on the team or race that makes the sprayer vexed.

IF YOU'RE PROUD TO BE A LEEDS FAN

Then, pushed for time, or fleeing some observer,
dodging between tall family vaults and trees
like his team's best-ever winger, dribbler, swerver,
fills every space he finds with versus Vs.

Vs sprayed on the run at such a lick,
the sprayer master of his flourished tool,
get short-armed on the left like that red tick
they never marked his work much with at school.

Half this skinhead's age but with approval
I helped whitewash a V on a brick wall.
No one clamoured in the press for its removal
or thought the sign, in wartime, rude at all.

These Vs are all the versuses of life
from LEEDS v. DERBY, Black/White
and (as I've known to my cost) man v. wife,
Communist v. Fascist, Left v. Right,

class v. class as bitter as before,
the unending violence of US and THEM,
personified in 1984
by Coal Board MacGregor and the NUM,

Hindu/Sikh, soul/body, heart v. mind,
East/West, male/female, and the ground
these fixtures are fought out on 's Man, resigned
to hope from his future what his past never found.

The prospects for the present aren't too grand
when a swastika with NF (National Front) 's
sprayed on a grave, to which another hand
has added, in a reddish colour, CUNTS.

Which is, I grant, the word that springs to mind,
when going to clear the weeds and rubbish thrown
on the family plot by football fans, I find
UNITED graffitied on my parents' stone.

'V.' BY TONY HARRISON

How many British graveyards now this May
are strewn with rubbish and choked up with weeds
since families and friends have gone away
for work or fuller lives, like me from Leeds?

When I first came here 40 years ago
with my dad to 'see my grandma' I was 7.
I helped dad with the flowers. He let me know
she'd gone to join my grandad up in Heaven.

My dad who came each week to bring fresh flowers
came home with clay stains on his trouser knees.
Since my parents' deaths I've spent 2 hours
made up of odd ten minutes such as these.

Flying visits once or twice a year,
and though I'm horrified just who's to blame
that I find instead of flowers cans of beer
and more than one grave sprayed with some skin's name?

Where there were flower urns and troughs of water
and mesh receptacles for withered flowers
are the HARP tins of some skinhead Leeds supporter.
It isn't all his fault though. Much is ours.

Five kids, with one in goal, play two-a-side.
When the ball bangs on the hawthorn that's one post
and petals fall they hum 'Here Comes the Bride'
though not so loud they'd want to rouse a ghost.

They boot the ball on purpose at the trunk
and make the tree shed showers of shrivelled may.
I look at this word graffitied by some drunk
and I'm in half a mind to let it stay.

(Though honesty demands that I say *if*
I'd wanted to take the necessary pains
to scrub the skin's inscription off
I only had an hour between trains.

So the feelings that I had as I stood gazing
and the significance I saw could be a sham,
mere excuses for not patiently erasing
the word sprayed on the grave of dad and mam.)

This pen's all I have of magic wand.
I know this world's so torn but want no other
except for dad who'd hoped from 'the beyond'
a better life than this one, *with* my mother.

Though I don't believe in afterlife at all
and know it's cheating it's hard *not* to make
a sort of furtive prayer from this skin's scrawl,
his UNITED mean 'in Heaven' for their sake,

an accident of meaning to redeem
an act intended as mere desecration
and make the thoughtless spraying of his team
apply to higher things, and to the nation.

Some, where kids use aerosols, use giant signs
to let the people know who's forged their fetters
like PRI CE O WALES above West Yorkshire mines
(no prizes for who nicked the missing letters!)

The big blue star for booze, tobacco ads,
the magnet's monogram, the royal crest,
insignia in neon dwarf the lads
who spray a few odd FUCKS when they're depressed.

Letters of transparent tubes and gas
in Düsseldorf are blue and flash out KRUPP.
Arms are hoisted for the British ruling class
and clandestine, genteel aggro keeps them up.

And there's HARRISON on some Leeds building sites
I've taken in fun as blazoning my name,
which I've also seen on books, in Broadway lights,
so why can't skins with spraycans do the same?

But why inscribe these *graves* with CUNT and SHIT?
Why choose neglected tombstones to disfigure?
This pitman's of last century daubed PAKI GIT,
this grocer Broadbent's aerosolled with NIGGER?

They're there to shock the living not arouse
the dead from their deep peace to lend support
for the causes skinhead spraycans could espouse.
The dead would want their desecrators caught!

Jobless though they are how can these kids,
even though their team's lost one more game,
believe that the 'Pakis', 'Niggers', even 'Yids'
sprayed on the tombstones here should bear the blame?

What is it that these crude words are revealing?
What is it that this aggro act implies?
Giving the dead their xenophobic feeling
or just a *cri-de-coeur* because man dies?

So what's a cri-de-coeur, *cunt? Can't you speak*
the language that yer mam spoke? Think of 'er!
Can yer only get yer tongue round fucking Greek?
Go and fuck yerself with cri-de-coeur!

'She didn't talk like you do for a start!'
I shouted, turning where I thought the voice had been.
'She didn't understand yer fucking "art"!
She thought yer fucking poetry obscene!'

I wish on this skin's word deep aspirations,
first the prayer for my parents I can't make
then a call to Britain and to all the nations
made in the name of love for peace's sake.

Aspirations, cunt! Folk on t' fucking dole
'ave got about as much scope to aspire
above the shit they're dumped in, cunt, as coal
aspires to be chucked on t'fucking fire.

IF YOU'RE PROUD TO BE A LEEDS FAN

OK, forget the aspirations. Look, I know
United's losing gets you fans incensed
and how far the HARP inside you makes you go
but *all* these Vs: against! against! against!

Ah'll tell yer then what really riles a bloke.
It's reading on their graves the jobs they did –
butcher, publican and baker. Me, I'll croak
doing t' same nowt ah do now as a kid.

'ard birth ah wor, mi mam says, almost killed 'er.
Death after life on t' dole won' t seem as 'ard!
Look at this cunt, Wordsworth, organ builder,
this fucking 'aberdasher Appleyard!

If mi mam's up there, don't want to meet 'er
listening to me list mi dirty deeds,
and 'ave to pipe up to St fucking Peter
ah've been on t'dole all mi life in fucking Leeds!

Then t' Alleluias stick in t' angels' gobs.
When dole-wallahs fuck off to the void
what'll t'mason carve up for their jobs?
The cunts who lieth 'ere wor unemployed?

This lot worked at one job all life through.
Byron, 'Tanner', 'Lieth 'ere interred'
They'll chisel fucking poet when they do you
and that, yer cunt, 's a crude four-letter word.

'Listen, cunt!' I said, 'before you start your jeering
the reason why I want this in a book
's to give ungrateful cunts like you a hearing!'
A book, yer stupid cunt, 's not worth a fuck!

'The only reason why I write this poem at all
on yobs like you who do the dirt on death
's to give some higher meaning to your scrawl.'
Don't fucking bother, cunt! Don't waste your breath!

'You piss-artist skinhead cunt, you wouldn't know
and it doesn't fucking matter if you do,
the skin and poet united fucking Rimbaud
but the *autre* that *je est* is fucking you.'

Ah've told yer, no more Greek . . . That's yer last warning!
Ah'll boot yer fucking balls to Kingdom Come.
They'll find yer cold on t'grave tomorrer morning.
So don't speak Greek. Don't treat me like I'm dumb.

'I've done my bits of mindless aggro too
not half a mile from where we're standing now.'
Yeah, ah bet yer wrote a poem, yer wanker you!
'No, shut yer gob a while. Ah'll tell yer 'ow . . .

'Herman Darewski's band played operetta
with a wobbly soprano warbling. Just why
I made my mind up that I'd got to get her
with the fire hose I can't say, but I'll try.

'It wasn't just the singing angered me.
At the same time half a crowd was jeering
as the smooth Hugh Gaitskell, our MP,
made promises the other half were cheering.

'What I hated in those high soprano ranges
was uplift beyond all reason and control
and in a world where you say nothing changes
it seemed a sort of prick-tease of the soul.

'I tell you when I heard high notes that rose
above Hugh Gaitskell's cool electioneering
straight from the warbling throat right up my nose
I had all your aggro in *my* jeering.

'And I hit the fire extinguisher ON knob
and covered orchestra and audience with spray.
I could run as fast as you then. A good job!
They yelled "damned vandal" after me that day . . .'

IF YOU'RE PROUD TO BE A LEEDS FAN

And then yer saw the light and gave up 'eavy!
And knew a man's not how much he can sup . . .
Yer reward for growing up's this super-bevvy,
a meths and champagne punch in t' FA Cup.

Ah've 'eard all that from old farts past their prime.
'ow now yer live wi' all yer once detested . . .
Old farts with not much left 'll give me time.
Fuckers like that get folks like me arrested.

Covet not thy neighbour's wife, thy neighbour's riches.
Vicar and cop who say, to save our souls,
Get thee behind me, Satan, drop their breeches
and get the Devil's dick right up their 'oles!

It was more a working marriage that I'd meant,
a blend of masculine and feminine.
Ignoring me, he started looking, bent
on some more aerosolling, for his tin.

'It was more a working marriage that I mean!'
Fuck, and save mi soul, eh? That suits me.
Then as if I'd egged him on to be obscene
he added a middle slit to one daubed V.

Don't talk to me of fucking representing
the class yer were born into any more.
Yer going to get 'urt and start resenting
It's not poetry we need in this class war.

Yer've given yerself toffee, cunt. Who needs
yer fucking poufy words. Ah write mi own.
Ah've got mi work on show all over Leeds
like this UNITED 'ere on some sod's stone.

'OK!' (thinking I had him trapped) 'OK!
If you're so proud of it then sign your name
when next you're full of HARP and armed with spray,
next time you take this short cut from the game.'

'V.' BY TONY HARRISON

He took the can, contemptuous, unhurried
and cleared the nozzle and prepared to sign
the UNITED sprayed where Mam and Dad were buried.
He aerosolled his name. And it was mine.

The boy footballers bawl *Here Comes the Bride*
and drifting blossoms fall onto my head.
One half of me 's alive but one half died
when the skin half-sprayed my name among the dead.

Half versus half, the enemies within
the heart that can't be whole till they unite.
As I stoop to grab the crushed HARP lager tin
the day's already dusk, half dark, half light.

That UNITED that I'd wished onto the nation
or as reunion for dead parents soon recedes.
The word's once more a mindless desecration
by some HARPoholic yob supporting Leeds.

Almost the time for ghosts I'd better scram.
Though not given much to fears of spooky scaring
I don't fancy an encounter with my mam
playing Hamlet with me for this swearing.

Though I've a train to catch my step is slow.
I walk on the grass and graves with wary tread
over these subsidences, these shifts below
the life of Leeds supported by the dead.

Further underneath's that cavernous hollow
that makes the gravestones lean towards the town.
A matter of mere time and it will swallow
this place of rest and all the resters down.

I tell myself I've got, say, 30 years.
At 75 this place will suit me fine.
I've never feared the grave but what I fear's
that great worked-out black hollow under mine.

IF YOU'RE PROUD TO BE A LEEDS FAN

Not train departure time, and not Town Hall
with the great white clock face I can see,
coal, that began, with no man here at all,
as 300 million-year-old plant debris.

Five kids still play at making blossoms fall
and humming as they do *Here Comes the Bride*.
They never seem to tire of their ball
though I hear a woman's voice call one inside.

Two larking boys play bawdy bride and groom.
Three boys in Leeds strip la-la *Lohengrin*.
I hear them as I go through growing gloom
still years away from being skald or skin.

The ground's carpeted with petals as I throw
the aerosol, the HARP can, the cleared weeds
on top of Dad's dead daffodils, then go,
with not one glance behind, away from Leeds.

The bus to the station's still the no. 1
but goes by routes that I don't recognise.
I look out for known landmarks as the sun
reddens the swabs of cloud in darkening skies.

Home, home, home, to my woman as the red
darkens from a fresh blood to a dried.
Home, home to my woman, home to bed
where opposites seem sometimes unified.

A pensioner in turban taps his stick
along the pavement past the corner shop,
that sells samosas now not beer on tick,
to the Kashmir Muslim Club that was the Co-op.

House after house FOR SALE where we'd played cricket
with white roses cut from flour-sacks on our caps,
with stumps chalked on the coal-grate for our wicket,
and every one bought now by 'coloured chaps',

'V.' BY TONY HARRISON

Dad's most liberal label as he felt
squeezed by the unfamiliar, and fear
of foreign food and faces, when he smelt
curry in the shop where he'd bought beer.

And growing frailer, 'wobbly on his pins'
the shops he felt familiar with withdrew
which meant much longer tiring treks for tins
that had a label on them that he knew.

And as the shops that stocked his favourites receded
whereas he'd fancied beans and popped next door,
he found that four long treks a week were needed
till he wondered what he bothered eating for.

The supermarket made him feel embarrassed.
Where people bought whole lambs for family freezers
he bought baked beans from check-out girls too harassed
to smile or swap a joke with sad old geezers.

But when he bought his cigs he'd have a chat,
his week's one conversation, truth to tell,
but time also came and put a stop to that
when old Wattsy got bought out by M. Patel.

And there, 'Time like an ever-rolling stream' 's
what I once trilled behind that boarded front.
A 1,000 ages made coal-bearing seams
and even more the hand that sprayed this CUNT

on both Methodist and C of E billboards
once divided in their fight for local souls.
Whichever house more truly was the Lord's
both's pews are filled with cut-price toilet rolls.

Home, home to my woman, never to return
till sexton or survivor has to cram
the bits of clinker scooped out of my urn
down through the rose-roots to my dad and mam.

IF YOU'RE PROUD TO BE A LEEDS FAN

Home, home to my woman, where the fire's lit
these still chilly mid-May evenings, home to you,
and perished vegetation from the pit
escaping insubstantial up the flue.

Listening to *Lulu,* in our hearth we burn,
as we hear the high Cs rise in stereo,
what was lush swamp club-moss and tree-fern
at least 300 million years ago.

Shilbottle cobbles, Alban Berg high D
lifted from a source that bears your name,
the one we hear decay, the one we see,
the fern from the foetid forest, as brief flame.

This world, with far too many people in,
starts on the TV logo as a taw,
then ping-pong, tennis, football; then one spin
to show us all, then shots of the Gulf War.

As the coal with reddish dust cools in the grate
on the late-night national news we see
police v. pickets at a coke-plant gate,
old violence and old disunity.

The map that's colour-coded Ulster/Eire's
flashed on again as almost every night.
Behind a tiny coffin with two bearers
men in masks with arms show off their might.

The day's last images recede to first a glow
and then a ball that shrinks back to blank screen.
Turning to love, and sleep's oblivion, I know
what the UNITED that the skin sprayed *has* to mean.

Hanging my clothes up, from my parka hood
may and apple petals, browned and creased,
fall onto the carpet and bring back the flood
of feelings their first falling had released.

'V.' BY TONY HARRISON

I hear like ghosts from all Leeds matches humming
with one concerted voice the bride, the bride
I feel united to, *my* bride is coming
into the bedroom, naked, to my side.

The ones we choose to love become our anchor
when the hawser of the blood-tie's hacked, or frays.
But a voice that scorns chorales is yelling: Wanker!
It's the aerosolling skin I met today's.

My alter ego wouldn't want to know it,
his aerosol vocab would baulk at LOVE,
the skin's UNITED underwrites the poet,
the measures carved below the ones above.

I doubt if 30 years of bleak Leeds weather
and 30 falls of apple and of may
will erode the UNITED binding us together.
And now it's your decision: does it stay?

Next millennium you'll have to search quite hard
to find out where I'm buried but I'm near
the grave of haberdasher Appleyard,
the pile of HARPs, or some new neonned beer.

Find Byron, Wordsworth, or turn left between
one grave marked Broadbent, one marked Richardson.
Bring some solution with you that can clean
whatever new crude words have been sprayed on.

If love of art, or love, gives you affront
that the grave I'm in's graffitied then, maybe,
erase the more offensive FUCK and CUNT
but leave, with the worn UNITED, one small v.

victory? For vast, slow, coal-creating forces
that hew the body's seams to get the soul.
Will Earth run out of her 'diurnal courses'
before repeating her creation of black coal?

IF YOU'RE PROUD TO BE A LEEDS FAN

But choose a day like I chose in mid-May
or earlier when apple and hawthorn tree,
no matter if boys boot their ball all day,
cling to their blossoms and won't shake them free.

If, having come this far, somebody reads
these verses, and he/she wants to understand,
face this grave on Beeston Hill, your back to Leeds,
and read the chiselled epitaph I've planned:

Beneath your feet's a poet, then a pit.
Poetry supporter, if you're here to find
how poems can grow from (beat you to it!) SHIT
find the beef, the beer, the bread, then look behind.

'v.' by Tony Harrison is published on its own (with press articles) by
Bloodaxe Books (1989) and is included in *Selected Poems by Tony
Harrison* published by Penguin Books (1987)